ENERGY CRISIS IN AMERICA?

ENERGY CRISIS IN AMERICA?

ROLAND V. BARNES (EDITOR)

Nova Science Publishers, Inc.
Huntington, NY

Editorial Production: Susan Boriotti and Donna Dennis
Office Manager: Annette Hellinger
Graphics: Wanda Serrano
Information Editor: Tatiana Shohov
Book Production: Jonathan Rose, Jennifer Vogt, Matthew Kozlowski,,
                     and Lynette Van Helden
Circulation: Cathy DeGregory Ave Maria Gonzalez, Ron Hedges, and Andre Tillman

Library of Congress Cataloging-in-Publication Data
Available Upon Request

ISBN 1-59033-006-4.

Copyright © 2001 by Nova Science Publishers, Inc.
            227 Main Street, Suite 100
            Huntington, New York 11743
            Tele. 631-424-6682   Fax 631-425-5933
            E Mail Novascil@aol.com; Novascience@earthlink.net

Printed in the United States of America

CONTENTS

PREFACE

Shortly after assuming office, President George W. Bush and his administration began drawing attention to a national energy crisis, which his critics claim only he can detect. They say President Bush and Vice President Dick Cheney are exaggerating and distorting the extent and causes of energy problems for the sole purpose of benefiting their "cronies" in the energy and oil industries. The most glaring example of this energy crisis is California, which underwent rolling blackouts and skyrocketing energy prices. Bush's opponents prefer to vilify energy companies as price gougers, rather than criticize California's skewered deregulation process – a system that refused to let the increased costs of energy distributors be passed on to consumers and hindered the construction of new power plants and supply lines to meet growing demand. For its part, the Bush administration says that California's, and the nation's, problems are chiefly the result of the lack of a national energy policy, a position the papers in this book prove to be an overstatement.

The states, by and large, have undergone population explosions, causing more demand for energy, but have often failed to permit the construction of new power plants and distribution lines to keep up. Instead of recognizing the supply and demand nature of the American economy, many politicians and activists choose only to address the demand. They excoriate those who use more than their "fair share" of energy – even though these "abusers" pay for their use – and implore us to sacrifice certain amenities in order to keep prices down. They will not let the supply side of the equation be addressed – no building is allowed, because it would damage the environment. However, technologies exist today with which we can supply electricity, oil, and other energy sources in environmentally safe ways. Even nuclear power is a viable option, as it is a "clean technology" that is safer than many of its opponents would have the public believe. Conservation, as Vice President Cheney said, is certainly a "personal virtue," but cannot on its own ease energy supply problems. The nation must also develop alternative fuel sources (water, solar, wind, geothermal, etc.) so that one day we will not be reliant on dirtier, conventional materials like coal and oil. However, until those alternate technologies can be feasibly applied and are in popular demand, we must continue using our current resources, under the system of American capitalism. The free market, with a hint of governmental oversight, has proven more than capable of riding out energy storms in the past and can certainly do so now and in the future.

The papers in this book analyze the energy situation in America now, from the questions of state deregulation to the possibility of national oil independence. Reading these works makes it clear that America has had and still does have varied energy policies, and they are the best place to start looking for solutions to any current problems the affecting nation.

Jonathan T. Rose
August 13, 2001

ENERGY EFFICIENCY: BUDGET, CLIMATE CHANGE, AND ELECTRICITY RESTRUCTURING ISSUES

Fred Sissine

SUMMARY

Debate in the second session of the 106th Congress cover the funding and direction of energy efficiency programs was focused on FY2001 spending request, the Clinton Administration's Climate Change Technology Initiative (CCTI), oil conservation options, and proposals for restructuring the electricity industry. Recent oil price increases have brought energy security back to the forefront as an issue for federal energy efficiency programs. The Persian Gulf remains volatile and oil imports make up one-fifth of the balance of trade deficit.

On the other hand, worldwide emphasis on environmental problems of air and water pollution and global climate change, and the related development of clean energy technologies in western Europe and Japan especially, have emerged as important influences on energy efficiency policymaking. The Clinton Administration views energy efficiency as the flagship of its energy policy, both for environmental and technology competitiveness reasons.

At the 1998 Fourth Conference of Parties (COP-4) in Buenos Aires, the Administration signed the United Nations' Kyoto Protocol on climate change. It calls upon the United States to cut greenhouse gas (GHG) emissions to 7% below the 1990 level during the period from 2008 to 2012. If the agreement is ratified, the Administration projects that energy efficient could play a large, if not the largest, role in achieving emissions reduction.

Accompanying the FY2001 budget request, CCTI sought $4 billion of tax incentives over the next 5 years to "encourage energy efficiency and the use of cleaner energy sources," plus a number of energy efficiency programs, notably at the Environmental Protection Agency (EPA) and the Department of Energy (DOE).

P.L. 106-291 (H.R. 4578; H. Rpt. 106-914 appropriates $814.9 million (excluding a $2 million prior year biomass transfer) for the FY2001 DOE Energy Efficiency Program. Relative to the FY2000 appropriation, the FY2001 level increases spending by $94.7 million, or 13%. This includes $49.2 million, or 9%, more for R&D and $22.5 million, or 13%, more for grants.

For EPA's FY2001 CCTI energy efficiency activities, P.L. 106-377 (H.R. 4635) appropriates $123.2 million. Relative to the FY2000 level, the FY2001 appropriation increases spending by

$19.9 million, which includes $10.1 million more for Buildings and $10.0 million more for Industry (See Table 1).

After the FY2001 appropriations were enacted, DOE released *Scenarios for a Clean Energy Future*, a study that shows the potential for advanced energy efficiency and other measures to reduce U.S. carbon emissions to the 1990 level by 2010. At the recent COP-6 meeting in The Hague, however, the United States was accused of trying to avoid making real efforts – for example, through greatly increased energy efficient efforts – to reduce emissions in order to address the Kyoto Protocol.

BACKGROUND AND ANALYSIS

Energy Efficiency Concept

Energy efficiency is increased when an energy conversion device, such as a household appliance engine, or steam turbine, undergoes a technical change that enables it to provide the same service (lighting, heating, motor drive) while using less energy. The energy-saving result of the efficiency improvement is often called "energy conservation." The energy efficiency of buildings can be improved through the use of certain materials such as attic insulation, components such as insulated windows, and design aspects such as solar orientation and shade tree landscaping. Further, the energy efficiency of communities and cities can be improved through architectural design, transportation system design, and land use planning. Thus, energy efficiency involves all aspects of energy production, distribution, and end-use.

These ideas of "efficiency" and "conservation" contrast with energy curtailment, which involves a decrease in output (e.g., turning down the thermostat) or services (e.g., driving less) to curb energy use. That is, energy curtailment occurs when saving energy causes a reduction in services or sacrifice of comfort. Curtailment is often employed as an emergency measure.

Energy efficiency is often viewed as a resource option like coal, oil or natural gas. In contrast to supply options, however, energy efficiency puts a downward pressure on energy prices by curbing demand instead of increasing supply. This means that energy efficiency provides additional economic value by preserving the resource base and reducing pollution.

History

From 1974 through 1992, Congress established several complementary programs, primarily at the Department of Energy (DOE), to implement energy saving measures in virtually every sector of societal activity. These energy efficiency and energy conservation programs were created originally in response to national oil import security and economic stability concerns. In the early 1980s, states and utilities took an active role in promoting energy efficiency as a cost-saving "demand-side management" tool for avoiding expensive power plant construction. Since 1988, national interest in energy efficiency has focused increasingly on energy efficiency as a tool for mitigating environmental problems such as air pollution and global climate change. This aspect spawned new programs at DOE and at several other agencies including the EPA, the Agency for International Development (AID), and the World Bank's Global Environment Facility (GEG). Energy efficiency is increasingly viewed as a critical element of sustainable development and economic growth.

The DOE energy efficiency program includes R&D funding, grants to state and local governments, and a regulatory framework of appliance efficiency standards and voluntary guidelines for energy-efficient design in buildings. In addition, its budget supports regulatory programs for energy efficiency goals in federal agencies and standards for consumer products. (Detailed descriptions of DOE programs appear in DOE's *FY2001 Congressional Budget Request, DOE/CR-0068-5, v.5, February 2000; which appears at* [http://www.cfo.doe.gov/budget/01budget/]).

From FY1993 through FY1998, DOE spent about $8.0 billion in 1999 constant dollars for energy efficient R&D, which amounts to about 10% of the total federal spending for energy supply R&D during that period. In 1999 constant dollars, energy efficiency R&D funding declined from $745 million in FY1979 to $213 million in FY1988 and then climbed to $521 million in FY1994. For FY1999, $526 million was appropriated, which is $5 million, or 1%, above the FY1994 mark in 1999 constant (real) dollars. Also, in 1999 constant dollars, since FY1973, DOE has spent about $7.4 billion on grants for state and local conservation programs.

This spending history can be viewed within the context of DOE spending for the three major energy supply R&D programs: nuclear, fossil, and renewable energy R&D. From FY1948 through FY1972, in 1999 constant dollars, the federal government spent about $22.4 billion for nuclear (fission and fusion) energy R&D and about $5.1 billion for fossil energy R&D. From FY1973 through FY1998, the federal government spent $43.2 billion for nuclear (fission and fusion), $21.1 billion for fossil, $11.7 billion for renewables, and $8.0 billion for energy efficiency. Total energy R&D spending from FY1948-FY1998, in 1999 constant dollars, reached $111.5 billion, including $66 billion, or 59%, for nuclear, $26 billion, or 23%, for fossil, $12 billion, or 11%, for renewables, and $8 billion, or 7%, for energy efficiency.

Since 1985, national energy use has climbed about 20Q (quads – quadrillion Btus, British thermal units), reaching a record high of 94 Q in 1998. DOE's 1995 report *Energy Conservation Trends* finds that energy efficiency and conservation activities from 1973 through 1991 curbed the pre-1973 growth trend in primary energy use by about 18 Q, an 18% reduction. In 1992, this was saving the economy abut $150 billion annually in total U.S. energy expenditures, a one-fourth reduction from the previous trend. Further, assuming fossil and other fuels were displaced in proportion to their actual use in 1992, then energy efficiency and conservation were providing about 300 million metric tons of carbon (MMTC) emission reductions that year.

DOE's Strategic and Performance Goals

Government Performance and Results Act (GPRA, P.L. 103-62) requires each federal agency to produce and update a strategic plan linked to annual performance plans. DOE's active *Strategic Plan* was issued in 1997. On February 18, 2000, DOE issued a new *Draft Strategic Plan* [http://www.cfo.doe.gov/stratmgt/plan/doesplan.htm]. Energy efficiency objectives and strategies appear under strategic goal #1, "Energy Resources." In the *DOE Annual Performance Plan for FY2001,* [http://www.cfo.doe.gov/budget/01budget/AnPerfP1/app-final.pdf] strategic objective ER2 aims to "Promote reliable, affordable electricity supplies that are generated with acceptable environmental impacts." Goals for 2010 are: (1) for electricity, increase distributed power to 20% of new annual capacity additions, (2) for buildings, reduce annual energy use by 2 Q, (3) for federal buildings, increase energy efficiency by 35% relative to 1985, (4) for industry reduce energy intensity to 25% below its 1990 level by 2010, and (5) for transportation, increase the fuel efficiency of new light vehicles by 5.4 mpg by 2010 and have 10 million vehicles on the road with light weight materials. Also, in April 2000, the Office of Energy Efficiency and Renewable

Energy (EERE) released its draft strategic plan, *Clean Energy for the 21ˢᵗ Century*. It reasserts the five goals noted above and offers others for 2010, including (1) double the amount of combined heat and power, and (2) achieve $3 billion in annual export sales of energy efficiency technologies. Related goals for 2001 include: (1) weatherize 75,000 homes, (2) recruit 500 new Energy Star partners, (3) achieve a 22% improvement in federal buildings energy efficiency relative to 1985, (4) conduct 750 industrial energy waste and productivity assessments, and (5) complete test of a fuel-flexible 50-kw fuel cell system for vehicles. Further, in early 2000, the National Academy of Public Administration issued *A Review of Management in the Office of Energy Efficiency and Renewable Energy* [www.napawash.org].

DOE Budget, FY2001

Interior Appropriations Bill

The House Appropriations Committee recommended $752.7 million (excluding a $2 million prior year biomass transfer). However, the Sununu floor amendment (#30, passed 214-211) cut $126.5 million from the Partnership for a New Generation of Vehicles (PNGV) under the Transportation Program. Further, the Sanders amendment (#28, passed by voice vote) added $21.5 million through an offsetting reduction in the Fossil Energy Program. Thus, the House-passed bill includes $647.7 million, a cut of $48.6 million, or 7%, below the FY2000 level. This includes $472.6 million for R&D programs, a decrease of $92.4 million, or 16% in current dollar terms. Also, the recommendation includes $177.0 million for grants programs, including $140 million for Weatherization grants. However, the House recommendation for Weatherization grants assumes that a $19 million advance appropriation in the Emergency Supplemental bill (H.R. 3908) would be approved beforehand.

Relative to the request, the House seeks a net decrease of $200.9 million, or 24%. This includes $186.9 million, or 28%, less for R&D programs and $14 million less for the Weatherization grant program. Also, the House recommends an increase of $6.0 million for Cooperative Programs with States and an increase of $11.7 million for the Energy Efficiency Science Initiative.

The FY2001 request for DOE's Energy Efficiency Program proposes to boost funding to $848.5 million (excluding a $2 million prior year biomass transfer) – an increase of $152.3 million, or 22%, over the FY2000 level of $696.2 million (excluding a $49 million prior year biomass transfer). This includes $659.5 million for research and development (R&D) programs, an increase of $82.8 million, or 14%. The R&D increase includes $24.7 million more for Buildings research and technology development programs, $56.6 million more for Federal Energy Management Programs (FEMP), $28.2 million more for Industry Programs, $24.0 million more for Transportation Programs, and $3.5 million more for Policy and Management. Also, the request includes $191.0 million for grants programs, an increase of $22.5 million, or 13%. Most of this increase, $19 million, is for the Weatherization Program.

For the Buildings R&D Program, the requested increase includes $16.8 million more for Equipment, Materials, and Tools and $9.3 million more for Community Energy Programs, which covers programs such as Rebuild America, Partnership for Advanced Technologies in Housing (PATH), and Energy Smart Schools. The requested increase for FEMP includes $2.8 million more for renewable energy technical guidance and $1.0 million more for water conservation and green power procurement.

Under Industry Programs, the requested increase includes $9.0 million more for the Agriculture Industry Program, which would support research on bio-based industrial feedstocks and the Vioenergy/Bioproducts Initiative, which aims to co-produce power, fuels, chemicals, and other bio-based products from crops, trees, and wastes. Also, the requested increase includes $5.0 million more for the Forest & Paper Industry Programs, which support this Initiative. This would support R&D on energy extraction from waste streams and sustainable forestry techniques.

The request for the Transportation Program seeks $4.8 million more for Hybrid Vehicles, $4.5 million more for Fuel Cell Vehicles, and $6.1 million more for Advanced Combustion Engine Vehicles.

The Clinton Administration sees energy (and renewable energy) as a key technology for curbing air pollution and global climate change, while contributing to the nation's economic strength and technology competitiveness. The President's State of the Union address reaffirmed these themes. (Budget appendix, p. 408).

EPA Budget, FY2001

The FY2001 EPA request for its share of programs under the Climate Change Technology Initiative (CCTI) was $227.3 million (See Table 1.) The conference committee approved $123.2 million, a $19.9 million, or 19% increase over the FY2000 level. The State of the Union address identified investment to spur "clean" energy technologies as a key strategy to address global warming. In further justification for its requested increase, EPA noted that its program strategy aimed to reduce emissions consistent with voluntary international commitments under the 9192 United Nations Framework Convention on Climate Change (UNFCC), which the United States has signed and ratified.

FY2001 is the third year of the Administration's CCTI effort. EPA conducts its CCTI programs under the Office of Environmental Programs and Management (EPM) and the Office of Science and Technology (S&T). EPA's CCTI programs are focused primarily on deploying energy-efficient technologies. These programs include Green Lights, Energy Star Buildings, Energy Star Products, Climate Wise, and Transportation Partners. They involve public-private partnerships that promote energy-efficient lighting, buildings, and office equipment. Efforts also include information dissemination and other activities to overcome market barriers.

The conference report (H. Rept. 106-988) noted that none of the funds appropriated shall be used to issue rules, regulations, or other orders to implement the Kyoto Protocol. However it notes further that this restriction shall not apply to the "conduct of education activities and seminars" nor to climate change-related activities that contribute to national energy security, energy efficiency, cost savings, environmental assessments, and general emission improvements.

**Table 1. EPA Funding for Climate Change Energy Efficiency Programs
($ millions current)**

	FY1999 Apprn.	FY2000 Apprn.	FY2001 Request	FY2001 House	FY2001 Senate	FY2001 Conf.
CCTI Buildings	38.8	42.6	80.1	42.7	-----	52.7
CCTI Transportation	31.8	29.6	65.1	27.0	-----	29.5
CCTI Industry	18.6	22.0	63.7	22.0	-----	32.0
CCTI Carbon Removal	0.0	1.0	3.4	1.0	-----	1.0
CCTI State & Local	5.0	2.5	4.5	2.5	-----	2.5
CCTI International Capacity	5.6	5.6	10.6	5.5	-----	5.5
CCTI, SUBTOTAL	99.8	103.3	227.3	100.7	101.3	123.2
Climate Change Research	22.8	20.6	22.7	20.6	22.7	22.7
TOTAL	122.6	123.9	250.0	121.3	124.0	145.9

Source: H. Rept. 106-988 (p. 121 & 129); S.Rept. 106-410; H.Rept.106-674, p. 47-49; EPA
FY2001 Congressional Justification, p. 67-73

Oil Conservation

On March 9, the House Commerce Committee's Subcommittee on Energy and Power held a hearing on *Price Fluctuations in Oil Markets*. Dr. John Cook of EIA testified that during the past year, crude oil prices rose from $12 per barrel to $34 per barrel, but noted that the historic high in 1981 reached $70 per barrel. Also, he noted that net oil imports supplied about 52% of U.S. oil use in 1998. Mr. Mark Mazur of DOE testified that the Administration relies primarily on market forces to manage long-term energy prices, but noted several program and policy actions DOE has taken in response to the recent increase in oil prices – including requests for increased funding for the Weatherization Grants Program. Further, he noted that DOE has several R&D programs that aim to cut long-term oil use, such as the Partnership for a New Generation of Vehicles (PNGV), recent initiatives to increase the fuel economy of light trucks and heavy trucks, and tax credits for hybrid electric vehicles.

The U.S. consumes about 17.2 million barrels of oil per day (mb/d), of which about 11.5 mb/d is used for transportation and about 3.8 mb/d is used in cars and 2.5 mb/d is used in light trucks. Corporate average fuel economy (CAFÉ) standard sets an efficiency requirement for new cars at 27.5 miles per gallon (mpg). However, the national fleet fuel economy for cars ha been very flat, moving only from 21.2 mpg in 1991 to 21.4 mpg in 1998. Short-term conservation measures that could reduce oil use in transportation include increased use of public transit, carpooling and ridesharing, and telecommuting. Long-term efficiency measures that could reduce transportation oil use include the PNGV program to develop an 80 mpg car and a variety of other DOE vehicle

R&D programs. In a 1996 report, *Energy Security: Evaluating U.S. Vulnerability to Oil Supply Disruptions and Options for Mitigating Their Efforts,* the General Accounting Office (GAO) cities DOE estimates that a variety of transportation and industry R&D programs could reduce oil use by 2.1 mb/d by 2010.

Climate Change

Energy Efficiency's Role

DOE's 1995 report, *Energy Conservation Trends*, shows that energy efficiency due to both high energy prices and federal programs has reduced long-term rates of fossil energy use and thereby curbed emissions of CO_2 significantly. Based on this finding, the Clinton Administration has repeatedly sought increased funding for energy efficiency as a strategy to further reduce emissions and help combat climate change.

Assuming no major future policy actions, the Business-As-Usual scenario in the EIA's Annual Energy Outlook projects a large growth in CO_2 emissions by 2010. Because CO_2 contributes the largest share of greenhouse gas emission impact, it has been the focus of studies of the potential for reducing emissions through energy efficiency and other means. A DOE report by five national laboratories entitled *Scenarios of U.S. Carbon Reutins: Potential Impacts of Energy Technologies by 2010 and Beyond*, also known as the *Five-Lab Study,* projects that emissions would reach 1,730 MMTC in 2010 – an increase of about 384 MMTC, or 29%. The *Five-Lab Study* anticipates that energy efficiency would be the single largest contributor, accounting for 50% to 90% of the projected emissions reduction in 2010. However, in a 1998 report, *Impacts of the Kyoto Protocol on U.S. Energy Markets and Economic Activity,* EIA finds problems with several key assumptions in the *Five-Lab Study* about the use of new energy-efficient technologies to reduce emissions.

Climate Change Technology Initiative, 2001

The Administration has made energy efficiency a key element of its strategy for curbing carbon dioxide and other greenhouse gas emissions, as reflected in its past CCTI proposals. In his January 27, 2000, State of the Union Address, President Clinton reaffirmed this, saying, "The greatest environmental challenge of the new century is global warming ... If we fail to reduce the emission of greenhouse gases, deadly heat waves and droughts will become more frequent, coastal areas will flood, and economies will be disrupted. This going to happen, unless we act. Many people ... still believe you cannot cut greenhouse gas emissions without slowing economic growth. In the Industrial Age that may well have been true. But in this digital economy, it is not true anymore. New technologies make it possible to cut harmful emissions and provide even more growth."

Thus, the Administration's Climate Change Technology Initiative (CCTI) for FY2001 proposes tax incentives in buildings, transportation, and industry sectors. First, it proposes a $1,000 credit for new homes purchased through 2003 that are 30% more efficient than the standard and a $2,000 credit through 2005 for new homes that 50% more efficient. Second, it provides a 20% investment credit through 2004 for fuel cells, natural gas heat pumps, and electric heat pump water heaters in residential and commercial buildings. Third, for electric vehicles and fuel cell vehicles, it extends a 10% tax credit (capped at $4,000) through 2006. Fourth, for hybrid vehicles, it creates a new tax credit (capped at $3,000) effective from 2003 through 2006. Fifth, CCTI proposes an accelerated 15-year depreciation schedule for distributed power equipment at industrial sites with a rated capacity under 500 kilowatts (or 12,500 pounds per of steam). This incentive is focused primarily on energy efficient system equipment. (The CCTI tax proposals an accelerated 15-year depreciation schedule for distributed power equipment at industrial sites with a rated capacity under 500 kilowatts (or 12,500 pounds per of steam). This incentive is focused primarily on energy efficient system equipment. (The CCTI tax proposals are available on the White House web site [http://www.pub.whitehouse.gov/retrieve-documents.html].) The Clinton Administration has estimated the impacts of CCTI credits on revenue at the Department of the Treasury. This is shown in the table below:

Table 2. CCTI Tax Credits: Projected Revenue Reduction at Treasury Department ($millions)

	FY2001	Total
Buildings Sector: New Energy Efficiency Homes, Residential, and Commercial Equipment	82 18	633 201
Transportation Sector: Extension for Electric and Fuel Cell Vehicles, New credit for Hybrid Vehicles	0	2,078
Industry Sector: Accelerated Depreciation for Distributed Power Equipment (all types)	1	10
Total	101	2,922

Source: White House Fact Sheet on CCTI Tax Incentives. Feb. 3, 2000

Also, the FY2001 CCTI has some funding increases for energy efficiency R&D and programs. The funding increases for DOE's Energy Efficiency Programs are described in the above section on *DOE Budget, FY2001*; they include increased spending for PNGV and PATH and new funding for the Bioenergy Initiative and the International Clean Energy Initiative (ICEI). The ICEI includes an increase of $39 million for DOE programs, $30 million more for programs at the U.S. Agency for International Development, and $15 million more for programs at the Export-Import Bank. Further, the funding increases for EPA's CCTI Programs are described in the above section on EPA Budget, 2001; they include new funding for the Clean Air Partnership Fund.

Legislation

Some bills have been introduced in the 106th Congress that address directly the role for energy efficiency in reducing emissions. For example, H.R. 2380 creates tax incentives for CCTI-related energy efficiency measures. S.882 proposes R&D funding increases for energy efficiency and other energy technologies as an alternative to the CCTI. It provides $200 million per year over 10 years to accelerate development of energy efficiency, fossil energy, nuclear energy, and renewable energy R&D. Through this means, the bill focuses on a long-term strategy for curbing greenhouse gas emissions. Also, some contend that it would be costly to implement the 7% reduction in U.S.

greenhouse emissions called for in the Protocol. Further, EIA contends that the CCTI provisions would provide a minimal impact on greenhouse emissions. In contrast, EPA and DOE stress the urgency of action, noting that CCTI provisions would provide immediate savings in energy, costs, and emissions.

Electric Industry Restructuring

Bills intended to ensure a continuing role for energy efficiency have been introduced in the 106th congress that include a public benefits fund (PBF), incentives for home energy efficiency, and/or an information disclosure requirement that identifies the sources of power for consumers. Some states and electric utility companies have already instituted such measures. Debate is focused on whether there should be a federal role in restructuring generally and in creating incentives for energy efficiency specifically.

The Administration's bill, "Comprehensive Electricity Competition Act," introduced by request as S. 1047 and H.R. 1828, includes a public benefits fund that supports energy efficiency and other elements of the policies mentioned above. Also, H.R. 2050 and S. 1369 set some provisions for energy efficiency support. In recent years, state restructuring actions have reduced both state and utility support for energy efficiency programs.

Under traditional regulation, electric company profit incentives link directly to increasing sales volume rather than lowering customer bills, which worked against energy efficiency improvements that shrink demand. Nevertheless, in response to rising power plant construction costs and environmental concerns, many states and electric utility companies created demand-side management (DSM) programs during the 1980s to promote energy efficiency and other activities as a less costly alternative to new supply. DSM has become a significant part of the nation's energy efficiency effort. DOE data show DS energy savings peaked in 1996 at 61 billion kilowatt-hours, which is about 0.66 Q, or the equivalent of the output from 12 one-gigawatt power plants. Utility DSM spending peaked in 1994 at $2.7 billion, about 1% of total electric utility operating expenses.

However, after California issued its first proposal for electric industry restructuring in 1994, utilities began downsizing DSM efforts. By 1998, DSM spending fell to about $1.4 billion, a 48% (or 51% real) drop from the 1994 level. There are concerns that a federal initiative to restructure the industry could cause DSM efforts to decline further, because DSM will no longer earn a rate of return in a market-based industry. Some note that the most appropriate way to promote energy efficiency is to build the environmental costs of energy supply sources into their power costs. This approach was debated in the early 1990s, but never implemented comprehensively. With restructuring now underway, the environmental cost dimension has been redirected toward the creation of public benefit funds to support energy efficiency, renewable energy, and other broad purposes.

At least 24 states have implemented some form of electric industry restructuring. Some of these states, such as California, include provisions for energy efficiency and conservation. California's law (A.B. 1890, Article 7) places a charge on all electricity bills from 1998 through 2001 that would provide $872 million for "cost effective" energy efficiency and conservation programs. Other states, such as Pennsylvania, have few if any provisions for energy efficiency. Some representatives of states with restructuring policy in place prefer that their policy remain undistributed and hope that Congress will not set any federal policy requirements.

Environmental groups and some energy producers raise concerns that federal efforts to restructure the electric industry could lead to reduced use of "clean" energy resources and increased pollution. They cite the recent drop in utility spending for energy efficiency and demand-side management in anticipation of state-based retail competition and other restructuring policies. This is noted in *Federal Research: Changes in Electricity-Related R&D Funding,* where GAO reports that spending on energy efficiency R&D by states and utilities has dropped rapidly. Second, they also observe that the environmental costs of pollution from supply sources are not included in the price of electric power.

In contrast to the environmentalists' view, a report by the Heritage Foundation, *Energizing America: A Blueprint for Deregulating the Electricity Market,* suggests that restructuring the industry by itself will help the environment because "deregulation forces power companies to meet higher standards of efficiency and cleanliness to ensure that local communities are provided the power they want without increased pollution." Further, some are opposed to utility bill charges to create a "public benefit" fund that supports a broad variety of purposes, which often include energy efficiency. They argue that such charges are taxes in disguise or that more market-oriented solutions should be pursued.

EPA's March 1997 position paper contended that "the new market must support and recognize the economic and environmental benefits of energy efficiency and demand side management." EPA also called for the use of emission caps to "internalize the cost of pollution" from the electric sector. This provision, it said, would address both air pollution and carbon dioxide emissions.

Some in Congress believe that state policy actions would create such an uneven regulatory patchwork or other inequities that a federal policy role is justified.

LEGISLATION

P.L. 106-74 (H.R. 2684)

FY2000 EPA (VA, HUD) Appropriations bill. House reported (H.Rept. 106-286) August 3, 1999. Passed House September 9. Senate reported (S.Rept. 106-161) September 16. Passed Senate September 24. Conference reported (H. Rept. 106-379) October 13. Signed into law October 20.

P.L. 106-113 (H.R. 3194)

Consolidated Appropriations Act for FY2000. Incorporates H.R. 3423, Interior Appropriations Bill. Introduced November 2, 1999. Passed House November 18. Conference reported (H.Rept. 106-479) November 18. Signed into law November 29.

P.L. 106-291 (H.R. 4578)

FY2001 Interior Appropriations bill. Makes appropriations for DOE Energy Efficiency Program. Reported (H.Rept. 106-646) June 1, 2000. Passed House (204-172), amended, June 16. Senate Committee on Appropriations reported (S.Rept. 106-312) June 22, 2000. Passed Senate, amended, July 18. Conference Committee reported (H.Rept. 106-914) September 29. House approved Conference report October 3 and Senate approved the report October 5. Signed into law October 11.

P.L. 106-377 (H.R. 4635)

FY2001 EPA (VA, HUD) Appropriations bill. Makes appropriations for Climate Change Energy Efficiency Programs. Reported (H.Rept. 106-674) June 12. Passed House (265-169), amended June 21. Senate Committee on Appropriations reported (S.Rept. 106-410 September 13. Passed Senate October 12, amended. Conference reported (H.Rept. 106-988) October 18. House and Senate approved conference report October 19. Signed into law October 27.

H.R. 1655 (Calvert)

DOE Civilian R&D Programs Authorization Bill, FY200 and 2001. Introduced June 3, 1999; referred to House Science Committee. Reported (H.Rept. 106-243) July 20. Passed House September 15.

H.R. 2050(Largent)

Electric Consumers' Power to Choose Act. Provides for a more competitive electric power industry. Creates tax credits for home energy efficiency and for combined heat and power. Introduced June 8, 1999; referred to Committee on Commerce, and to the Committees on Ways and Means, Transportation and Infrastructure, and Resources. The Commerce Subcommittee on Energy and Power held a hearing on July 22.

H.R. 2380 (Matsui)

Energy Efficient Technology Tax Act. Amends Internal Revenue Code to create tax incentives for energy efficiency and renewable energy measures. Introduced June 29, 1999; referred to Committee on Ways and means.

H.R. 2466 (Regula)/S. 1292 (Gorton)

FY2000 Interior Appropriations bill. Senate report (S.Rept. 106-99) June 28, 1999. H.R. 2466 brought to Senate floor July 27. House reported (H.Rept. 106-222) July 1. Passed House July 15 with H. Amdt. 258, that added $13 million to Weatherization grants. Passed Senate September 23. Conference reported (H.Rept. 106-406) October 20.

H.R. 2944 (Barton)

Electricity Competition and Reliability Act. Section 531 repeals PURPA Section 210 provision that requires utilities to purchase power from new qualifying cogeneration and small power (renewable energy) production facilities. Introduced September 24, 1999; referred jointly to Committees on Commerce, Transportation and Infrastructure, and Ways and Means. Commerce Committee's Subcommittee on Energy and Power held hearings September 27 and October 6.

H.R. 3908 (Young)

Emergency Supplemental Appropriations for FY2000. Title IV, Chapter 2 appropriates $19 million to the DOE Weatherization grant program for FY2001. Reported (H.Rept. 106-521) March 14, 2000. Passed House March 30. Sent to Senate.

H.R. 5176 (Billbray)

Energy Efficient Building Incentives Act. Provides tax incentives for energy efficiency improvements in new and existing buildings, including energy and renewable energy equipment. Introduced September 14; referred to Committee on Ways and Means.

H.R. 5339 (Johnson)

Provides income tax credit through 2005 for fuel cells used in residential and commercial buildings. Introduced September 28, 2000; referred to Committee on Ways and Means.

H.R. 5613 (Knollenberg)

Extends comment period for DOE proposed rule to raise energy efficiency standards for clothes washers and central air conditioners. Introduced November 1, 2000; referred to Commerce Committee, Subcommittee on Energy and Power.

S. 882 (Murkowski)

Energy and Climate Policy Act of 1999. Establishes new Office of Global Climate Change at DOE and authorizes $2 billion over 10 years to fund energy efficiency and other energy technology programs. Introduced April 27, 1999; referred to Committee on Energy and Natural Resources. Hearing held March 30, 2000.

S.1047 (Murkowski)/H.R. 1828 (Bliley)

Comprehensive Electricity Competition Act (The Administration's proposed bill). Senate bill introduced May 13, 1999; referred to Committee on Energy and Natural Resources. Hearing held July 15. House bill introduced May 17, 1999; referred to Committee on Commerce, and to the committees on Resources, Agriculture, Transportation and Infrastructure, and the Judiciary. House Commerce Subcommittee on Energy and Power held hearing July 22.

S.1369 (Jeffords)

Clean Energy Act of 1999. Creates PBF and other incentives to support energy efficiency, renewable energy, and other measures under electricity restructuring. Introduced July 14, 1999; referred to Committee on Energy and Natural Resources.

S. 1776(Craig)

Climate Change Energy Policy Response Act. To reduce greenhouse gas emissions, the bill provides financial incentives for deployment of energy efficiency equipment outside the United States, and it provides for research on demand management and other means of reducing traffic congestion. Introduced October 25, 1000; referred to Committee on Energy and Natural Resources. Hearing held March 30, 2000.

S. 2098 (Murkowski)

Electric Power Competition and Reliability Act. Section 201 repeals a PURPA Section 210 provision that requires utilities to purchase power for new qualifying cogeneration and small power (renewable energy) production facilities. Introduced February 24, 2000; referred to Committee on Energy and Natural Resources. Hearings held April 11, 13 and 27.

S. 2557 (Lott)

National Energy Security Act. Includes provisions to conserve energy resources, support renewable energy, and improve energy efficiency. It would raise the materials spending cap and change the materials spending share under the DOE Weatherization Program, authorize $25 million in FY2001 for competitive energy efficiency research grants, and extend the tax credit for electricity from steel cogeneration. Introduced May 16, 2000; placed on Calendar as #552. Motion to proceed passed September 22.

S. 2718 (Smith)/H.R. 5345 (Cunningham)

Energy Efficient Building Incentives Act. Provides tax incentives for energy efficiency improvements in new and existing buildings, including energy-efficient and renewable energy equipment. Senate bill introduced June 13, 2000; referred to Committee on Finance. House bill introduced September 29; referred to Committee on Ways and Means.

S. 3152 (Roth)

Community Renewal and New Markets Act. Section 604 creates an income tax credit for energy-efficient equipment in commercial buildings through 2003. Section 606 creates an incomes tax credit for qualified hybrid vehicles from 2003 through 2005. Introduced October 3, 2000; placed on calendar.

Table 3. DOE Energy Efficiency Budget for FY1999-FY2001
(Selected programs, $ millions)

	FY1999 Apprn.	FY2000 Est.	FY2001 Request	FY2001 House	FY2001 Senate	FY2001 Conf.
BUILDINGS	261.1	284.0	339.8	291.5	295.6	317.2
Research and Standards	60.3	75.4	100.1	74.9	85.4	86.7
Tech. Assistance*	187.3	189.5	225.0	197.4	195.0	211.5
Weatherizn. (grants)*	133.0	135.0	154.0	140.0	140.0	153.0
State Energy (grants)	33.0	33.5	37.0	37.0	34.0	38.0
Management & Plng	13.5	13.2	14.7	13.2	13.2	13.2
FED. ENG. MGMT.	23.8	23.9	29.5	24.4	25.7	25.7
INDUSTRY	162.8	161.7	184.0	167.2	167.0	174.7
Forest & Paper	11.8	12.1	17.1	----	12.1	12.1
Aluminum	7.9	11.2	11.0	----	11.2	11.2
Mining	2.0	3.0	4.0	----	3.8	3.8
Agriculture	2.0	4.0	13.0	----	7.0	3.0
Crosscutting	98.1	890.9	90.8	84.1	83.6	87.1
Distributed Generation	50.1	27.3	17.3	15.3	17.3	18.3
Management & Plng	8.2	8.9	9.3	8.9	9.1	9.1
TRANSPORTATION	198.7	232.8	250.9	227.7	248.2	256.0
Vehicle Technologies	123.7	141.4	161.2	138.2	156.9	160.3
Hybrid Systems	41.4	43.0	47.8	44.0	47.0	50.0
Fine Cell	32.9	37.0	41.5	38.6	41.5	41.5
Adv. Combustion Engine	37.0	47.8	53.9	48.3	51.8	52.3
Fuels Utilization R&D	17.5	21.6	24.5	22.6	23.1	23.6
Materials Technologies	36.8	42.5	38.5	39.6	42.5	45.5
Tech. Deployment	12.7	12.8	17.0	12.8	15.1	15.1
Management & Plng	7.9	8.5	9.7	8.5	8.5	8.5
Coop. Program with States	----	6.0	0.0	6.0	6.0	6.0

Energy Eff. Science Initiative	----	11.7	0.0	11.7	0.0	11.7
POLICY & MGMT.	38.0	42.9	46.4	43.9	42.5	43.4
R&D SUBTOTAL	518.4	576.7	659.5	472.6	604.9	625.9
GRANTS SUBTOTAL	166.0	168.5	191.0	177.0	174.0	191.0
GROSS TOTAL	684.4	745.2	850.5	649.7	778.9	816.9
House Floor PNGV Reduction	----	----	----	-126.5	----	----
House Floor Increase	----	----	----	21.5	----	----
Biomass Dev. Fund	----	-25.0	-2.0	-2.0	-2.0	-2.0
Prior Year Balances	-66.4	----	----	----	-15.0	----
ADJUSTED TOTAL	618.0	720.2	848.5	647.7	761.9	814.9

*Committee mark excludes $19 million advance appropriation in H.R. 3908.

Source: DOE FY2001 Cong. Bud.Request. Feb. 2000; H.Rept. 106-646; S.Rept. 106-312; House Support Table, July 27; H.Rept. 106-914.

ELECTRIC UTILITY RESTRUCTURING: OVERVIEW OF BASIC POLICY QUESTIONS

Larry B. Parker

INTRODUCTION: SEGMENTING AN INTEGRATED INDUSTRY[1]

After many decades of operating in a comprehensive, regulated market structure, the electric utility industry is facing significant change, both from new generating and transmission technology and shifting policy perspectives with respect to competition and regulation.[2] The continuing policy response to this change is likely to affect just about every consumer in the country. The industry is massive, with 1996 assets totaling $696 billion retail sales of $212 billion, and wholesale sales (sales of resale) of $47 billion. It consists of 3,196 utilities – 243 investor-owned, 2010 publicly owned, 932 cooperatives, and 10 federal entities. It is difficult to overestimate the importance of electric service to the country's economy and individuals' quality of life. In 1996, the average residential customer paid $861 to buy 9,784 kilowatt-hours (815 Kwh monthly) of electricity.[3]

---

[1] For related information on electric utility restructuring, see CRS Electronic Briefing Book at [www.congress.gov/brbk/html/ebeletop.html].

[2] The advent of new generating technologies, particularly gas-fired combined cycle, has both lowered entry barriers to competitors of traditional utilities and lowered the marginal costs of those competitors below that of some traditional utilities. As noted by FERC, smaller and more efficient gas-fired, combined cycle generation plants can produce power on the grid for between 3 cents and 5 cents a kilowatt-hour (Kwh). This is typically less than for the larger coal-fired (4-7 cents a Kwh) or nuclear (9-15 cents a Kwh) plants built by traditional utilities over the past decade. Indeed, it is less than the average costs of some utilities. Coupled with advances in generating technology have been advances in transmission technology that permit long distance transmission economically and permit increased coordinated operations and reduced reserve margins

This technological advancement has been combined with legislative initiatives, such as the *Energy Policy Act of 1992* (EPACT), to encourage the introduction of competitive forces into the electric generating sector. This shift in policy continues with the promulgation of FERC Order 888 and individual states implementation of retail wheeling initiatives.

[3] For residential customers of investor-owned utilities, based on revenues. For publicly owned utilities, the average residential customer paid $729 to buy 10,425 kilowatt-hours (869 Kwh monthly) of electricity.

The policy shift underlying the changes occurring in the electric utility industry is a growing belief that the rationale for the current economic regulation of electric utilities at both the federal and state levels – that electric utilities are natural monopolies – is being overtaken by events, and that market forces can and should replace some of the current regulatory structure. Regulation and rate-of-return ratemaking arguably exist as a partial substitute for the marketplace. The emerging trend in the industry suggests that regulation is an imperfect substitute for the marketplace and that with emerging new generating and transmission technology, real self-regulating market forces are now able to replace government regulation in many instances. This substitution could result in a more efficient allocation of the country's resources, and provide consumers with more accurate price signals regarding the actual cost of electricity.

The restructuring effort attempts to reduce and alter the role of government in electric utility regulation by identifying transactions, industry segments, regions, or specific activities that might no longer be the subject of economic regulation. In those areas where the marketplace cannot supplant regulation, existing regulation could remain as it is or be modified to be more performance-based. Thus, the government's role in regulation of electricity would play a more limited role in identified areas, such as antitrust enforcement. The current focus of the restructuring effort is the electric generating sector where experience under the *Public Utility Regulatory Policies Act of 1978* (PURPA) and the *Energy Policy Act of 1992* (EPACT) suggests that competition is possible.

The purpose of restructuring the electric utility is to promote economic efficiency, not simply to create competitive markets. As noted by former Federal Energy Regulatory Commission (FERC) Commissioner Charles G. Stalon: "Competitive markets are not ends in themselves."[4] Competitive markets are a vehicle to increase economic efficiency by relating costs and prices. Proponents argues that the events of the last 15-20 years demonstrate the regulatory system has not provided consumers with the proper price signal regarding the current relationship between costs and prices.[5] Restructuring those segments of the electric system that can sustain viable competitive markets would at least partially restore the necessary price signal to consumers and suppliers.

With enactment of PURPA, the federal government unwittingly opened up the restructuring debate by listing barriers in the electric generating market to non-utility entrants; by 1994, non-utility generating capacity was about 8% of the U.S. total. Introducing competition in the wholesale generation market was formalized by Congress with the passage of EPACT. This

---

Statistics from Energy Information Administration. *Financial Statistics of Major U.S. Investor-Owned Electric Utilities: 1996.* Washington, D.C.: DOE/EIA-0437(96)/1, December 1997; and Energy Information Administration. *Statistics of Major U.S. Publicly Owned Electric Utilities: 1996.* Washington, D.C.: DOE/EIA-437(96)/2, March 1998.

[4] Stalon, Charles G., "Wheeling, Competition, and Economic Efficiency," *Energy Systems and Policy*, 1986, p. 77.

[5] Electricity pricing under the current regulatory system is based on the concept of "just and reasonable" rates. Rates are derived from a utility's "revenue requirement" that is determined by the state public utility commission based on the utility's costs (operating expenses and current depreciation on facilities) and a "fair" rate of return on the utility's investment (the original cost of construction plus any improvements minus accumulated depreciation). This "embedded cost" method of determining rate insulates consumers' rates from sudden increases (or decreases) resulting in changes in new construction costs (i.e., the marginal cost of electricity) because any new costs are averaged into the existing revenue requirements. In contrast, market pricing based on marginal costs would inform the consumer quickly about changes in new construction costs, sending the consumers a more economically accurate price signal with respect to the cost of electricity.

process continues with FERC Orders 888 and 889, which provide for open access to the transmission grid at the wholesale level for all generators, and for recovery of costs incurred under the existing regulatory regime that may not be recoverable in a more competitive market (i.e. "stranded cost" recovery). Concurrently with these actions at the federal level, some states have began addressing restructuring issues at the retail level, with some states moving aggressively toward retail competition (also known as retail wheeling) and other choosing not to actively pursue such a course.

BACKGROUND: HOW WE GOT WHERE WE ARE

The *Federal Power Act* (FPA) and the *Public Utility Holding Company Act of 1935* (PUHCA) established a regime of regulating electric utilities that gives specific and separate powers to the states and the federal government. State regulatory commissions address intrastate utility activities, including wholesale and retail rate-making. State authority currently tends to be as broad and as varied as the states are diverse. At the least, a state public utility commission will have authority over retail rates, and often over investment and debt. Some state regulatory bodies also oversee any facets of utility operation. Despite this diversity, the essential mission of the state regulator is the establishment of retail electric prices. This is accomplished through an adversarial hearing process. The central issues in such cases are the total amount of money the utility will be permitted to collect and how the burden of the revenue requirement will be distributed among the various customer classes (residential, commercial, and industrial).

Under the *Federal Power Act*, federal economic regulation addresses wholesale transactions and rates for electric power flowing an interstate commerce. Federal regulation followed state regulation and is premised on the need to fill the regulatory vacuum resulting from the constitutional inability of states to regulate interstate commerce. In this bifurcation of regulatory jurisdiction, federal regulation is limited and conceived to supplement state regulation. The Federal Energy Regulatory Commission (FERC) has the principal functions at the federal level for the economic regulation of the electricity utility industry, including financial transactions, wholesale rate regulation, interconnection and wheeling of wholesale electricity, and ensuring adequate and reliable service. In addition, to prevent a recurrence of the abusive practices of the 1920s (e.g., cross-subsidization, self-dealing, pyramiding, etc.), the Securities and Exchange commission (SEC) regulates utilities' corporate structure and business ventures under the *Public Utility Holding Company Act* (PUHCA, Title 1 of the *Federal Utility Act*).[6]

This regulatory regime changed little between 1935 and 1978. Beginning in 1978, primarily in response to the energy crisis, laws were passed to encourage the development of alternative sources of power. The *Public Utility Regulatory Policies Act of 1978* (PURPA) was enacted in part to augment electric utility generation with more efficiently produced electricity and to provide equitable rates to electric consumers.[7] Specifically, PURPA encouraged the development of small power production and cogeneration of electricity and steam (called qualifying facilities or QFs). In addition to PURPA, the *Fuel Use Act of 1978* (FUA) helped QFs become established. Under FUA, utilities were not permitted to use natural gas to fuel new generating technology. QFs,

---

[6] For background information on PUHCA, see: Abel, Amy. *Electricity Restructuring Background: The Public Utility Holding Company Act of 1935 (PUHCA)*. CRS Report RS20015, January 7, 1999.

[7] For background information on PURPA, see Abel, Amy. *Electricity Restructuring Background: The Public Utility Regulatory Policies Act of 1978 and the Energy Policy Act of 1992*. CRS Report for Congress 98-419 ENR, May 4, 1998.

which are by definition not utilities, were able to combine the availability of natural gas and new, more efficient generating technology, such as combined-cycle, with a regulatory system (specifically, section 219 of PURPA) that provided them with a captive market that priced their product at their local utility's "avoided cost."[8] The introduction of new generating technologies lowered the financial threshold for entrance into the electricity generation business a well as shortened the lead time for constructing new plants. FUA was repealed in 1987, but by this time QFs and small power producers had already gained a portion of the total electric generating capacity.

This influx of QF power challenged the cost-based rates that previously guided wholesale transactions. Before implementation of PURPA, FERC approved wholesale interstate electricity transactions based on the seller's costs to generate and transmit the power. As more nonutility generators entered the market in the 1980s, these cost-based rates were challenged. Since nonutility generators typically do not have enough market power to influence the rates they charge, FERC began approving certain wholesale transactions whose rates were a result of a competitive bidding process. These rates are called market-based rates.

The *Energy Policy Act of 1992* removed several regulatory barriers to entry into electricity generation to further competition of wholesale electricity supply.[9] Specifically, EPACT provides for the creation of new entities, called "exempt wholesale generators" (EWGs), that can generate and sell electricity at wholesale without being regulated as utilities under PUHCA. Under EPACT, these EWGs are also provided with regulatory support to assure transmission of their wholesale power to a wholesale purchaser. However, EPACT does not permit FERC to mandate that utilities to transmit EWG power to retail consumers (commonly called "retail wheeling"), an activity that remains under the jurisdiction of state public utility commissions.

In line with EPACT, FERC issued a Notice of Proposed Rulemaking (NOPR), that proposed ending the utilities' transmission dominance to allow more wholesale competition in the generation sector. On April 24, 1996, FERC issued two final rules on transmission access – Orders 888 and 889. In issuing its final rules, FERC concluded that these Orders would "remedy undue discrimination in transmission services in interstate commerce and provide an orderly and fair transition to competitive bulk power markets." Under Order 888, the Open Access Rule, transmission owners are required to offer both point-to-point and network transmission services under terms and conditions comparable to those they provide for themselves. The Rule provides a single tariff providing minimum conditions for both network and point-to-point services and the non-price terms and conditions for providing these services and ancillary services.

This Rule also allows for full recovery of so-called stranded costs. Stranded costs can be viewed as a transition problem resulting from the movement from a comprehensive regulatory regime to a more competitively based electric generating sector. The utilities' current investments in electric generating facilities are based on an implied "regulatory bargain" between regulated utilities and their regulators,[10] a situation upset by the emergence of competitive forces in the

---

[8] Departing from traditional utility rate regulation, PURPA shifted the price basis for electricity from the seller's cost to the purchaser's cost. FERC adopted rules under PURPA to define avoided cost: the likely costs for both energy and facilities that would have been incurred by the purchasing utility if that utility had to provide its own generating capacity. State regulators have wide latitude in establishing the procedure to assign avoided costs.

[9] For background information on EPACT, se Abel, Amy. *Electricity Restructuring Background: The Public Utility Regulatory Policies Acts of 1978 and the Energy Policy Act of 1992.* CRS Report for Congress 98-419 ENR, May 4, 1998.

[10] The "regulatory bargain" refers to the typical situation where utilities are obligated to serve wholesale customers through contractual arrangements and obligated to serve retail customers through their

electric generating system. As a result, some utilities have costs that were prudently incurred under the current system that are uneconomic or "stranded" by the transition to a more competitive electric generation market. FERC Order 888 provides for utilities to recovery these wholesale stranded costs with those costs being paid by wholesale customers wishing to leave their current supply arrangements.

Order 889, the Open Access Same-time Information System (OASIS) rule, establishes standards of conduct to ensure a level playing field. The Rule requires utilities to separate their wholesale power marketing and transmission operation function, but does required corporate unbundling or divestiture of assets.

Retail competition (also called retail wheeling) refers to the ability of retail consumers to obtain their electric services from any one they choose. Currently, retail competition involves a competitive generation market, but a transmission and distribution system that is regulated so as to provide customers access to that competitively based generation on a reasonable and nondiscriminatory basis.[11] FERC Orders 888 and 889 represents FERC's attempt to achieve this competition on a wholesale level. However, FERC does not have jurisdiction over retail competition, as explicitly stated in EPACT. Currently, that is under the jurisdiction of the states. As of January 1999, 19 states have moved aggressively toward implementing retail wheeling; however, other states, such as Idaho, have decided not to move in this direction at this time. Forty-four states are currently conducting formal or informal procedures with respect to electric utility restructuring, illustrating that the issue is a dynamic one with momentum at the state level that is not dependent on congressional action. However, the diversity of responses coming from those differing processes may be an impetus for some to consider a uniform, national response to the issue.

BASIC POLICY QUESTIONS

The questions now are whether further legislative action is desirable to encourage competition in the electric utility sector and how a transition between a comprehensive regulatory regime to a more competitive electric utility sector could be made with the least amount of economic and service disruption.[12] Determining those segments of the electric system amendable to competitive forces and who should make those determinations is the crux of the restructuring debate. The task falls into five categories that are discussed below.

---

monopoly franchise rights. In return for providing service on demand, the regulatory authorities ensured financial integrity by permitting the utilities to recover prudently incurred costs plus a reasonable rate of return.

[11] Thus, retail wheeling involves the unbounding of electricity rates into three components: (1) a generation rate resulting from a consumer's choice of supplier, (2) a FERC approved transmission rate, and (3) a state public utility commission approved distribution rate. Like wholesale competition under FERC Order 888, retail competition would require the transmission entity or entities to wheel power from any supplier the retail consumer chooses at non-discriminatory rates.

[12] For a review of congressional electricity restructuring activities, see: Abel, Amy and Larry Parker. *Electricity: The Road Toward Restructuring.* CRS Issue Brief 96003, updated regularly.

Who should determine the boundaries and pace of restructuring efforts?[13]

The restructuring of the industry challenges the current state-federal division of regulatory responsibilities because of the magnitude of potential impacts and the dynamic nature of events. About 55% of total investor-owned electric utility plant assets are involved in generating electricity (the remainder supports transmission and distribution activities).[14] Any change in the manner in which those assets are valued would have a major effect on the rates that consumers would pay. Moving from a traditional embedded-cost valuation scheme to a market valuation would increase the value of some generating capacity and decrease the value of other generating capacity. Competition would tend to move the value of generating capacity to the marginal cost of constructing new capacity, generally represented at the current time by a new natural gas-fired, combined-cycle facility. In general, older facilities that have been fully depreciated would tend to have market values greater than their current book value under regulation; whereas, newer, capital intensive facilities (such as some nuclear plants) would have market values less than their current book value. Case-by-case valuation would be affected by location, availability of alternatives, and electricity demand. Thus, at least in the short-term, a specific locate could have higher or lower electric rates resulting from a more competitive system, if its current generating capacity is particularly expensive or inexpensive because of age, fuel source, or other cost-related variable.

Currently, 80% to 90% of generating assets are under state jurisdiction. Given the stakes involved, it is not surprising that state regulatory bodies believe they are the most qualified to oversee any transition to a more competitive generating sector. Transitional issues vary among states, and states believe that they should have the flexibility to resolve those issues within their own context. Indeed, some states have determined that the beset transition for them is no transition, while other states have moved aggressively to further restructuring.[15]

Proponents of comprehensive generating competition argue that maximum economic efficiency requires a national market and that a piecemeal approach is inefficient. For them, federal legislation is necessary to preempt the state role in regulation, if states are unwilling to move on their own. So the first decision point for restructuring is "Who is going to take the lead?" FERC's Order 888 uses an expansive interpretation of existing authority to justify its wholesale open access and stranded cost provisions.[16] With FERC prohibited by the *Energy Policy Act of*

---

[13] For a further flavor of the jurisdictional debate, see: Federal Energy Regulatory Commission. *Promoting Wholesale Competition Through Open Access Non-Discriminatory Transmission Services by Public Utilities; Recovery of Stranded Costs by Public Utilities and Transmitting Utilities.* 61 *Federal Register* 21619-21627 [Hereafter referred to as FERC Order 888]; Kemezis, Paul. "Who Controls the 'Last Inch'?" *Electric World,* January, 1996, pp. 25-28; Stagliano, Vito. "Electric Restructuring: Not by FERC alone," *Public Utilities Fortnightly,* October 15, 1995, pp. 30-33; Glazer, Craig A. "Jurisdictional Gridlock: A Pathway Out of Darkness," *Public Utilities Fortnightly,* January 1 1996, pp. 29-31; Hanger, John. "Four Olive Branches: What the FERC Bestowed on PUCs in Order 888," *Public Utilities Fortnightly,* October 1, 1996, pp. 38-41; and, Flippen, Edward L. "Radical Restructuring? Not for My State," *Public Utilities Fortnightly,* August 1996, pp. 11-12.

[14] Energy Information Administration. *Financial Statistics of Major U.S. Investor-Owned Electric Utilities: 1996.* Washington D.C.: U.S. Govt. Print. Off., 1997. DOE/EIA-0437(961)/1, p. 43.

[15] State level electric restructuring activities are tracked by several journals, including *LEAP Letter* (William A. Spratley & Associates, published bimonthly) and *Retail Wheeling & Restructuring Report* (Edison Electric Institute, published quarterly).

[16] Some argue that FERC has gone too far in its interpretation of the *Federal Power Act.* For example, see Craven, Donald B. and Shelley, Anthony F. "Mandatory Wheeling: Is FERC Overstepping its Bounds?"

1992 (EPACT) from ordering retail competition, new legislation would appear necessary for FERC to expand its role in retail issues. Arguably, to the extent that individual states continue to work out their own solutions to restructuring challenges, broad federal legislation arguably becomes either less draconian or less necessary.

The challenge is made more complex because the jurisdictional situation is not static. The "bright line" between federal and state responsibilities is becoming increasingly blurred by events. With increased competition, interstate transactions are expected to increase, potentially increasing the amount of electric transactions under the purview of FERC. On a more fundamental level, the basic concept of a contract path – the transmission lines that power is contracted to flow over – has always been a legal fiction, as electrons follow the path of least resistance and do not respect political boundaries.[17] With an increasingly dynamic market situation, it is not clear that regulatory jurisdictions can be based on the assumption that they do. Thus, the issue of who is going to control the transition is not a simple either-or; indeed, the "bright line" between the two may have to be completely re-evaluation and redrawn. Judging by state reactions to FERC's attempt to clarify the bright line in FERC Order 888, this could be a difficult and contentious task.[18]

How should "stranded costs" and other transitional issues be handled?"[19]

Changing the economic and regulatory conditions under which electricity has been priced and provided for the last 60 years raises several transitional issues. Perhaps the most contentious issue facing the policy community is the recovery of so-called "stranded costs." Stranded costs are defined by recovery proponents as those costs that were legitimately and prudently incurred under

---

Public Utilities Fortnightly, October 15, 1995, pp. 27-29. For FERC's legal justification, see FERC Order 888, 61 *Federal Register* 92, May 10, 1996. Pp. 21560-21570.

[17] For a further discussion of this phenomenon in the context of electricity restructuring, see Hogan, William. Electricity Transmission and Emerging Competition. Prepared for Public Utility Research Center Annual Conference entitled: "Market and Technological Convergence: Implications for Regulation." Published by John F. Kennedy School of Government, Harvard University, April 27, 1995.

[18] For example, see Glazer, Craig A. "Jurisdictional Gridlock: A Pathway Out of Darkness," *Public Utilities Fortnightly,* January 1, 1996, pp. 29-31; and, Stagliano, Vito, "Electric Restructuring: Not By FERC Alone," *Public Utilities Fortnightly,* October 1, 1996, pp. 38-41.

[19] There is a massive amount of literature on transitional costs, particularly stranded costs. For detailed discussions, see Federal Energy Regulatory Commission, Promoting Wholesale Competition Through Open Access Non-Discriminatory Transmission Services by Public Utilities; Recovery of Stranded Costs by Public Utilities and Transmitting Utilities. 61 *Federal Register* 92, Pay 10, 1996. Pp. 21628-21664. (Hereafter referred to as FERC Order 888); Congressional Budget Office, *Electric Utilities: Deregulation and Stranded Costs.* DBO Papers, October 1998; Hempling, Scott, Rose, Kenneth, and Burns, Robert E. *The Regulatory Treatment of Embedded Costs Exceeding Market Prices: Transition to a Competitive Electric Generation Market.* Unpublished Monograph, November 7, 1994; and Rose, Kenneth. *An Economic and Legal Perspective on Electric Utility Transition Costs.* Columbus: National Regulatory Research Institute, July 1996. For a more general discussion, see Stelzer, Irwin M. *Stranded Investment: Who Pays the Bill?* Washington, D.C.: American Enterprise Institute for Public Policy Research, March 30, 1994; (unattributed) "US Electric Utilities and Stranded Costs," *Energy Economist,* August 1996 pp. 16-23; Hill, Lawrence J., and Brown, Matthew H. "Strandable Commitments in the Electric Industry," Denver: National Conference of State Legislatures, December 1995; and, James T. Rhodes, et al., "Who Should Pay for 'Stranded Investments,' and Why?" *Public Utilities Fortnightly,* June 1, 1994, pp. 34-48.

the "old" regulatory regime that are not economically recoverable under the "new" competitive regime that the industry is entering. They view the utility as blameless, having made good faith investment decisions to construct generating capacity and to make other commitments the cost of which is now "stranded" by customers suddenly seeking to avoid the cost of that capacity by demanding that the utility wheel them lower cost power supplied by an outside competitor. In contrast, opponents of stranded cost recovery believe that such costs are not "stranded" by customers seeking a better deal on power rates, but rather represent poor foresight and business decisions on the part of some utilities for which customers should not be held responsible. The magnitude of stranded costs is disputed; FERC cities stranded cost estimates that range from "billions" to $200 billion.

FERC Order 888 agrees with the proponents of full stranded cost recovery, and requires that those costs be recovered directly from the customers whose decision to leave the utility system is stranding the costs; this calculation is based on a "revenues lost" formula. However, FERC Order 888 focuses on wholesale stranded costs and leaves retail stranded costs to state regulatory bodies (except for municipalization). Wholesale stranded costs may comprise only a few percent of the total amount.

Thus, unless federal legislation pre-empts current state authority, the primary regulatory body responsible for potential stranded cost recovery would be state regulatory commissions. The states have proposed or implemented alternatives for stranded cost recovery that range from full recovery paid for by all consumers (California) to recovery limited by regional electricity cost considerations (New Hampshire). In addition, states have proposed different bases for valuating stranded costs than FERC's "lost revenue" approach; for example, California defines stranded cost as the net book value of uneconomic generation resources.

Although much of the debate on stranded costs revolves around uneconomic generation plants, utilities have incurred other commitments or expenses in the delivery of service to customers. Utility balance sheets contain a variety of "regulatory assets," such as nuclear decommissioning assessments; "liabilities," such as PURPA section 210 contracts, and "social costs," such as low-income assistance programs.[20] The ability to recover costs for these categories of stranded costs are potentially endangered by the transition to a more competitive system, particularly if competition is extended to the retail level.

In addition, utilities are not the only participants in the restructuring effort that may face transition costs because of the revaluation of generating assets. Because of the guaranteed pass-through of taxes, regulated utilities made good tax collectors for state and local governments. Power plants can also represent a sizeable source of property taxes for some communities, taxes generally based on the plant's book value. In addition, some utilities have gross-receipts taxes. Competition would change the assumption of automatic pass-through in the case of the generating sector, a power plant's value, and a utility's gross receipts. State and local government will have to decide how to respond.

How should the market be structured to ensure a smooth operating electric system in its hybrid competitive-regulated form?

Fundamental to the new more competitive electricity system is the notion that electricity can be treated as a commodity that is transported to consumers, and not as a service provided

---

[20] Del Roccili, John A. "Stranded Cost Recovery Presents Stumbling Block to Open Access," *Electric Light & Power*, April 1996. Pp. 15, 18-20.

consumers through an integrated generation-transmission-distribution system.[21] This approach presumes that the product can be distinguished from the service network, even through the physics of the network intertwines the commodity and its delivery system into a fully integrated and indistinguishable whole.   In addition, this approach presumes it can deliver electricity more efficiently than the regulated "natural monopoly" that it would replace. In short, electricity would enter the world of markets and contracts and exit the world of integrated service and natural monopolies.

Treating electricity as a commodity has several difficulties, primarily resulting from the control requirements necessary to operate the system successfully. Electricity is difficult to store for any period of time, requiring precise supply-demand coordination; electricity is heavily depending on a network infrastructure that must be maintained within acceptable operating parameters to avoid overheating and sagging of lines (thermal limits), loss of voltage stability from inadequate supply of reactive power (voltage stability limits), and loss of system synchronization (power stability limits); electricity does not follow contracted paths, but flows through the path of least resistance, causing unintended loop flows; and, electricity is sent instantaneously to market.[22] These operational limitations are made more acute in a more dynamic market situation because the system's infrastructure is designed to maintain reliability on a local level, not to promote large scale transfers between different parties.

Thus, the need for system coordination tempers the desire for direct, bilateral competition in the electricity debate, resulting in the proposed segmented industry of competitive generation, but regulated, natural monopoly transmission and distribution. The question is what balance between competition and control the new market should embody. Under a hybrid system, the necessary control requirements to operate the system successfully fall to the transmission entity to maintain. Several proposals have been suggested for this entity, called by a variety of names, including "PoolCo," Independent System Operators (ISO), and "Transcos."[23] Some proposals focus on a mandatory spot market that all generators must sell to and all consumers buy from. Others focus on bilateral transactions between generators and consumers along with intermediaries, such as brokers. Transmission entities would also have the responsibility and authority to ensure reliability (involving services such as spinning reserves and coordinating transmission capacity expansions), and coordinating grid operation (to manage congestion and avoid system overloads). Such control under any proposal places a stress on insulating the "regulated" transmission entity

---

[21] Hunt, Sally, and Shuttleworth, Graham. "Unlocking the GRID," *IEEE Spectrum*, July 1996, pp. 20-25.

[22] See Fuldner, Arthur H. "Upgrading Transmission Capacity for Wholesale Electric Power Trade," *Electric Power Monthly*, June 1996, pp. xi-xxii; Douglas, John. "The Challenges of Open Access," *EPRI Journal*, September 1994, pp. 6-15; Stauffer, Hoff. "Less Discussed Issues that Matter of the Retail Wheeling Debate," Presentation to Energy Policy Forum, American Enterprise Institute, May 16-17, 1995; Hogan, William W. "Electricity Transmission and Emerging Competition," Presentation to Energy Policy Forum, American Enterprise Institute, May 16-17, 1995; and, (unattributed Special Report), "Competition, deregulation: Is the US Rushing into the Dark," *Electrical World*, October 1996. Pp. 17-29.

[23] See FERC Order 888, pp. 21579-21597; Stalon, Charles G. "To Pool or Not to Pool? Toward a New System of Governance," *Public Utilities Fortnightly*, March 1, 1996, pp. 16-20; Staffuer, Hoff. "Less Discussed Issues that Matter of the Retail Wheeling Debate," Presentation to Energy Policy Forum, American Enterprise Institute, May 16-17, 1995; Hogan, William W. "Electricity Transmission and Emerging Competition," Presentation to Energy Policy Forum, American Enterprise Institute, May 16-17, 1995; Barkovich, Barbara R., and Hawk, Dianne V. "Charting a New Course in California," *IEEE Spectrum*, July 1996, pp. 26-31; Falkenberg, Randall J. "PoolCo and Market Dominance." *Public*

from the "competitive" generators. Thus, the physical control issues that must be addressed by a hybrid system have implications for the industry structure issues that it must also address.

This need for coordination and reliability is complicated by the current system's somewhat informal means of addressing the issue. There are an estimated 30 voluntary utility groups designed to improve reliability, promote coordinated planning and development, and encourage economic dispatch. These groups range from informal pools based on simple cooperation to fully integrated tight power pools. These groups are supplemented by the North American Electric Reliability Council (NERC), an organization formed by the electric utility industry to help coordinate planning and assess system reliability. Whether this system is adequate for a new, more fragmented industry is unclear.

How should the electric utility industry be structured or restructured to encourage and safeguard a more competitive system?

In several ways, the existing regulatory structure is the outcome of a previously less regulated electric system's failure to maintain competitive forces against the threat of monopolistic practices, and to preserve financial solvency against the threat of unsound business practices. Arguably, the success of the current system for over 50 years is a testament to the *Federal Power Act* and the *Public Utility Holding Company Act* in structuring a system that regulators could effectively oversee. The current challenge is to maintain this success while transitioning to new industry structures.

Segmenting the industry into competitive and regulated components raises new issues with respect to industry structure and regulatory oversight. As identified above, substantial tension between the different functional components, which must coordinate their activities but not engage in anti-competitive practices, could exist under a segmented system. However, besides the issue of network control discussed above, this complex situation, involving unregulated, competitive generators and regulated transmitters and distributors, raises the question of what should be considered acceptable ownership patters between the different entities. FERC has determined that "functional unbundling" of wholesale generation and transmission services along with a code of conduct, is sufficient to protect non-discriminatory open access transmission.[24] Whether this arrangement would be sufficient under a more comprehensive retail competition scheme is arguable. More aggressive options to prevent market abuses through industry structure could include complete divestiture of generation or transmission/distribution assets or requiring separate corporate affiliates for each function.[25] The decisions depend on one's evaluation of the states' and federal government's ability to oversee financial transactions within each of the possible

---

Utilities Fortnightly, December 1995, pp. 26-29; Budhraja, Vikram S. A Competitive Electricity Market with POOLCO. Presentation to Hedging Electricity Pricing Risk, AIC Conference, April 27, 1995.

[24] FERC defines functional unbundling as involving a utility: (1) taking transmission services for all its sales and purchases under the same tariff of general applicability as do others; (2) stating separate rates for wholesale generation, transmission, and ancillary services; and (3) relying on the same information network that its transmission customers rely on to obtain information about its transmission system when buying or selling power. FERC rule also contains a "code of conduct" as a safeguard against market abuses. See FERC Order 888, p. 21552.

[25] For a review of how state public utility commissions have attempted to deal with potential abuse practices from affiliate transactions, see Harunuzzaman, Mohammad, and Costello, Kenneth. *State Commission Regulation of Self-Dealing Power Transactions*. Columbus: National Regulatory Research Institute, January 1996.

corporate structures that may evolve as the industry becomes more competitive. In one sense, unbundling raises the question of what kind of "PUHCA-like" legislation is necessary under the new system.

Using competition as the determinant of electric generating rates places a high premium on maintaining full and effective competition in that sector, and preventing anti-competitive interactions between it and the regulated segments. Thus a reappraisal of antitrust provisions and their implementation may also be appropriate in determining acceptable industry structures.[26] In particular, as noted by FERC: "The most likely route to market power in today's electric utility industry lies through ownership or control of transmission facilities."[27] Thus, part of the review of industry structure policy may involve a re-evaluation of merger and acquisition policy as embodied in PUHCA and FERC policy.[28]

Developing legislation to guide corporate structure raises the question of what to do with the old legislation – PUHCA. If new legislation adequately dealt with possible market abuses arising from corporate structures under the new segmented system, the existing PUHCA could arguably be eliminated with respect to electric utilities.[29] If a less aggressive approach is chosen, then decisions must be made on how much of the current PUHCA is appropriate to a more competitive environment, and whether conditions should be placed on its repeal.[30]

Likewise, a more competitive environment raises questions about the need for PURPA, particularly the mandatory purchase requirement (section 210). If the generation sector is structured competitively, any guaranteed access to generation markets must be questioned as to whether the benefits it provides outweigh the resulting distortion in the competitive market. Section 210 provides such access and thus raises the question whether it is needed any longer or under what conditions it might be modified or repealed.

The current structure of the electric industry includes investor-owned, customer-owned (co-ops), and publicly owned entities generating, transmitting, and distributing electricity. Among other things, the customer-owned and publicly owned entities receive preference to low-cost federal hydropower through the Power Marketing Administrations (PMAs). In addition, FERC has only limited authority over non-jurisdictional utilities such as municipal power authorities or PMAs. A new, more competitive market structure raises the question as to how much buyers of power should be on the same footing. In particular, increased competition in the generation section brings into focus public power's federal hydropower preference. Arguably, if the generation market is competitive, low-cost federal hydropower should not be reserved for publicly and customer-owned entities (all else being equal). Instead, like any other electric generator, the federal government should simply sell its power to the higher bidder regardless of that entity's ownership structure. Indeed, some public power entities might gain more from being able to competitively bid for their power supplies than to maintain their federal hydropower preference

---

[26] For a general discussion of anti-trust concerns, see Meeks, James E. *Antitrust Concerns in the Modern Public Utility Environment.* Columbus: The National Regulatory Research Institute, April 1996.

[27] FERC Order 888, p. 21546.

[28] For some considerations with respect to competition and merger policy, see Moot, John S. "A New FERC Policy for Electric Utility Mergers?" 17 *Energy Law Journal*, pp. 139-161; Michaels, Robert J. "Mergers and Market Power: Should Antitrust Rule?" *Public Utilities Fortnightly*, October 15, 1996. Pp. 42-44; and, Legato, Carmen, D. "Electric Mergers: Transmission Pricing, Market, Size, and Effects on Competition," *Public Utilities Fortnightly*, June 1, 1996 pp. 23-28.

[29] See Hogan, Joris M., and Howard, Rodrigo J. "Why Now, More than Ever, PUHCA Should be Repealed," *Electrical World*, May, 1996 pp. 55-57.

[30] Hawes, Douglas W. "Whither PUHCA: Repeal or Re-Deal?" *Public Utilities Fortnightly*, July 15, 1995 pp. 34-38.

and current supply arrangements.[31] Any attempt to address the federal hydropower preference issue is likely to be very contentious.[32]

How should non-economic regulatory factors be integrated into the envisioned hybrid system?[33]

Over the past 25 years, electric utilities have acquired a number of important non-economic tasks, including environmental controls and programs, consumer-oriented programs (demand-side management, conservation incentives), and encouraging alternative sources of energy.[34]   In addition, there are social welfare aspects of electric supply that are unavoidable when dealing with a service that affect people's livelihoods, such as uncollectible expenses from customers who are unable or unwilling to pay their bills.[35] The status and future of these activities would have to be reassessed under a more competitive system. Several alternatives exist to address these tasks, depending on the specific function.[36] For some functions, such as demand-side management, the still-regulated transmission or distribution entity could be required to take the lead, with possible financial assistance from local or state governments. Another possibility would be to develop new programs that work with the new competitive markets to provide appropriate incentives for the desired result. For example, in order to encourage renewable energy generation, several bills introduced in the 105th Congress provided for a set-aside program with tradable credits to ensure that a small percentage of U.S. generation came from such sources.[37] Finally, a review could indicate that a particular function should be redefined as a government function (such as

---

[31] The percentage of a public policy entity's generation supply that it receives via the PMA varies greatly, from a few percent to virtually all. A competitive generation market may permit a entity with a small percent of federal hydropower to save more by obtaining its supplemental supplies at lower competitive prices than it would lose from the increased price of its federal hydropower. The situation is likely to be case-specific. Obviously, the best of both worlds for public power would be to maintain the preference clause and competitively obtain its necessary supplemental supplies (including the possibility of reselling federal hydropower to the highest bidder).

[32] For a broader discussion in the context of attempts to sell the PMAs, see Parker, Larry. *Power Marketing Administrations: A Time for Change?* CRS Report for Congress 95-356 ENR, March 7, 1995.

[33] For a further discussion, see Brown, Matthew H., and Hill, Lawrence J. "Competing Utilities and Energy Efficiency, Renewable Energy and Low-Income Customers," Denver: National Conference of State Legislators, December 1995; and, Hirst, Eric, and Tonn, Bruce. "Social Goals and Electric-Utility Deregulation," *Issues in Science and Technology,* Spring, 1996 pp. 43-47.

[34] Hirst, Eric, and Tonn, Bruce. "Social Goals and Electric-Utility Deregulation. Issues in Science and Technology, Spring 1996 pp. 43-47.

[35] Kretschmer, Ruth K. "Electric Restructuring: Asking the Right Questions," Public Utilities fortnightly, February 15, 1996 pp. 12-14; and, Brown, Matthew H., and Hill, Lawrence J. "Competing Utilities and Energy Efficiency, Renewable Energy and Low-Income Customers," Denver: National Conference of State Legislators, December 1995.

[36] For other alternatives see: Brown, Matthew H., and Hill, Lawrence J. "Competing Utilities and Energy Efficiency, Renewable Energy and Low-Income Customers," Denver: National Conference of State Legislators, December 1995.

[37] These included S. 1401, H.R. 655, H.R. 1960, and S. 2287. For a side-by-side comparison of six comprehensive restructuring bills introduced in the 105h Congress, see Parker, Larry. *Electricity Restructuring: Comparison of S. 1401, H.R. 655, H.SR. 1230, S. 772, H.R. 1960, and S. 2287.* CRS Report for Congress 97-504 ENR, July 16, 1998.

uncollectible expenses) or eliminated as unnecessary. Some would put section 210 of PURPA in the latter category.

In addition to affecting the above social goals, deregulation is creating new social concerns as its direct impacts on other values, such as clean air, are evaluated. As noted previously, a competitive market would introduce new consideration in power plant operations. That older, fully depreciated power plants, could be more fully utilized under a more competitive generating sector would affect emissions of certain air pollutants. In general, the Clean Air Act imposes its most stringent pollution controls on new power plant construction, permitting existing capacity to meet less stringent and less costly standards. This decision may give some older facilities a competitive operating cost advantage to compliment its low, depreciated, cost basis. It also draws into further question an implied assumption of the Clean Air Act that existing capacity would be retired after a fixed number of years (usually 30 years) and replaced with new, less polluting, equipment. However, this is not definite, because the economic and environmental advantages of new technology, such as natural-gas-fired, combined-cycle technology (a very clean technology may be sufficient in some cases to overcome the existing plant's advantages identified above.

Analysis suggesting that emissions of nitrogen oxides (NOx), a precursor to ozone formation, could increase under FERC Order 888 resulted in substantial controversy and to proposed legislation that would prevent implementation of the Order until the environmental problem was addressed.[38] The controversy is likely to become more contentious as the debate expands into the area of retail competition, and whether the issue should be addressed in the context of electricity restructuring or in the context of Clean Air Act reauthorization.[39]

FINAL OBSERVATIONS

Over its 100-plus-year history, the electric utility industry has evolved as technology, economics, and regulatory policies have converged to force a re-examination of the industry. These forces are at work again, creating a dynamism that is changing the way in which the industry is structured and operated. The re-examination is already underway. At the federal level, the passage of EPACT and the promulgation of FERC Order 888 are moving to open up the wholesale generation sector to market forces. At the state level, most sates are reviewing their electricity policies, with each state determining for itself the most appropriate response for its utilities and their ratepayers.

At the federal level, this phenomenon raises two fundamental issues. First, who will determine the pace and boundaries of any response to these forces? Electric service is a vital component of a modern economy; national interests are at stake in what direction restructuring

---

[38] For the case for remediation, see: Alliance for Affordable Energy, et al., Joint Comment on Draft Environmental Impact Statement. Comment on Docket Nos. RM95-8-000 and RM94-7-001 before the Federal Energy Regulatory Commission. Submitted February 1, 1996; and, Environmental Protection Agency. Comments on Draft Environmental Impact Statement. Comment on Docket Nos. RM95-8-00 and RM94-7-001 before the Federal Energy Regulatory Commission. Submitted February 21, 1996. For FERC's response to calls for remediation, see Federal Energy Regulatory Commission. Promoting Wholesale Competition Through Open Access Non-Discriminatory Transmission Services by Public Utilities (RM95-8-000) and recovery of Stranded Costs by Public Utilities and Transmitting Utilities (RM94-8-001): Final Environmental Impact Statement. Washington D.C.: FERC/EIS-0096, April, 1996.

[39] For a further discussion, see: Parker, Larry and John Blodgett. *Electricity Restructuring: The Implications for Air Quality*. CRS Report for Congress 98-615 ENR, July 10, 1998.

takes. Concerns about economic efficiency and the treatment of various participants (such as electric utilities) may suggest to some that the federal government provide direction to current state initiatives. In contrast, others argue that states, who have traditionally had responsibility over retail electricity issues, have more of the expertise and experience necessary to handle the situation, and that the national interest in electricity supply is neither threatened by state initiatives nor a justification for federal pre-exemption of states' rights. Congress may wish to consider whether the time is ripe for federal intervention in the continuing evolution of the electric utility industry or whether a "wait and see" attitude toward state proceeding is more appropriate at this point.

Second, are there any national values threatened by the restructuring, that Congress may want to address? Restructuring the electric utility industry may affect environmental efforts, research and development and other energy-related programs, and the quality of life for lower-income individuals. Electricity is more than a commodity, it is a necessity of modern life. The system of environmental, energy, and low income assistance programs are premised on electric utilities providing a service, not just a commodity. Regardless of whether the federal government decides to take a leading role in the restructuring efforts, it may have to examine many of its programs to determine their appropriateness under a more competitive system and decide whether those programs or the structure of the new electric system and decide whether those programs or the structure of the new electric system needs to be altered to accomplish stated goals. As a corollary to this decision, Congress may wish to consider whether these examinations should occur as part of the restructuring debate, or in the legislative context in which those concerns arise (e.g., Clean Air Act, Low-Income Home Energy Assistance program (LIHEAP), etc.).

ELECTRICITY: THE ROAD TOWARD RESTRUCTURING

Amy Abel and Larry Parker

SUMMARY

The Public Utility Holding Company Act of 1935 (PUHCA) and the Federal Power Act (FPA) were enacted to eliminate unfair practices and other abuses by electricity and gas holding companies by requiring federal control and regulation of interstate public utility holding companies. Prior to PUHCA, electricity holding companies were characterized as having excessive consumer rates, high debt-to-equity ratios, and unreliable service. PUHCA remained virtually unchanged for 50 years until enactment of the Public Utility Regulatory Policies Act of 1978 (PURPA, P.L. 95-617). PURPA was, in part, intended to augment electric utility generation with more efficiently produced electricity and to provide equitable rates to electric consumers. Utilities are required to buy all power produced by qualifying facilities (QFs) at avoided cost (the amount it would cost the utility to produce that same amount of electricity; rates are set by state public utility commissions or through a bidding process). QFs are exempt from regulation under PUHCA and the FPA.

Electricity regulation was changed again in 1992 with the passage of the Energy Policy Act (EPACT, P.L. 102-486). The intent of Title 7 of EPACT is to increase competition in the electric generating sector by creating new entities, called "exempt wholesale generators" (EWGs) that can generate and sell electricity at wholesale without being regulated as utilities under PUHCA. This title also provides EWGs with a way to assure transmission of their wholesale power to its purchaser. The effect of this Act on the electric supply system is potentially more far-reaching than PURPA.

On April 24, 19996, the Federal Energy Regulatory Commission (FERC) issued two final rules on transmission access (Orders 888 and 889). FERC believed these rules would remedy undue discrimination in transmission services in interstate commerce and provide an orderly and fair transition to competitive bulk power markets.

In addition to stand-alone PURPA reform bills, comprehensive legislation to reduce electricity regulation has been introduced in the 106th Congress. Comprehensive legislation involves three issues. The first is PUHCA reform. Some electric utilities want PUHCA changed so they can more easily diversify their assets. State regulators have expressed concerns that increased diversification could lead to abuses including cross-subsidization. Consumer groups have expressed concern that a repeal of PUHCA could exacerbate market power abuses in a monopolistic industry where true competition does not yet exist.

The second is PURPA's mandatory purchase requirement provisions. Many investor-owned utilities support repeal of these provisions. They argue that their state regulators' "misguided" implementation of PURPA has forced them to pay contractually high prices for power that they do not need. Opponents of this legislation argue that it will decrease competition and impede development of renewable energy.

The third is retail wheeling. It involves allowing retail customers to choose their electric generation from any source they want and having their local utility deliver it to them. Currently, this is under state jurisdiction, and 25 states have moved toward retail wheeling. However, some have argued that the federal government should act as a backstop to ensure that all states introduce retail wheeling, pre-empting state authority if necessary.

BACKGROUND AND ANALYSIS

Historically, electricity service has been defined as a natural monopoly, meaning that the industry has (1) an inherent tendency toward declining long-term costs, (2) high threshold investment, and (3) technological conditions that limit the number of potential entrants. In addition, many regulators have considered unified control of generation, transmission, and distribution as the most efficient means of providing service. As a result, most people (about 75%) are currently served by a vertically integrated, investor-owned utility.

As the electric utility industry has evolved, however, there has been a growing belief that the historic classification of electric utilities as natural monopolies has been overtaken by events and that market focus can and should replace some of the traditional economic regulatory structure. For example, the existence of utilities that do not own all of their generating facilities, primarily cooperatives and publicly owned utilities, has provided evidence that vertical integration has not been necessary for providing efficient electric service. Moreover, recent changes in electric utility regulation and improved technologies have allowed additional generating capacity to be provided by independent firms rather than utilities.

The Public Utility Holding Company Act (PUHCA) and the Federal Power Act (FPA) of 1935 (Title I and Title II of the Public Utility Act) established a regime of regulating electric utilities that gave specific and separate powers to the states and the federal government. A regulatory bargain was made between the government and utilities. In exchange for an exclusive franchise service territory, utilities must provide electricity to all users as reasonable, regulated rates. State regulatory commissions address intrastate utility activities, including wholesale and retail rate-making. State authority currently tends to be as broad and as varied as the states are diverse. At the least, a state public utility commission will have authority over retail rates, and often over investment and debt. At the other end of the spectrum, the state regulatory body will oversee many facets of utility operation. Despite this diversity, the essential mission of the state regulator is the establishment of retail electric prices. This is accomplished through an adversarial hearing process. The central issues in such cases are the total amount of money the utility will be permitted to collect and how the burden of the revenue requirement will be distributed among the various customer classes (residential, commercial, and industrial.)

Under the FPA, federal economic regulation addresses wholesale transactions and rates for electric power flowing in interstate commerce. Federal regulation followed state regulation and is premised on the need to fill the regulatory vacuum resulting from the constitutional inability of states to regulate interstate commerce. In this bifurcation of regulatory jurisdiction, federal regulation is limited and conceived to supplement state regulation. The Federal Energy Regulatory Commission (FERC) has the principal functions at the federal level for the economic regulation, interconnection and wheeling of wholesale electricity, and ensuring adequate and reliable service. In addition, to prevent a recurrence of the abusive practices of the 1920s (e.g., cross-subsidization, self-dealing, pyramiding, etc.), the Securities and Exchange Commission (SEC) regulates utilities' corporate structure and business ventures under PUHCA.

The electric utility industry has been in the process of transformation. During the past two decades, there has been a major change in direction concerning generation. First, improved technologies have reduced the cost of generating electricity as well as the size of generating facilities. Prior preference for large-scale – often nuclear or coal-fired – power plants has been supplanted by a preference for small-scale production facilities that can be brought online more quickly and cheaply, with fewer regulatory impediments. Second, this has lowered the entry barrier to electricity generation and permitted non-utility entities to build profitable facilities. Recent changes in electric utility regulation and improved technologies have allowed additional generating capacity to be provided by independent first rather than utilities.

The oil embargoes of the 1970s created concerns about the security of the nation's electricity supply and led to enactment of the Public Utility Regulatory Policies Act of 1978 (PURPA, P.L. 95-617). For the first time, utilities were required to purchase power from outside sources. PURPA was established in part to augment electric utility generation with more efficiently produced electricity and to provide equitable rates to electric consumers.

In addition to PURPA, the Fuel Use Act of 1978 (FUA, P.L. 95-620) helped qualifying facilities (QFs) become established. Under FUA, utilities were not permitted to use natural gas to fuel new generating technology. QFs, which are by definition not utilities, were able to take advantage of abundant natural gas as well as new generating technology, such as combined-cycle that uses hot gases from combustion turbines to generate additional power. These technologies lowered the financial threshold for entrance into the electricity generation business as well as shortened the lead time for constructing new plants. FUA was repealed in 1987, but by this time QFs and small power producers had gained a portion of the total electricity supply.

This influx of QF power challenged the cost-based rates that previously guided wholesale transactions. Before implementation of PURPA, FERC approved wholesale interstate electricity transactions based on the seller's costs to generate and transmit the power. As more non-utility generators entered the market in the 1980s, these cost-based rates were challenged. Since non-utility generators typically do not have enough market power to influence the rates they charge, FERC began approving certain wholesale transactions whose rates were a result of a competitive bidding process. These rates are called market-based rates.

This first incremental change to traditional electricity regulation started a movement toward a market-oriented approach to electricity supply. Following the enactment of PURPA, two basic issues stimulated calls for further reform: whether to encourage nonutility generation and whether to permit utilities to diversify into non-regulated activities.

The Energy Policy Act of 1992 (EPACT, P.L. 102-486) removed several regulatory barriers to entry into electricity generation to increase competition of electricity supply. Specifically, EPACT provides for the creation of new entities, called "exempt wholesale generators" (EWGs), that can generate and sell electricity at wholesale without being regulated as utilities under PUHCA. Under EPACT, these EWGs are also provided with a way to assure transmission of their wholesale power to a wholesale purchaser. However, EPACT does not permit FERC to mandate that utilities transmit EWG power to retail consumers (commonly called "retail wheeling" or "retail competition"), and activity that remains under the jurisdiction of state public utility commissions. PURPA began to shift more regulatory responsibilities to the federal government, and EPACT continued that shift away from the states by creating new options for utilities and regulators to meet electricity demand.

The question now is whether further federal legislative action is desirable to encourage competition in the electric utility sector and if so at what speed this change would occur. Currently, 25 states have moved toward retail wheeling (23 states and the District of Columbia have enacted restructuring legislation, and 1 state has issued a comprehensive regulatory). Issues discussed here include repeal or alteration of both PUHCA and PURPA, transmission access and FERC's Orders 888 and 889, stranded cots, environmental impact, and issues related to utility diversification.

Transmission Issues

In addition to creating a new type of wholesale electricity generator, Exempt Wholesale Generators (EWGs), the Energy Policy Act (EPACT) provides EWGs with a system to assure transmission of their wholesale power to its purchaser. However, EPACT did not solve all of the issues relating to transmission access. As a result of EPACT, on April 24, 1996, FERC issued Orders 888 and 889. In issuing its final rules, FERC concluded that these Orders will "remedy undue discrimination in transmission services interstate commerce and provide an orderly and fair transition to competitive bulk power markets." Under Order 888, the Open Access Rule, transmission line owners are required to offer both point-to-point and network transmission services under comparable terms and conditions that they provide for themselves. The Rule provides a single tariff providing minimum conditions for both network and point-to-point services and the non-price terms and conditions for providing these services and ancillary services. This Rule also allows for full recovery of so-called stranded costs with those costs being paid by wholesale customers wishing to leave their current supply arrangements. The rule encourages but does not require creation of Independent System Operators (ISOs) to coordinate intercompany transmission of electricity.

Order 889, the Open Access Same-time Information System (OASIS) rule, establishes standards of conduct to ensure a level playing field. The Rule requires utilities to separate their wholesale power marketing and transmission operation functions, but does not require corporate unbundling or divestiture of assets. Utilities are still allowed to own transmission, distribution and generation facilities but must maintain separate books and records.

FERC estimated that Orders 888 and 889 will result in an annual cost savings of $3.8 to $5.4 billion. FERC also expects other non-quantifiable benefits, including better use of existing institutions and assets; technical innovation; and less rate distortion.

On December 20, 1999, FERC issued Order 2000 that described the minimum characteristics and functions of regional transmission organizations (RTOs) [http://www.ferc.fed.us/news1/rules/pages/rulemake.htm]. In FERC's NOPR, four primary characteristics and eight functions are described as essential for Commission approval of an RTO. The required characteristics are: the RTO must be independent from market participants; it must serve a region of sufficient size to permit the RTO to perform effectively; an RTO will be responsible for operational control; and it will be responsible for maintaining the short-term reliability of the grid. The required functions of an RTO outlined in Order 2000 are: it must administer its own transmission tariff; it must ensure the development and operation of market mechanisms to manage congestion; it must address parallel flow issues both within and outside its region; it will serve as supplier of last resort for all ancillary services; it must administer an Open

Access Same-Time Information System; it must monitor markets to identify design flaws and market power and propose appropriate remedial actions; it must provide for interregional coordination; and an RTO must plan necessary transmission additions and upgrades.

Order 2000 does not require RTO participation, set out RTO boundaries, or mandate the acceptable RTO structure. RTOs will be able to file with FERC as an independent system operation (ISO), a for-profit transmission company (transco) or another type of entity that has not yet been proposed. Although RTO participation is voluntary under Order 2000, FERC built in guidelines and safeguards to ensure independent operation of the transmission grid. RTO's are required to conduct independent audits to ensure that owners do not exert undue influence over RTO operation.

FERC Order 2000 requires the existing ISOs to submit to FERC by January 1, 2001 a plan to describe whether their transmission organization meets the criteria established in the RTO rulemaking. Electric utilities not currently members of an ISO had to file plans with FERC by October 1, 2000. The order does not mandate RTO formation, but if an individual utility opts not to join an RTO, the utility is required to prove why it would be harmed by joining such an entity.

On May 14, 1999, the United States Court of Appeals for the Eighth Circuit ruled in a case between FERC and Northern States Power. The court held that the Commission over stepped its authority when it ordered Northern States Power Company to treat wholesale customers the same as it treats native load customers in making electricity curtailment decisions. This decision raises federal-state jurisdictional questions, particularly a state's right to guarantee system reliability.

Stranded Costs and Takings

With the introduction of competition, utilities have been concerned that construction costs that they incurred under their monopoly service territory agreements may not be recovered and will be "stranded" by consumers leaving their system for less expensive power elsewhere. The issue of stranded costs is one of the larger transitional issues facing the electric utility industry as it moves towards competition. Stranded costs are defined by recovery proponents as those costs that were legitimately and prudently incurred under the "old" regulatory regime that are not economically recoverable under the "new" competitive regime that is being entered. Alternatively, opponents characterize stranded costs as unrecoverable business investments that were known to the utilities. Examples of stranded costs include uneconomic nuclear power plant investments and above-market electricity supply contracts under PURPA. The magnitude of potential stranded costs is uncertain. FERC estimates total retail and wholesale stranded costs to be as high as $200 billion.

In terms of a retail customer's ability to attract competing electricity suppliers, a major determinant, at least in the short-term, will be the magnitude of a customer's demand for electricity. Assuming that direct contracts with outside generators were allowed under a further restructured supply system, larger electricity consumers, such as industrial activities, would be more able to make direct deals with outside generators than smaller entities, such as residential customers. This situation would split users, with some able to leave a utility system for an outside generator while others remain captive to the local utility. This split would magnify issues raised by the FERC Orders, particularly recovery of stranded costs. It has been estimated that 90% of potential stranded cost from electricity restructuring would come from retail, rather than wholesale, open access. This situation greatly raises the stakes for state public utility commissions in terms of who pays for such costs. In addition, retail wheeling may strand other investments, such as demand-side management, (e.g., energy conservation programs) commonly called "stranded benefits") that increase the complexity of state decision-making.

FERC Order 888 allows public utilities and transmitting utilities to fully recover stranded costs from those customers wishing to leave their current supply arrangements. "We [FERC] continue to believe that utilities that entered into contracts to make wholesale requirements sales under an entirely regulatory regime should have an opportunity to recover stranded costs that occur as a result of customers leaving the utilities' generation system..."

This "fairness" argument is countered by others who argue that ratepayers should not have to pay for the uneconomic decisions made by some utilities. In addition, they argue that stranded cost recovery would delay the benefits of a more competitive generating sector for many years and be a disincentive to the creation of that more competitive generation sector. According to them, the competitive market handwriting has been on the wall for many years, and utilities have simply chosen to ignore it. However, if any cost reconvey is determined to be justified under specific circumstances, opponents of stranded cost recovery argue that the regulatory body should not allow 100% reconvey, but rather require some sharing of the burden with the stockholders of the individual utilities.

PURPA Contracts. Two major sources of stranded costs are: §210 PURPA contracts and investment in power generating facilities. Under §210, PURPA utilities are required to purchase power from qualifying power production facilities and qualifying cogeneration facilities at a price set by state public utility commissions. Following the enactment of PURPA, contracts were formed between the utilities and independent power producers (IPPs) pursuant to §210. These contracts require generally that the utilities pay the IPPs for the costs the utilities would have incurred had they generated the energy themselves. These costs are defined as "avoided costs." The amounts to be paid to the IPPs are fixed for the length of the contracts. Although the cost of generating power has decreased, the contracts require the utilities to pay above-market prices to the IPPs. In a restructured environment that promotes lower market prices, the utilities could be subject to even greater losses.

Restructuring legislation that eliminated prospective mandatory purchase obligations, maintained existing contracts between the utilities and IPPs. At the state level, utilities attempting to alter the terms of existing contracts have been unsuccessful in the courts. Congress' interest in maintaining existing contracts arguably does little to alter the settled expectations of the utilities and IPPs that executed contracts pursuant to §210.

Generating Facilities. The second situation giving rise to the issue of stranded costs involves the investments made by utilities in their power plants. Under current rate base regulation, a utility is entitled to recover the market cost of its investment by charging a price that is equal to the average cost of producing power. In a restructured environment, the market price available to the utility could be less than its average cost of producing power. If that occurred, a significant portion of the utility's investment could become stranded.

While it has been argued that states should have the authority to decide how retail stranded costs are to be recovered for the utilities in each state, others maintain that the interstate nature of the electric utility industry permits Congress to legislate broadly for the recovery of such costs. The limits of federal and state jurisdiction are further complicated by the states' role in implementing federal regulation of the utilities. For example, state regulatory authorities were given discretion to set rates and terms in the contracts that were formed pursuant to §210 of PURPA. Repeal or reform of PURPA would likely affect this authority.

Takings. The utilities' current investments in electric generating facilities are arguably based on a "regulatory bargain" in which utilities are obligated to serve wholesale customers through contractual arrangements and obligated to serve retail customers through their monopoly franchise rights. In return for providing service on demand, the regulatory authorities ensured financial integrity by permitting the utilities to recover prudently incurred costs plus a reasonable rate of return. This system has been upset by the emergence of competitive forces in the electric generating system prompting outside parties to build facilities that can generate electricity at lower cost than many utilities' embedded generating costs, competitive forces that national policy is nurturing and encouraging.

Prompted by the possibility that they will be unable to recover their stranded costs, the utilities have attempted to argue that a failure to compensate them would constitute a "taking" of their property. Under the Takings Clause of the Fifth Amendment, private property may not be taken for public use without just compensation. The utilities contend that a "regulatory compact" was executed between legislators and the utilities; that compact gave the utilities an exclusive customer base and any possible return on their investments is being taken.

The validity of a "regulatory compact" has been widely challenged. Many argue that the Takings Clause does not guarantee compensation in a restructured environment. Critics of this approach say that private entities do not have a constitutional right to profit from their investments. They view the failure to receive full compensation as an investment risk that was known to the utilities prior to their investment in the generating facilities. The utilities' argument so far has been unsuccessful in the courts.

Environmental Questions and Proposed Responses

The electric industry is a major source of air pollution as well as of greenhouse gases. Therefore, changes underway are being closely examined for their potential environmental effects. At issue is whether proposed legislation to restructure the industry should include environmental protections.

Future electricity demand and implementation for air quality regulations will determine air emissions impacts from electricity restructuring. Projected increases in electricity demand in the short- to mid-term suggest that restructuring may further encourage utilities to renovate a sizeable amount of existing coal-fired capacity, which generally produces more air pollutants and greenhouse gases than alternative types of generation. Renovating older coal-fired facilities is often very cost-effective compared with building new, less polluting plants, portending the potential for an increase in emissions of some air pollutants, especially nitrogen oxides, and of carbon dioxide, a greenhouse gas.

The Clean Air Act regulates emissions of conventional air pollutants from electric utilities. While it has historically focused on new construction in applying its most stringent standards, several current and prospective regulations would significantly increase controls on existing, coal-fired facilities. These controls may diminish the attractiveness of renovating older, more polluting facilities, but the effectiveness of the regulations in coping with a restructured industry remains to be seen. In addition, greenhouse gas emissions are not regulated, so any increases in carbon dioxide would not be controlled under existing authorities.

Thus, the environmental effects of restructuring depend on whether, for conventional air pollutants, the existing regulatory regimen will work effectively as the industry structure changes. For some pollutants, such as sulfur oxides, a nationwide emissions "cap" seems secure; but for others, particularly nitrogen oxides, the state-led implementation process may have difficulty coping with regional disparities in emissions. For carbon dioxide, any controls would be contingent on future ratification of the Kyoto Agreement to curtail emissions and on domestic legislation. Suggested options to mitigate possible air pollution impacts from electric utility restructuring include: (1) "cap and trade" programs to prevent increases in pollution levels; (2) "green price" to encourage consumes to choose less polluting sources of electricity; (3) renewable portfolio standards to require a percentage of electricity generated to come from renewable, non-polluting, sources.

Among the comprehensive electricity restructuring bills introduced, only the Administration's proposal (H.R. 1828/S. 1047/S. 1048) contains provision with respect to "cap and trade" programs. The Administration's bill authorizes EPA to establish regional "cap and trade" programs to implement nitrogen oxide (NOx) reduction programs. With respect to green pricing, the Administration's bill, H.R. 2944 and H.R. 2050 require electricity suppliers to inform consumers as to the energy source used for generating their electricity and its environmental characteristics. Finally, both the Administration's bill and H.R. 2050 have renewable portfolio standards, although they differ significantly.

Several stand-alone bills to reduce emissions from utility plants have been introduced in the 106th Congress. These bills focus on reducing emissions of at least sulfur dioxide and nitrogen oxide emissions from power plants, with some including carbon dioxide and mercury emissions as well.

Calls for Additional Electric Regulatory Reform

PUHCA

One argument for additional PUHCA reform has been made by electric utilities that want to further diversify their assets. Currently under PUHCA, a holding company can acquire securities or utility assets only if the SEC finds that such a purchase will improve the economic efficiency and service of an integrated public utility system. It has been argued that reform to allow diversification would improve the risk profile of electric utilities in much the same way as in other businesses: The risk of any one investment is diluted by the risk associate with all investments. Utilities have also argued that diversification would lead to better use of under-utilized resources (due to seasonal nature of electric demand). Utility holding companies that have been exempt from SEC regulation argue that PUHCA discourages diversification because the SEC could repeal exempt status if exemption would be "detrimental to the public interest."

State regulators have expressed concerns that increased diversification could lead to abuses, including cross-subsidization: a regulated company subsidizing an unregulated affiliate. Cross-subsidization was a major argument against the creation of EWGs and has reemerged as an argument against further PUHCA reform. In the case of electric and gas companies, non-utility ventures that are undertaken as a result of diversification may benefit from the regulated utilities' allowed rate of return. Moneymaking non-utility enterprises would contribute to the overall financial health of a holding company. However, unsuccessful ventures could harm the entire holding company, including utility subsidiaries. In this situation, utilities would not be penalized for failure in terms of reduced access to new capital, because they could increase retail rates.

Several consumer and environmental public interest groups, as well as state legislators, have expressed concerns about PUHCA repeal. PUHCA repeal, such groups argue, could only exacerbate market power abuses in which they see as a monopolistic industry where true competition does not yet exist. The national Rural Electric Cooperative Association also opposes stand-alone changes to PUHCA.

Several bills would repeal PUHCA and give FERC additional authority. Some bills give FERC jurisdiction over utility mergers, and these bills authorize FERC to remedy market power problems in wholesale markets.

PURPA

The comprehensive bills and several stand-alone bills would reform PURPA. All bills except H.R. 971 would prospectively repeal §210 of PURPA, the mandatory purchase requirement provisions. Proponents of such stand-alone bills – primarily investor-owned utilities (IOUs) located in the Northeast and in California – argue that their state regulators' "misguided" implementation of PURPA in the early 1980s has forced them to pay contractually high prices for power they do not need. They argue that, given the current environment for cost-conscious competition, PURPA is outdated. The PURPA Reform Group, which promotes IOU interests, strongly supports such bills by contending that the current law's mandatory purchase obligation was anti-competitive and anti-consumer.

Opponents of these types of bills (IPPs, industrial power customers, most segments of the natural gas industry, the renewable energy industry, and environmental groups) have many reasons to support PURPA as it stands. Mainly, their argument is that PURPA introduced competition in the electric generating sector and, at the same time, helped promote wider use of cleaner, alternative fuels to generate electricity. Since the electric generating sector is not yet fully competitive, they argue, repeal of PURPA would decrease competition and impede the development of the renewable energy industry. The Competitive Power Council, a group representing IPP interests, argues that PURPA repeal would create less competition and greater utility monopoly control over the electric industry. The Electric Generation and the National Independent Energy Producers also want comprehensive legislation to look at all aspects of electricity regulation. State regulators are concerned that this legislation would prevent them from deciding matters currently under their jurisdiction. The National Association of Regulatory Utility Commissioners has opposed legislation that would allow FERC to protect utilities from costs associated with PURPA contracts.

Comprehensive Reform Proposals: Retail Wheeling

Many analysts believe the next logical step in restructuring is retail competition. Encouraging competition in the electric supply system is already occurring as some states allow generating utilities to arrange for transmission of electricity from its sources to a retail consumer whether or not this transaction occurs within their service territory. EPACT expressly prevents FERC from ordering retail competition (retail wheeling). Such transactions remain under state regulatory control; FERC's open access Orders address wheeling at the wholesale level only. However, it is clear that FERC hopes that its Orders will pave the way for states to permit retail customers to shop for their electricity needs anywhere they want, rather than being limited to buying electricity from their local utility.

Indeed, we should determine the pace of boundaries of retail wheeling efforts is a fundamental issue. Electric service is a vital component of a modern economy; thus, national interests are at stake in what direction the restructuring debate takes. Concerns about economic efficiency and the treatment of various participants (such as electric utilities) may suggest to some that the federal government provide direction to current state initiatives. In contrast, others argue that the states, which have traditionally had responsibility over retail electricity issues, have the expertise and experience necessary to handle the situation (more so than the federal government) and that the national interest in electricity supply is neither threatened by state initiatives nor a justification for federal preemption of states' rights. Currently, retail choice is under state jurisdiction, and 25 states have moved toward retail wheeling (23 states and the District of

Columbia have enacted restructuring legislation, and 1 state has issued a comprehensive regulatory). Congress may consider whether expanding federal jurisdiction is warranted in the continuing evolution of the electric utility industry or whether a "wait and see" attitude toward state proceedings is more appropriate at this point.

Administration Proposal

On April 15, 1999, the Clinton Administration issued its Comprehensive Electricity Competition Plan. The plan, introduced by request as S. 1048, S. 1047, and H.R. 1828, addresses retail competition, consumer protection, transmission system reliability, promotion of public benefits, and clarification of federal and state authority. This plan is based on a bill submitted by the Administration in the 105th Congress (S. 2287).

The plan encourages, but does not require, states to implement retail choice by January 1, 2003. The "flexible mandate" would permit states to opt out of the competition mandate if they find through public proceedings that consumers in the state would be better served by an alternative policy such as state-crafted retail competition plan or the current monopoly system.

Under this proposal, electricity suppliers would be required to provide consumers uniform information on price, terms, and conditions of their electric product. In addition, the Federal Trade Commission would be authorized to establish and enforce requirements to prevent slamming and cramming. This proposal would also establish a Public Benefits Fund to support energy conservation and efficiency measures as well as affordable electricity service to low-income customers. Retail suppliers of electricity would be required to provide net metering service for all customers.

FERC would be given additional authority to order corporate divestiture of generation facilities to mitigate market power and to clear jurisdiction over mergers and consolidations of electric utility holding companies and generation-only companies.

The Administration plans to strengthen the transmission system by allowing FERC to require independent system operations (ISOs). The Federal Power Act would be amended to require FERC to approve and oversee an organization that establishes and enforces mandatory reliability standards. The Administration also propose to codify Order 888 and amend substantive requirements of PUHCA and PURPA.

Under the current proposal, as of January 1, 2003, the Tennessee Valley Authority (TVA) would be permitted to sell electricity at wholesale without restrictions. With significant restrictions, TVA would also be able to sell to retail consumers outside its current retail service territory. Other utilities would be able to sell wholesale and retail power in the TVA region beginning January 1, 2003. TVA would be able to recover stranded costs. FERC would be given jurisdiction over transmission rates for the Bonneville Power Administration (BPA), the Western Area Power Administration (WAPA) and the Southwestern Power Administration (SWPA). In addition, FERC would be given authority to require BPA, WAPA, and SWPA to turn over operational control of their transmission facilities to an independent regional system operator.

One of the most divisive issues for the Administration has been whether to include environmental provisions with market reforms. The proposal codifies EPA's authority to create a cap-and-trade program to reduce nitrogen oxide emissions (a precursor to smog), but does not address sulfur dioxide or mercury emissions or the goals of the Kyoto Global Climate Change Treaty. Another environmental provision mandates that renewable resources other than hydropower will account for at least 7.5% of each supplier's portfolio by the year 2010. A credit trading program is suggested as a means of reducing the costs of this provision.

The plan addresses a large public power issue by prohibiting public power companies from issuing tax-exempt bonds for new transmission and generation facilities. Municipalities would still be able to issue tax-exempt bonds for new electricity distribution facilities. Outstanding tax-exempt bonds for municipal utilities would be grandfathered.

LEGISLATION

H.R. 25 (Boehlert)
Requires nationwide reductions in nitrogen oxides and sulfur dioxide emissions from utility sources. Includes provisions to study and control emissions of mercury from utility and major industry sources. Introduced January 6, 1999; referred to Committee on Commerce.

H.R. 341 (Andrews)
Establishes a fund for environmental priorities to be funded by a portion of the consumer savings resulting from retail competition. Introduced January 19, 1999; referred to Committee on Commerce with subsequent referral to the Committee on Transportation.

H.R. 657 (Sweeney)
Requires nationwide reductions in NOx and SO2 emissions from utility sources. Includes provisions to study and control emissions of mercury from utility and major industry sources. Introduced February 9, 1999; referred to Committee on Commerce.

H.R. 667 (Burr)
Comprehensive electric utility restructuring legislation. Prospectively repeals Section 210 PURPA. Repeals PUHCA 12 months after date of enactment but maintains FERC and state public utility commission access to utility books and records. States that have provided for the recovery of stranded costs may not modify or repeal such provisions for seven years as a condition of receiving federal energy assistance. States may permit a transmitting utility to deny access to transmission and local distribution facilities to any utility attempting to wheel power from states that maintain exclusive franchise market areas. Introduced February 10, 1999; referred to Committee on Commerce.

H.R. 971 (Walsh)
Existing PURPA contracts could be amended by state regulatory authorities to reflect current incremental cost of the purchasing utility. States could require that future PURPA contracts reflected varying incremental costs of the purchasing utility. Introduced March 3, 1999; referred to Committee on Commerce.

H.R. 1138 (Stearns)
Prospective repeal of §210 of PURPA. Contracts in effect on January 6, 1999, would not be affected. Stranded costs associated with PURPA contracts can be recovered. Introduced March 16, 1999; referred to Committee on Commerce.

H.R. 1486 (Franks)
Requires that rules are promulgated within 2 years enactment that would allow the Federal Power Marketing Administrations and the Tennessee Valley Authority to sell electricity at market

prices. Introduced April 20, 1999; referred to Committees on Resources, Transportation and Infrastructure, and Commerce.

H.R. 1587 (Stearns)

Comprehensive electric utility restructuring legislation. Introduced April 27, 1999; referred to Committees on Commerce, Resources, and Transportation and Resources.

H.R. 1828 (Bliley, by request)

Administration's comprehensive electricity restructuring legislation. Introduced May 17, 1999; referred to Committees on Commerce, Resources, Agriculture, Transportation and Infrastructure, and the Judiciary. Commerce Committee hearing held June 17, 1999.

H.R. 2363 (Tauten)

Repeals the Public Utility Holding Company Act of 1935 and replaces it with limited state and FERC access to utility records. Introduced June 25, 1999; referred to Committee on Commerce. Subcommittee on Energy and Power hearing held on July 22, 1999.

H.R. 2050 (Largent)

Comprehensive electricity restructuring legislation. Introduced June 8, 1999; referred to Committees on Commerce, Ways and Means, Transportation and Infrastructure, and Resources.

H.R. 2569 (Pollen)

Provides for a comprehensive system of performance standards and emissions caps to control emissions of NOx, SO_2 CO_2, and Hg from generating facilities. Other provisions encourage renewable energy and efficiency programs and repeal Section 210 of PURPA. Introduced July 20, 1999; referred to Committee on Commerce.

H.R. 2602 (Wynn)

Amends the Federal Power Act with respect to electric reliability and oversight. Introduced July 22, 1999; referred to Committee on Commerce.

H.R. 2645 (Kucinich)

Allows retail choice. Includes provisions on consumer protection and environmental protection. Introduced July 29, 1999; referred to Committee on Commerce.

H.R. 2734 (Brown, S.)

Allows local government entities to serve as non-profit aggregators of electricity services. Introduced August 5, 1999; referred to Committee on Commerce.

H.R. 2786 (Sawyer)

Repeals Section 203 of the FPA. FERC is given authority over membership in voluntary RTOs. Introduced August 5, 1999; referred to Committee on Commerce.

H.R. 2900 (Waxman)

Requires reductions in nitrogen oxides, sulfur dioxide, carbon dioxide, and mercury emissions. Introduced September 21, 1999; referred to Committee on Commerce.

H.R. 2944 (Barton)
A comprehensive electricity restructuring bill. Introduced September 24, 1999; referred to Committee on Commerce, and in addition to the Committees on Transportation and Infrastructure, Resources, and Ways and Means. The House Commerce Committee, Subcommittee on Energy and Power held a markup session on October 27, 1999. See, [http://www.house.gov/garton/discussindraftpage1.html] for a summary. On October 28, 1999, H.R. 2944 was forwarded by subcommittee to full committee (amended).

H.R. 2947 (Inslee)
Allows the use of net metering by distributed power. Introduced September 24, 1999; referred to the Commerce Committee, Subcommittee on Energy and Power.

H.R. 2980 (Allen)
Clean Power Plant Act of 1999. Amends the Clean Air Act to Require reduction in emissions of sulfur dioxide, nitrogen oxides, mercury, carbon dioxide, and hazardous air pollutants from electric power plants and to provide assistance for workers and communities adversely affected by reduced consumption of coal. Introduced September 30, 1999; referred to Committees on Commerce, Education and the Workforce, Transportation and Infrastructure, Banking and Financial Services, and Science.

H.R. 4861 (Lazzio/Boehlert)
Requires nationwide reductions in nitrogen oxides, carbon dioxide and sulfur dioxide emissions from utility sources. Includes an emissions cap of mercury. Includes a renewable portfolio standard and net metering provisions. Introduced July 13, 2000; referred to the Commerce Committee, Subcommittee on Energy and Power.

H.R. 4941 (Wynn)
Establishes a reliability organization and standards for transmission of bulk power. Introduced July 24, 2000; referred to the Commerce Committee.

S. 161 (Moynihan)
Requires that the Federal Power Marketing Administrations and the Tennessee Valley Authority sell electricity at market prices within 2 years of enactment. Introduced January 19, 1999; referred to Committee on Energy and Natural Resources.

S. 172 (Moynihan)
Requires nationwide reductions in nitrogen oxides and sulfur dioxide emissions from utility sources. Includes provisions to study and control emissions of mercury from utility and major industry sources. Introduced January 19, 1999; referred to Committee on Environmental and Public Works.

S. 282 (Mack)
Prospectively repeals Section 210 of PURPA. Stranded costs associated with PURPA contracts would be fully recoverable. Introduced January 21, 1999; referred to Committee on Energy and Natural Resources.

S.313 (Shelby)

Repeals the Public Utility Holding Company Act of 1935. States and the Federal Energy Regulatory Commission maintain limited access to specific utility books and records. Introduced January 27, 1999; referred to Committee on Banking, Housing, and Urban Affairs. Reported to Senate without amendment March 2, 1999 (S.Rept. 106-7).

S. 516 (Thomas)

Comprehensive electric utility restructuring legislation. Prospectively repeals Section 210 PURPA. Repeals PUHCA 18 months after date of enactment but maintains FERC and state public utility commission access to utility books and records. States may choose to impose charges for stranded cost recovery. Provides for a FERC-sanctioned Electric Reliability Organization. States may assess charges to fund public benefit programs. Introduced March 3, 1999; referred to Committee and Energy and Natural Resources.

S. 673 (Leahy)

Proposes a comprehensive control program to reduce mercury emissions from utility plants and other sources. Introduced March 19, 1999; referred to Committee on Environment and Public Works.

S. 1047 (Murkowski, by request)

Administration's comprehensive electricity restructuring proposal. Includes all administration provisions except the tax provisions (see S. 1048). Introduced May 13, 1999; referred to Committee on Energy and Natural Resources.

S. 1048 (Murkowski, by request)

Tax provisions of the Administration's comprehensive electricity restructuring proposal (see, S. 1047). Introduced May 13, 1999; referred to Committee on Finance.

S. 1273 (Bingaman)

Amends §210 of PURPA, amends Federal Power Act to facilitate a transition to more competitive electric power markets. Introduced June 24, 1999; referred to Committee on Energy and Natural Resources.

S. 1284 (Nickles)

Repeals PUHCA, prospective repeal of §210 of PURPA, amends Federal Power Act so that no state can discriminate against any consumer who seeks to purchase electric energy in interstate commerce from any supplier. Introduced June 24, 1999; referred to Committee on Energy and Natural Resources.

S. 1369 (Jeffords)

Provides for a comprehensive system of performance standards and emissions caps to control emissions of nitrogen oxides, sulfur dioxide, carbon dioxide, and mercury from generating facilities. Other provisions encourage renewable energy and efficiency programs and repeal Section 210 of PURPA. Introduced July 14, 1999; referred to Committee on Energy and Natural Resources.

S. 1949 (Leahy)

Establishes a comprehensive system of performance standards emissions caps from mercury, carbon dioxide, nitrogen oxides, and sulfur dioxide. Promotes use of clean coal technologies, fuel cells, and renewable energy sources. Introduced November 17, 1999; referred to Committee on Finance.

S. 2071 (Gordon)

Establishes a reliability organization and standards for transmission of bulk power. Introduced February 10, 2000; referred to Committee on Energy and Natural Resources. On June 21, 2000, S. 2071 was substituted for the language of S. 2098 and reported out of Committee. On June 20, 2000, passed Senate with an amended by Unanimous Consent (consideration: CR S6293-6295; text: CR 7/10/2000 S6352-6356).

S. 2098 (Murkowski)

Introduced as comprehensive electric restructuring legislation that would encourage utilities to form regional transmission organizations (RTO) and allow utilities to have active ownership in the RTO. As introduced, it would create an Electric Reliability Organization. It would give the federal government eminent domain rights to cite new transmission lines. It would prospectively repeal of Section 210 of PURPA and repeal PUHCA one year after books and records. Introduced February 24, 2000; referred to Committee on Energy and Natural Resources. Amended on June 21, 2000 and reported out of Committee by substituting the language of S. 2071, stand-alone reliability legislation.

S. 2886 (Gramm/Schumer)

Comprehensive electric restructuring legislation. Requires each state to implement retail competition by January 1, 2002, enforceable by appeal to federal court. FERC is authorized to establish and enforce reliability standards implemented by regional transmission organizations. Prospective repeal of PURPA. PUHCA is repealed and replaced by enhanced federal and state access to company records. Introduced July 18, 2000.

ELECTRICITY RESTRUCTURING: THE IMPLICATIONS FOR AIR QUALITY

Larry Parker and John Blodgett

INTRODUCTION

Electricity generation is a major source of air pollution as well as of greenhouse gases. As a result, changes in the electric utility industry raise concern about environmental consequences. Such changes are currently in the offing, both from new generating and transmission technologies and from shifting policy perspectives with respect to competition and regulation. Whether legislation to restructure the industry should include environmental protections has become an issue. Several bills were introduced in the 106th Congress to incorporate such protections into any potential federal restructuring legislation.[1] More legislative proposals are expected to be introduced in the 107th Congress.

This paper reviews the changes now underway in the utility industry from the perspective of their environmental implications – specifically, the potential for electric utility restructuring to increase emissions of air pollutants regulated by the Clean Air Act (CAA) and of greenhouse gases that could be affected by the Kyoto agreement to address climate change.[2] The paper is divided into six parts.

- The *Overview* provides background on the electric utility industry and current restructuring efforts, the industry's emissions, and the fundamental argument with respect to current restructuring activities and potential air pollutant effects. It identifies electricity demand and air quality regulation as critical to determining air emission impacts from electricity restructuring.

---

[1] For a current review of legislation, see Larry Parker and Amy Abel, *Electricity: The Road Toward Restructuring,* Issue Brief IB10006, updated regularly. For a comparison of initiatives introduced in the 106th Congress, see: Larry Parker, *Electricity Restructuring and Air Quality: Comparison of Proposed Legislation,* CRS Report RS20326, updated July 26, 2000.

[2] For current information on the status of the Kyoto agreement and related legislation, see Wayne A. Morrissey and John R. Justus, *Global Climate Change,* Issue Brief IB89005.

- *The Utility Industry* examines the electricity demand component in more detail. Estimating electricity demand increases in the short- to mid-term and discussing the implications of transmission capacity for interregional electricity transfers, the analysis suggests that restructuring may encourage current trends among utilities to renovate a sizeable amount of existing coal-fired electricity, which generally produces more air pollution and greenhouse gases than alternative kinds of electricity generation.
- *Environmental Regulation* provides background on current air pollution regulations affecting electric utilities and on the resulting complex system of federal and state, pollutant-by-pollutant controls. It discusses regulatory implications for existing capacity and new construction, noting that while the CAA has historically focused on new construction in applying its most stringent standards, several current and prospective regulations would significantly increase controls on existing, coal-fired facilities. It also notes that an increasingly competitive generating market may present significant challenges to the state-directed environmental regimen of the CAA.
- *The Effects of Restructuring and Environmental Actions on Emissions* analyzes the cost-effectiveness of existing coal-fired facilities versus new construction and the environmental effects of increased utilization of existing coal-fired facilities. The analysis indicates that renovating existing coal-fired facilities is generally very cost-effective compared with new, less polluting construction, pointing to a potential for increasing emissions of some air pollutants, especially nitrogen oxides, depending on regulatory actions, and of the greenhouse gas carbon dioxide, which is not regulated.
- *Assessing the Impacts of Restructuring* examines the Federal Energy Regulatory Commission's attempt to estimate the environmental impacts of introducing competition into the wholesale electricity market, and reactions to that analysis. It notes the considerable difficulties in attempting to isolate the potential impact on emissions of restructuring the electricity generation from other technological and policy trends occurring in the industry.
- The *Conclusion* reviews possible responses to potential risks to the environment arising from electricity restructuring. Critical issues are: (1) For conventional air pollutants, whether the existing regulatory regimen will work effectively as the industry structure changes; for some pollutants, such as sulfur oxides, a nationwide emissions "cap" seems secure, but for others, particularly nitrogen oxides, the state-led implementation process may find it difficult to cope with increasingly regional utility industry and environmental challenges. And (2) for greenhouse gases, any controls are contingent on future ratification of the Kyoto Agreement to curtail emissions and on domestic implementation legislation.

OVERVIEW

The Electric Utility Industry and Air Emissions

The industry is massive, with 1996 assets totaling $696 billion, retail sales of $121 billion, and wholesale sales (sales of resale) of $47 billion. It consists of 3,195 utilities – 243 investor-owned, 2010 publicly owned, 932 cooperatives, and 10 federal entities. It is difficult to overestimate the importance of electric service to the nation's economy and individuals' quality of life. In 1996, the average residential customer paid $861 to buy 9,707 kilowatt-hours (809 Kwh monthly) of electricity.[3]

The industry is also a major source of air pollution. The combustion of fossil fuels, which account for 67% of electricity generation, results in the emission of a stream of gases. These gases include several pollutants that directly pose risks to human health and welfare, including sulfur oxides (SO_2), nitrogen oxides (NO_x), particulate matter (PM), volatile organic compounds (VOCs), carbon monoxide (CO), and various heavy metals, including lead and mercury (Hg). Other gases may pose indirect risks, notably carbon dioxide (CO_2), which may contribute to global warming.[4] (See table 1.)

Of the fossil-fired steam generators, coal-fired facilities contribute a disproportionately large share of these gases. While coal accounts for about 84% of fossil-fuel fired electricity generated, it accounts for 90% or more of the gases listed in table 1 (99% of the Hg). Besides the fuel, the location of a generator can also have important consequences for air pollution impacts (for CO_2 source location is immaterial). Location can be important both with respect to local ambient conditions and, because of long-range transport, to downwind areas. For example, with prevailing air movement from west to east, nonattainment of the ozone air pollution standard in the Northeast has directed attention to the concentration of coal-fired generating facilities in the Midwest as possible contributing sources, particularly of NO_x, which is a precursor of smog-forming ozone, among other effects.

Utilities are currently subject to an array of environmental regulations, which differentially affect both the cost of operating existing generating facilities and of constructing new ones. In particular, air pollution controls impact the construction and operating costs of fossil-fuel fired facilities – hydropower, nuclear, solar, wind, and other nonfossil-fueled fired electricity sources produce essentially zero air pollutants (although they have other environmental impacts). Generally, air quality regulations impose the greatest costs on coal-fired facilities and the least on natural gas-fired ones. This disparity would become greater if the U.S. were to accept the greenhouse gas reduction goals of the Kyoto Agreement Table 2 illustrates the variation among fossil fuels for emissions of NO_x and CO_2

The Argument about Restructuring and the Environment

After many decades of operating in a comprehensive, regulated market structure, the electric utility industry is facing significant change, both from new generating and transmission

---

[3] Based on revenues. Statistics from: Energy Information Administration, *Financial Statistics of Major U.S. Investor-Owned Electric Utilities: 1996,* DOE/EIA-0437(96)/1 (Washington, D.C.: December 1997); and Energy Information Administration, *Statistics of Major U.S. Publicly Owned Electric Utilities: 1996,* DOE/EIA-437(96)/2 (Washington, D.C.: March 1998).

[4] Steam-electric utilities produce only minor amounts of VOCs, CO, and lead – on the order of 2% or less of all sources.

technology and shifting policy perspectives with respect to competition and regulation. At issue is whether these changes will increase air pollution emissions.

Table 1: National Estimated Emissions from Fossil-Fuel, Steam-Electric Utilities – 1996

	CO2		NOx		PM10		SO2		Hg	
	1000 short tons	% all sources	1000 short tons	% all sources	10000 short tons	% all sources	1000 short tons	% all sources	Tons	% all sources
Electric Utilities	2,209,287	36	6,103	25	302	11	13,217	67	52	33
Coal	1,911,627		5,395		273		12,426		51.6	
Oil	100,895		208		9		730		0.2	
Gas	195,868		344		1		2			
Other/ Internal Combustion	897		156		19		60			

Sources: CO2 – DOE, Energy Information Administration, *Electric Power Annual 1998*, Vol. II, p. 42; NOx, PM10, SO2 – EPA, *National Air Quality and Emissions Trends Report, 1998* EPA 454/R-00-003 (March 2000), Tables A-4, A-6 and A-8 [http://www.epa.gov/oar/aqtrnd98/fr_table.html]; Hg – EPA, *Mercury Study Report to Congress*, Vol. 1, "Executive Summary" EPA-452/R-97-003 (December 1997), p. 3-6 [Hg data estimated annual emissions 1994/1995].

Table 2: NOx and CO2 Emission Rates by Fuel Source

Fuel	NOx Emissions (Lb./mmBtu)	CO2 Emissions (lbs. Carbon/mmuBtu)
Coal	0.1 - >2	55.9
Natural Gas	0.005 - >1	31.7
Residual Fuel Oil	0.05 - >1	46.8

Range for NOx reflects the difference between best available control technology and emissions from an uncontrolled existing power plant.

Sources: NOx - Larry Parker, Nitrogen Oxides and Electric Utilities: Revising the NSPS, CRS Report 96-737, July 25, 1997; CO2 – EIA, Emissions of Greenhouse Gases in the United States: 1987-1992 (Washington, D.C., 1994), Appendix A; and EIA, Emissions of Greenhouse Gases in the United States: 1987-1994 (Washington, D.C., 1995), p. 18.

Technology

The advent of new generating technologies, particularly natural gas-fired combined cycle, has both lowered entry barriers to competitors of traditional utilities and lowered the marginal costs of those competitors below that of some traditional utilities. As noted by the Federal Energy Regulatory Commission (FERC), smaller and more efficient natural gas-fired, combined cycle generation plants can produce power on the grid for between 3 cents and 5 cents per kilowatt-hour (Kwh). This is typically less than for the larger coal-fired (4-7 cents/Kwh) or nuclear (9-15 cents/Kwh) plants built by traditional utilities over the past decade.[5] Indeed, it is less than the average generating costs of some utilities. Coupled with advances in generating technology have been advances in transmission technology that permit long distance transmission economically and permit increasingly coordinated operations and reduced reserve margins.

This technological advancement has been combined with legislative initiatives, such as the Energy Policy Act of 1992 (EPACT), to encourage the introduction of competitive forces into the electric generating sector. This shift in policy continues with the promulgation of FERC Order 888 encouraging competition in the wholesale electricity market and implementation by some states of retail competition initiatives.

Restructuring

The policy shift underlying the changes occurring in the electric utility industry is a growing belief that the rationale for the current economic regulation of electric utilities at both the federal and state levels – that electric utilities are natural monopolies – is being overtaken by events, and that market forces can and should replace some of the current regulatory structure. Regulation and rate-of-return ratemaking[6] arguably exist as a partial substitute for the marketplace. The emerging

---

[5] FERC, "Promoting Wholesale Competition ... [Final Rule]," 61 *Federal Register* (May 10, 1996), 21544.

[6] Rate-of-return ratemaking means that a regulatory body allows the utility to obtain a guaranteed rate of return on investment. The regulatory body specifies a utility's legitimate costs and approves rates that allow the recovery of those costs plus a regulatorily determined acceptable profit. Wholesale sales are

trend in the industry suggests that regulation is an imperfect substitute for the marketplace and that with emerging new generating and transmission technologies, real self-regulating market forces are now able to replace government regulation in many instances. This substitution could result in a more efficient allocation of the country's resources and provide consumers with more accurate price signals regarding the actual cost of electricity.

The restructuring effort attempts to reduce and alter the role of government in electric utility regulation by identifying transactions, industry segments, regions, or specific activities that might no longer be the subject of economic regulation. Current proposals to increase competition in the electric utility industry involve segmenting electric functions (generation, transmission, distribution) that are currently integrated (or bundled) in most cases (both in terms of corporate and rate structures). The overall purpose of restructuring is to promote economic efficiency, which will presumably lead to lower overall rates.

Some argue that this singular focus on economic efficiency could come at the expense of other values that the regulatory system traditionally has balanced against economic efficiency, particularly equity and environmental considerations. The environmental concern with respect to restructuring is that the new economic signals being given by a competitive generation market could result in increased emissions of undesirable pollutants for two basic reasons: (1) lower baseload prices resulting from restructuring would increase electricity demand and, therefore, increase generation and emissions; and (2) the restructured generating market's revaluation of existing facilities to the marginal cost of constructing new capacity (along with their low operating costs) would encourage the rehabilitation and full utilization of these older, more polluting generating facilities.

Proponents of restructuring argue that it would increase efficiency and reduce electricity costs. To the extent greater competition and lower costs translate into lower prices, demand can be expected to rise (and incentives to conserve electricity and for new technologies such as renewable energy can be expected to decline). More demand would require more generation, resulting in more emissions. How much emissions might increase would depend on what facilities generate the additional power and on controls imposed by existing or prospective Clean Air Act requirements, as discussed below. Some cost studies indicate that the lion's share of cost savings from restructuring would come from the increased use of existing coal-fired capacity[7] – which is disproportionately more polluting than alternative sources of power. If true, then the need for new (cleaner) generating capacity could be delayed by restructuring, as production from existing capacity is maximized.

Based on the above, the general scenario goes as follows. A competitive generating sector would result in a revaluation of generating assets – i.e., moving from a traditional embedded-cost valuation scheme to a market valuation scheme, which would increase the value of some generating capacity and decrease the value of other generating capacity. Competition would tend to move the value of generating capacity to the marginal cost of constructing new capacity, generally represented at the current time by a new natural gas-fired, combined-cycle facility. In general, older facilities that have been fully depreciated would tend to have market values greater than their current book value under regulation; in contrast, newer, capital intensive facilities (such as some nuclear plants) would have market values less than their current book value. (Case -by-

---

regulated by FERC; retail sales are regulated by state Public Utilities Commissions, which may also regulate investment and debt.

[7]For example, see Michael T. Maloney and Robert E. McCormick, *Customer Choice, Consumer Value: An Analysis of Retail Competition in America's Electric Industry*, prepared for the Citizens for a Sound Economy Foundation (1996).

case valuation would be affected by location, availability of alternatives, and electricity demand.) In addition, the Clean Air Act typically imposes its most stringent pollution controls on new power plant construction, permitting existing capacity to meet less stringent and less costly standards. This differential impact may give some older facilities a competitive operating cost advantage to complement their low, depreciated cost basis.

The new valuation, combined with low operating costs, would encourage operators to maximize generation from their existing facilities. The trend toward increased utilization have already begun. In 1995, coal-fired facilities operated at a 62% capacity factor. By 1999, operation of coal-fired capacity had increased to 67%. The upper limit here is unclear – the economic and environmental advantages of new technology, such as natural gas-fired, combined-cycle technology (a very clean technology) may be sufficient in some cases to overcome the advantages of expanding use of existing plants.

Environmental Implications

It is this renewed attractiveness of existing capacity under restructuring, specifically of coal-fired capacity, along with the potential that demand for electricity may rise (and energy conservation slacken) if prices decline, that raises environmental concerns. Absent effective controls, burning more coal will produce more emissions than alternative sources of electricity generation – and much of that coal capacity is in the Midwest, which is currently a center of attention for reducing NOx emissions.

Except for CO_2, the regulatory regimen of the Clean Air Act provides authorities for controlling the potential increase in emissions – assuming they are effectively implemented. Existing controls "cap" SO_2 emissions in the 48 contiguous states and the District of Columbia, and there is on reason to question the effectiveness of the cap in the future, regardless of the changes underway in the utility industry. For NOx emissions, control and implementation is more complicated, primarily because implementation of much of the process lies with the states. Any increase in NOx emissions in the Midwest could complicate an already difficult process underway to reduce the region's NOx emissions, which contribute to ozone nonattainment in the Northwest.[8] How this regional, state-implemented process would be affected by restructuring is not certain.

CO_2 is not currently regulated. Any increase in fossil fuel-fired generation will increase CO_2 emissions, with coal producing about 75% more carbon emissions than natural gas on a Btu basis. If the U.S. were to ratify the Kyoto Agreement, which would require the U.S. to reduce greenhouse gas emissions to below 1990 levels, any increases would have to be rolled back or offset.[9] The effort required would be increased if restructuring differentially advantaged coal.

Ultimately, whether developments in electricity generation and demand lead to increased emissions of air pollutants depends on the implementation of the CAA (and on any new requirements that might be enacted); while for CO_2 increases are likely unless Congress ratifies the Kyoto Agreement and enacts implementing legislation (an uncertain prospect). Those who are focused on preventing environmental deterioration tend to take a precautionary stance, to propose immediate preventative measures, and to argue that such measures be attached to available legislative vehicles. In contrast, those who doubt that there will be significant environmental

---

[8] For a discussion of those efforts, see Larry Parker and John Blodgett, *Air Quality: EPA's Ozone Transport Rule, OTAG, and Section 126 Petitions – A Hazy Situation?* CRS Report 98-236, updated July 14, 2000.

[9] For a discussion of U.S. Global climate change policy, see Larry Parker and John Blodgett, *Global Climate Change Policy: From "No Regrets" to S. Res. 98,* CRS Report RL30024, January 12, 1999.

effects and/or who are focused on the substantial regulatory structure in place tend to take a wait-and-see position.

The current attention on increased emissions from coal-fired generation may address the clearest and most quantifiable risk to the environment from restructuring, but with so many changes underway, the ultimate outcome remains uncertain. Some trends are already manifest, such as renovation of existing coal-fired capacity. Others are just emerging, such as a "green market" in California, in which consumers can take into account environmental costs in their purchasing decisions. Some effects remain to be determined in the future, such as the implications of new price signals for demand and conservation; the implication of new cost valuations for the choice of new generating technologies; developments in transmission capacity; and the effectiveness of ongoing environmental programs. These complexities and their interactions are explored in more detail in the following discussions.

THE UTILITY INDUSTRY

Utility industry variables affecting emissions include: overall demand for electricity, which will respond to any changes in prices; the mix of fuels, which will be strongly affected by demand, especially for baseload capacity; and transmission capacity, which will affect what generators can respond to demand. Also crucial are environmental regulations that set limits on certain emissions and/or shift costs among generating facilities. This interactive matrix makes it difficult to separate out the environmental effects of any one component, such as restructuring.

Meeting Future Electricity Demand

In general, the United States has more electric generating capacity than it needs to maintain reliability. Currently, capacity margins[10] of between 12% and 17% are considered necessary to maintain adequate reliability.[11] Nationwide, U.S. capacity margins average 15% – varying from about 13% to 18% on a regional basis.[12] These capacity margins are expected to fall in the future as demand increases. The planned capacity margin in 2008 is 9.1%, unless announced new merchant plant capacity comes on line as intended. In that case, the 2008 capacity margin would be 15.6%.

On the surface, these numbers would suggest that there would be a general need for new capacity in the short- to mid-term (5-10 years), providing opportunities for different generating technologies, such as natural gas combined-cycle technology, coal-fired technologies, renewables, and nuclear power. However, this may not be the case for some regions. Much of the planned construction to meet the capacity growth needs identified above is designed to meet anticipated

---

[10] Capacity margins should not be confused with reserve margins. Capacity margin is the difference between generating capacity and peak load expressed as a percent of generating capacity. Reserve margin is the difference between generating capacity and peak load, expressed as a percent of peak load. Thus, a 17% capacity margin is roughly equivalent to a 20% reserve margin.

[11] Capacity margins are generally set according to a Loss of Load Probability (LOLP) calculation – a measure of the long-term expectation that a utility will be unable to meet demand. A 1 day in 10 year LOLP is typical.

[12] Data for 1999. North American Electric Reliability Council, *Reliability Assessment: 1999-2009* (Princeton, NJ: NERC, May, 2000), p.14.

peak load, not baseload needs.[13] Capacity that is not dispatchable on demand, such as some renewables and nuclear power, may not fit the demand curve over this time period. For example, utilities representing the southeastern U.S. estimate that nearly 90% of the projected 26,990 Mw of new capacity coming on line over the next 10 years will be non-baseload capacity. Similarly, the utilities representing the industrial Midwest estimate that 94% of the projected 13,500 MW of new capacity coming on line will be combustion turbines (a technology typically used for meeting peak load).[14]

This lack of planned construction for new baseload generating units reflects, in part, an existing surplus of baseload capacity, particularly coal-fired capacity.[15] In 1995, coal-fired capacity operated at a 62% capacity factor. By 1999, this had increased to 67%.[16] If demand and economics justified it, this average could improve to 75% or more. An increase to 75% capacity would be equivalent to about 23,000 Mw of baseload capacity – sufficient to meet increases in aggregate baseload demand for a couple of years, depending on transmission capacity constraints. (An increase to 85% capacity would be equivalent to about 53,000 Mw.) Thus, it would appear that under current expectations, existing baseload facilities, such as nuclear plants, and new baseload construction, such as natural gas combined-cycle, may in many cases be competing against existing coal-fired facilities for the next 5-10 years.

Transmission Capacity

The degree to which existing coal-fired capacity competes against other baseload technologies will be partially dependent on transmission capacity. Under ideal economic conditions, the price of providing baseload electricity would tend to levelize across the country, reflecting a nationwide market for such electricity. In reality, this is unlikely to occur until and unless substantial improvements are made in transmission capacity and the robustness of the transmission grid. An increase in market forces in the generating sector does not necessarily translate into the increased transmission capacity and robustness that would allow consumers to fully exploit potential generation savings.

Under current restructuring proposals, the transmission sector remains a monopoly controlled by rate-of-return regulation. The history of this approach to transmission planning has resulted in a system focused on and justified by local reliability concerns, not a system concerned with maximizing economic efficiency on a nationwide or even interregional basis. How well and how completely the regulatory structure can be changed to facilitate the dynamics of a deregulated generating sector is difficult to predict. Market prices may regionalize, reflecting the increasingly

---

[13] Baseload refers to the minimum amount of electric power delivered or required over a given period at a constant rate. Baseload power plants, like nuclear plants, are designed to operate whenever they are available (generally over 60% of the time).

[14] North American Electric Reliability Council, *Reliability Assessment: 1996-2005* (Princeton, NJ: NERC, October 1996).

[15] The lack of planning also reflects the shortening of lead-times for new construction, uncertainty about future demand, and uncertainty about the future structure of the generating sector.

[16] It is this trend in coal-fired generation utilization that caught the attention of EPA and the possibility for action under the New Source Review requirements of the Clean Air Act. For more information, see Larry B. Parker and John E. Blodgett, *Air Quality and Electricity: Enforcing New Source Review*, CRS Report RL 30432 (January 31, 2000).

regional control of transmission, but large-scale interregional transactions may be several years away.

If transmission barriers result in largely regional markets, marginal costs for baseload capacity may differ between regions. For example, regions with substantial excess coal-fired capacity may have low marginal costs based on the incremental costs of increased capacity utilization. Other regions, with substantial increasing demand, may have marginal costs based on new construction costs, such as building a natural gas-fired combined-cycle plant or a coal-fired fluidized bed combustor. Depending on price, a generating technology that is competitive "on average" may not be competitive within a specific region because of low-cost alternatives; likewise, a "higher cost" generating technology that is non-competitive "on average" may be competitive within a specific region because of the higher cost of alternatives.

Implications of Utility Developments

All of these factors will be summed up in the price for baseload power. It is generally assumed that deregulation of the generating sectors will encourage the development of marginal cost pricing.[17] In particular, deregulation will clearly expose the substantial cost differences between baseload generation and peak generation. While baseload facilities generally run at over 60 percent capacity, peak demand facilities run at under 20 percent capacity. This substantial difference in utilization, among other differences, means that peak power will cost more under restructuring than it does now, when the cost is generally rolled in with the less expensive baseload power.[18]

At least in the short-term, this stratification of electricity pricing may mean that the market price for baseload power will be considerably lower than the current average electricity price would indicate. This would encourage the use of existing baseload capacity with low operating costs (e.g., coal-fired capacity) and discourage constructing new baseload facilities, particularly those technologies requiring substantial investment (e.g., nuclear power). Low baseload prices may also discourage development of non-dispatchable power sources (e.g., some renewable technologies) and installation of some conservation technologies. Higher prices for peaking power would encourage technologies designed for such load (e.g., combustion turbines), and technologies designed to reduce such loads (e.g., load management techniques). In the long term, if prices for electricity decline, electricity use is likely to increase and incentives to conserve electricity are likely to decrease. Long-term declining prices could also reduce incentives for new technologies, including some renewable energy technologies.

How these different effects play out will determine the potential for increased emissions from restructuring. Although the overall effect on emissions is difficult to assess, involving several

---

[17] Marginal cost has been used by some public utility commissions to determine appropriate rates between different customer classes for several years, and utilities have also experimented with "time-of-day" rates that reflect marginal costs across time. Under restructuring, generating costs may move more in the direction of "time of day" pricing as more reflective of actual costs than the current average cost method.

[18] As stated by a study done for the American Gas Association study of future electric generation: "In principle, retail deregulation and retail wheeling, should radically change the current pricing structure for end-use electricity. Peak pricing will increase sharply and off-peak pricing will decrease sharply." Harry Chernoff, *Existing and Future Electric Generation: Implication for Natural Gas,* Study prepared for the American Gas Association, Policy Analysis Group, by Science Applications International Corporation (October 1996) p. 23.

currently unquantifiable variables, the most substantial environmental effect in the short- to mid-term is likely to come from enhanced cooperation of existing coal-fired capacity. Whether one can ascribe that effect strictly to restructuring is debatable, however.

ENVIRONMENTAL REGULATION

The Clean Air Act imposes a complex regulatory structure on air pollution sources. From an historical perspective, the regulatory environment for a major emission source, like an electric generating facility, has been largely dependent on two factors: (1) Where the facility is located (in an area meeting clean air standards, or in an area not attaining them) and, (2) How old the facility is (new or old source). Other factors, such as facility size and specific pollutants controlled, feed off these two factors. This framework is changing, however, as illustrated in the following case study on NOx.

Example: Nitrogen Oxide Control

Nitrogen oxides, both directly and because they contribute to formation of ozone, raise human health and environmental concerns that bring them under the purview of the CAA. Nitrogen dioxide (NO2), the index compound for nitrogen oxides, can irritate the lungs and lower human resistance to various respiratory infections, such as influenza. In combination with volatile organic compounds (VOCs) and in the presence of heat and sunlight, NOx forms ozone, for which human health concerns include lung damage, chest pain, coughing, nausea, throat irritation, and congestion. Ozone also exacerbates the effects of bronchitis, heart disease, emphysema, and asthma.[19] In addition, nitrogen oxides contribute to the formation of fine particulates, suspected of significant human mortality and morbidity effects and for which EPA recently set new standards that will become effective in 10 to 15 years.[20]

Environmental concerns about NOx emissions include its transformation into nitric acid, a component of acid precipitation; visibility impairment; and adverse effects of ozone on plant life.[21] In addition, EPA estimates that up to 40% of the nitrogen "loading" in the Chesapeake Bay, resulting in excessive nutrient enrichment, is the result of deposition of air-borne nitrogen oxides. In the West, nitrogen oxides contribute to visibility impairment, particularly in southern California.

These multiple effects result in multiple control measures under the Clean Air Act, as described below.

---

[19] For a discussion of human health effects of air pollution, see Morton Lippmann, "Health Benefits from Controlling Exposure to Criteria Air Pollutants," in John Blodgett, ed., *Health Benefits of Air Pollution Control: A Discussion,* CRS Report 89-161, February 27, 1989, pp. 75-144.

[20] John Blodgett, et al., *Air Quality Standards: EPA's Final Ozone and Particulate Matter Standards,* CRS Report 97-721 (Updated June 19, 1998).

[21] For a discussion of ozone and acid precipitation effects on vegetation, see David S. Shriner, et al., *Response of Vegetation to Atmospheric Deposition and Air Pollution: State of Science and Technology Report 18* (Washington, D.C.: National Acid Precipitation Assessment Program, December 1990).

Air Quality Regulations Impacting on Utilities

Primary National Ambient Air Quality Standard (NAAQS) set maximum levels of permitted pollution concentrations nationwide. NAAQS are federally enforceable with specific deadlines for compliance; they are required by Section 109 of the CAA to protect the public health with an "adequate margin of safety." They are periodically reviewed to take into account the most recent health data. Three NAAQS may result in NOx controls: NAAQS for nitrogen dioxide, ozone, and fine particulates.

In 1994, all monitoring locations in the U.S. were in compliance with the NO2 NAAQS; however, compliance with the ozone NAAQS remains elusive in several parts of the country, particularly in southern California, the Texas Gulf Coast, and the Northeast corridor (from Virginia to Maine). Because NOx is a precursor to ozone formation, NOx control represents an important component in reducing ozone pollution. In recognition of the multi-state nature of the ozone problem in the Northeast, the 1990 CAA Amendments created an Ozone Transport Commission (OTC) to development and coordinate emission reduction efforts for that area. In addition, in 1998, the EPA promulgated a new ozone transport rule that would control NOx emissions for 21 eastern states, and ten states petitioned the EPA to control NOx emissions in the Midwest under section 126 of the CAA.[22]

For areas in attainment with these NAAQS, the CAA mandates states to require new sources, such as power plants, to install Best Available Control Technology (BACT) as the minimum level of NOx control required of a new power plant.[23] State permitting agencies determine BACT on a case-by-case basis, taking into account energy, environmental and economic impacts. BACT can be much more stringent than the federal New Source Performance Standard (NSPS – described below), but can not be less stringent than NSPS. Existing sources are not required to install controls in attainment areas.

For areas not in attainment with one or more of these NAAQS, the CAA mandates states to require new sources to install Lowest Achievable Emissions Rate (LAER) technology. Along with offset rules, LAER ensures that overall emissions do not increase as a result of a new plant's operation. LAER is based on the most stringent emission rate of any state implementation plan or achieved in practice without regard to cost or energy use. It may not be less stringent than NSPS. Existing sources are required to install Reasonably Available Control Technology (RACT), a state determination based on federal guidelines.

A Prevention of Significant Deterioration (PSD) program (Part C of the CAA) forces on ambient concentrations of pollutants (including NO2) in "clean" air areas of the country (i.e., areas where air quality is better than the NAAQS). The provision allows some increase in clean areas' pollution concentrations depending on their classification. In general, historic or recreation areas (e.g., national parks) are classified class 1 with very little degradation allowed while most other areas are classified class 2 with moderate degradation allowed. Class 3 areas are permitted to degrade up to the NAAQS. New sources in PSD areas must undergo preconstruction review and must install BACT; state permitting agencies determine BACT on a case-by-case basis, taking into account energy, environmental, and economic impacts. More stringent controls can be required if

---

[22] For more information, see Larry Parker and John Blodgett, *Air Quality: EPA's Ozone Transport Rule, OTAG, and Section 126 Petitions – A Hazy Situation?* CRS Report 98-236, updated July 14, 2000. For recent activities with respect to these initiatives, see: Larry B. Parker and John E. Blodgett, *Air Quality and Electricity: Initiatives to Increase Pollution Controls,* CRS Report RS20553, December 28, 2000.

[23] More stringent controls can be required if modeling indicates that BACT is insufficient to avoid violating the NAAQS.

modeling indicates that BACT is insufficient to avoid violating PSD emission limitations, or the NAAQS itself.

A complement to the PSD program for existing sources is the regional haze program (section 169A) that focuses on "prevention of any future, and the remedying of any existing, impairment of visibility" resulting from manmade air pollution in national parks and wilderness areas.[24]   Among the pollutants that impair visibility are sulfates, organic matter, and nitrates. In 1999, the EPA promulgated a regional haze program, which, would entail more stringent controls on NOx and SO2. However, like the fine particulate NAAQS, it will be several years before any regional haze program might result in controls.

New Source Performance Standards (NSPS) are federal standards defining the minimum controls necessary for new sources regardless of their location – in contrast to the PSD and NAAQS standards that focus on ambient concentrations of pollutants.   EPA's NSPS determinations represent the floor for state BACT and LAER determinations in case-by-case situations.

Required under Section 111 of the CAA, NSPS require major new sources to install the best system of continuous emission reduction which has been adequately demonstrated. In making such an assessment, the CAA requires EPA to take into account "the cost of achieving such reduction and any non-air quality health and environmental impact and energy requirements." To keep controls abreast of technological innovations, the CAA originally required EPA to review and revise NSPS every four years. But at the time of enactment of the 1990 CAA Amendments, the last revision of the NOx NSPS for electric and non-electric steam generating units had occurred in 1979. With substantial technological improvements in controlling NOx having occurred during the 1980s, the 1990 Amendments (title IV, section 407(c)) required EPA to promulgate a new NOx NSPS for electric and non-electric steam generating units by 1994 – a deadline EPA did not meet. In September, 1998, EPA did promulgate a new NOx NSPS. It is considerably more stringent than the 1979 standard for coal-fired facilities, but not particularly stringent for natural gas or oil-fired facilities.[25]

The acid deposition control provisions of title IV of the 1990 Amendments focus on total emissions from existing sources of sulfur dioxide and nitrogen oxides. For nitrogen oxides, section 407 of title IV requires tangential- and wall-fired (dry bottom, not cell burner equipped) boilers (group 1 boilers) designated to meet 1995 phase 1 reductions to meet an emission limitation based on low-NOx burner technology. Regulations for phase 1 NOx reductions were finalized in 1995. For phase 2 in the y ear 2000, remaining group 1 boilers are required to meet the same standard (or more stringent if technology and costs permit) as those covered in phase 1, and boilers with other firing configurations (group 2 boilers) are required to meet standards based on available technology that is comparable in cost to low-NOx burners. EPA finalized regulations for phase 2 group 1 and group 2 boilers in 1996 (61 *Federal Register* 245, pp. 67112-67164).

Implications of Air Quality Regulations for Utilities

In the light of changes in the utility industry, this mix of air quality regulations has important consequences for (1) utilities' choices both for construction of new facilities and operation of

---

[24] See James McCarthy, et al., *Regional Haze: EPA's Proposal to Improve Visibility in National Parks and Wilderness Areas,* CRS Report 97-1010, updated July 9, 1998.

[25] See Larry Parker, *Nitrogen Oxides and Electric Utilities: Revising the NSPS,* CRS Report 96-737, updated October 13. 1998.

existing ones, and (2) the potential effectiveness by which federal and state air pollution controls apply to a changing industry structure.

New Construction and Existing Sources

For constructing new power plants, the CAA envisions the federal NSPS and the state PSD/BACT program as the baseline for control efforts in attainment areas, and the state-set LAER and federally-based offset requirements as the baseline in nonattainment areas. For SO2, federal offset requirements overlay these other requirements. The costs of installing NSPS (or BACT or LAER or obtaining offsets) on new construction fall most sharply on coal-fired facilities. This could disadvantage coal in choices among technologies for new generations.

At the same time, the historically less stringent controls on existing coal-fired facilities – none in attainment areas, RACT in nonattainment areas – have clearly advantaged existing sources, particularly coal, in competing with new sources for meeting generating needs. This may be changing. For existing facilities, especially coal-fired facilities, a host of new regulatory initiatives may result in more stringent controls for a number of possible pollutants.

In addition, in what could crucially affect the potential costs of reconditioning and extending the life of existing coal-fired plants, EPA, together with the Department of Justice, has initiated a New Source Review (NSR) enforcement process to reduce pollution from existing sources. The first overt action under process occurred November 3, 1999, when the Justice Department filed seven lawsuits against electric utilities in the Midwest and South, charging them with violations of the NSR requirements of the CAA. EPA also issued an administrative order against the Tennessee Valley Authority, alleging similar violations.

The crux of the enforcement actions is the "preconstruction" permitting process of the NSR, which is designed to ensure that newly constructed facilities, or substantially modified existing ones, do not result in violations of applicable air quality standards. The question the enforcement actions raise is whether the specified facilities engaged in rehabilitation actions that represent "major modifications" of the plants, in which case the CAA would require the installation of best available control technology – BACT.

The crucial definition of "major modification" derives from an EPA ruling that a life extension project by Wisconsin Electric Power Company (WEPCO) triggered NSR requirements. Since 1992, after considerable litigation and congressional debate, the "test" to determine the applicability of NSR compares whether a facility's projected actual emissions after the modification are more than its actual emissions before the modification. Utilities argue that the "modifications' EPA cites in the suits were just routine maintenance, which does not trigger NSR. If EPA's position in these suits is upheld, this could have the dual effects of increasing the costs to utilities of expanding the use of coal-fired utilities in the future and of reducing the emissions from coal-fired facilities.[26]

Table 3 identifies the range of environment actions that are beginning to affect or may in the future affect emissions from fossil-fuel fired facilities. As discussed in the next section, these controls could have a substantial influence on the cost of power from coal-fired facilities, making them less attractive in a competitive marketplace.

---

[26] On the NSR enforcement actions, see Larry B. Parker and John E. Blodgett, *Air Quality and Electricity: Enforcing New Source Review*, CRS Report RL30432, Jan. 13, 2000.

Table 3: Potential Control on Existing Sources

Pollutant	Potential Controls on Existing Sources
Nitrogen Oxides	Title IV, sec. 407 Ozone Transport Commission (OTC) Rules Ozone Transport Rule Section 126 Petitions Revised Ozone NAAQS Fine Particulate NAAQS New Source Review Enforcement Regional Haze Rule More stringent Legislation*
Sulfur Oxides	Title IV Fine Particulate NAAQS New Source Review Enforcement Regional Haze Rule More stringent Legislation*
Mercury	Potential EPA regulation as a HAP NE Action Plan on Mercury Potential Legislation*
Carbon Dioxide	Potential ratification of Kyoto Agreement Potential Legislation*

*For information on current legislative proposals relating restructuring to environmental controls, see Larry Parker and Amy Abel, *Electricity: The Road Toward Restructure,* CRS Issue Brief IB10006. For a review of legislation introduced in the 106th Congress, see: Larry Parker, *Electricity Restructuring: Comparison of Comprehensive Bills,* CRS Report RL30087, July 24, 2000; and, Larry Parker, *Electricity Restructuring and Air Quality: Comparison of Proposed Legislation,* CRS Report RS20326, July 26, 2000.

Implementation under Restructuring

The mix of regulatory authorities results in a complex federal-state process for regulating the industry. The state-regulated utility system meshed reasonably well with the state-implemented air quality controls. As the utility industry becomes more competitive and potentially more regional, and as air quality problems also become more regional (regional haze, long-range pollutant transport), state-directed controls on existing sources may prove less efficient and effective than previously.

These regional challenges may reprise the past inability of the state-led process to control acid rain, the result of long-range transport of SO2 for which utilities are a major source. As a result of the failure of the state-based process to address this problem, Congress in 1990 added the acid rain program to the CAA, which established a national "cap" on emissions. This has proven an efficient program; SO2 credits are not excessively expensive and the most popular technology for new construction – natural gas-fired combined-cycle technology – produces almost no SO2 emissions.[27] The flexibility and straight-forward compliance mechanism of this "cap and trade"

---

[27] U.S. Environmental Protection Agency, *1996 Compliance Report, Acid Rain Program,* EPA 430-R-97-025 (June 1997).

program would seem to mesh well with a flexible, competitive utility industry, so electricity restructuring would not appear to create any serious implementation problems for this SO2 control program.

However, the acid rain program is discrete; there is no comparable nationwide "cap and trade" program for other pollutants. For example, as noted earlier, the 1990 CAA Amendments did create an Ozone Transport Region in ten northeastern states for addressing ozone transport (and NOx, as a precursor) and it authorized EPA to create others. However, this effort may be inadequate to bring the Northeast into compliance with the Ozone NAAQS. To bring under control additional sources of long-range transport, EPA created a 21-state Midwest-Northeast region (where substantial coal-fired NOx emission increases could occur) subject to the promulgated Ozone Transport Rule, a feature of which is a voluntary, state-implemented NOx "cap and trade" program. However, EPA does not have authority to require the states within the region to act in concert or to impose uniform rules for cap and trade as in the acid rain program. Thus, how this regional effort to control NOx would work in practice remains to be seen; interstate disagreements have surfaced, and industry restructuring could change emissions patters in ways that could exacerbate them.[28]

The potential for diverse state requirements in the region could lead to inconsistent requirements that could pose barriers to restructuring the industry – or opportunities. Differing requirements could allow utilities to choose which state had the least stringent requirements, while the power could be transmitted to the location of demand; or inconsistent requirements – or uncertain ones – might be an added incentive for construction of generating capacity that is clean and hence not subject to them.

To the regulatory dynamic of the Clean Air Act has no direct consequence for potential increases in CO2 emissions under utility restructuring: CO2 is not subject to CAA regulation and any controls are prospective, contingent on U.S. ratification of the Kyoto Agreement and on domestic implementing legislation. The uncertainty of legislative action on CO2 compared to the potential for action on restructuring legislation in the next couple of years has led some to find in the restructuring issue a surrogate for a debate on CO2 controls and global climate change in general. This situation for a debate on CO2 controls and global climate change in general. This situation adds complexity to the restructuring debate.

THE EFFECTS OF RESTRUCTURING AND ENVIRONMENTAL ACTIONS ON EMISSIONS

As suggested previously, restructuring involves the interplay of many factors affecting emissions. As indicated above, some, such as renovating existing coal-fired capacity, represent a furthering of an existing trend. Others, such as green pricing, represent a new trend created by restructuring. Although the overall effect on emissions is difficult to assess, involving several currently unquantifiable variables, the most substantial environmental effect in the short- to mid-term arises from the potential for enhanced operation of existing coal-fired capacity. However, how much one should ascribe that effect to general trends in the industry vis a vis restructuring is debatable.

---

[28] For recent actions with respect to the Ozone Transport rule, see: Larry B. Parker and John E. Blodgett, *Air Quality and Electricity: Initiatives to Increase Pollution Control,* CRS Report RS 20553, December 28, 2000.

Economics and Coal-Fired Generation

A general trend in the electric utility industry for over a decade has been the renovation of existing capacity beyond its initial lifespan (especially coal-fired capacity) in lieu of constructing new capacity. If restructuring results in a stratification of electricity pricing in terms of baseload, intermediate, and peak power, the low price of baseload capacity could provide additional impetus to refurbish existing coal-fired capacity and to maximize operation of such power. Likewise, lower baseload prices would likely reduce incentives to conserve electricity and to develop new non-peaking technologies, including renewable energy. As noted above, substantial amounts of underused coal-fired capacity currently exist. The degree to which it is competitive over the next 5-10 years will depend primarily on two factors – cost of enhanced maintenance to extend the life of the facilities (life extension), and potential for additional pollution control costs (which is discussed in the next section).

Depending on the condition of an existing coal-fired facility, recondition can be a very economic means of adding baseload capacity.[29] This reconditioning process, called life extension, can help halt and partially reverse the deterioration of a power plant's efficiency and reliability during continued operation. Over time, the operation and maintenance (O&M) of a power plant increases, along with its heat rate. For example, based on FERC data, EPA assumes the median O&M costs for coal-fired facilities up to 10 years old is $17.60?Kw, compared with the median costs for a facility more than 30 years old of $31.20/KW.[30] However, EPA believes that much of this increase (about $9.40/Kw) represents continuous reconditioning efforts to extend the life of the plant – that "life extension" efforts increasingly represent a continuing upgrading process, rather than a one-time reconstruction of the power plant.[31]

Thus, one-time projections for life-extension costs overestimate the incremental cost of this effort. EPA estimates that the cost to extend power plant life from 40 to 65 years will be on the order of $8.8/Kw per year in additional O&M costs – or 1.4 mills/Kwh. Assuming the power plant has been well-maintained up to now, this cost would appear quite attractive for an additional 20-25 years of operation. Including estimated O&M and fuel costs, such power plants would generate electricity for about 2 cent/Kwh.[32] In general, the potential for rising fuel prices is considered small in the case of coal. There appears to be ample supply of coal available at current prices.

Against existing coal-fired capacity is newly constructed natural gas combined-cycle technology. Conventional wisdom within the industry is that, based on current trends in generating technology and fuel costs, the technology of choice for new construction will be natural gas-fired combined-cycle plants. To illustrate the sensitivity of new natural gas-fired facilities to fuel costs and technology improvements, four different cases were analyzed. The results are

---

[29] ICF Incorporated, *Repowering and Life Extension: Background Paper*, prepared for the Office of Atmospheric Programs and Office of Air Quality Planning and Standards, EPA (draft report) (February 1995).

[30] U.S. Environmental Protection Agency, Office of Air and Radiation, *Analyzing Electric Power Generation Under the CAAA* (July 1996), p. A3-11. Estimates in 1995$.

[31] Part of this represents a strategy by utilities to avoid having to comply with New Source Performance Standards (NSPS) at their existing facilities by not triggering the WEPCO rule, which requires existing facilities to achieve NSPS under some circumstances. It is this strategy that EPA and Department of Justice are attacking with the NSR enforcement actions discussed previously.

[32] Calculation assumes heat rate of 10,000 Btu/Kwh, fixed O&M costs of $31 Kw/yr (not including incremental life extension costs discussed in the text), fuel costs of $1.30 Btu/Kwh, and a 70% capacity factor.

presented in table 4. Estimates hold that the annual costs on a levelized basis for a natural gas combined-cycle plant at about 2.4-2.5 cents/Kwh, with costs rising to 3.4-3.5 cents/Kwh if natural bas prices rise to $3.50/mmBtu compared with $2.25/mmBtu assumed in the base-case calculations. While very competitive for new construction, it is not quite competitive, *in general*, to renovating existing coal-fired capacity.[33]

Table 4. Costs of New Natural Gas-fired Combined-cycle Facility
(1995 dollars)

	Base Case	High fuel cost case	Higher efficiency base case	Higher efficiency/high fuel costs case
Efficiency Assumption	7,300 Btu/Kwh	7,300 Btu/Kwh	6,800 Btu/Kwh	6,800 Btu/Kwh
Fuel Cost Assumption	$2.25/mmBtu	$3.50/mmBtu	$2.25/mmBtu	$3.50/mmBtu
Total Costs	2.5 cents/Kwh	3.4 cents/Kwh	2.4 cents/Kwh	3.3 cents/Kwh

Other assumptions include capital costs of $593/Kw, fixed O&M of $10/Kw/yr., variable O&M of 0.5 mills/Kwh, capacity factor of 85%, and a real capital charge of 10.4%.

SOURCES: Environmental Protection Act, Electricity Power Research Institute, CRS estimates.

As indicated, the analysis strongly suggests that natural gas pricing is the most important variable in determining generating costs from such plants. In the base-case analyses, fuel costs represent about two-thirds of the total costs (including capital charges). In the high costs analyses, fuel costs represent about three-fourths of the total costs. The importance of fuel costs is lessened a little by continuing improvements in generating efficiency. However, it is likely to remain the dominant cost factor over the time period discussed here. This variable would also have to be factored into any decision about existing coal-fired versus newly constructed natural gas-fired capacity.

Air Quality and Coal-fired Generation

If restructuring further encourages the increased utilization of existing coal-fired capacity in lieu of constructing new capacity and discourages energy conservation and development of cleaner technology because of low baseload pricing or other factors, the short- to mid-term effects could be increased air pollution. Operating an additional 23,000 Mw of coal-fired capacity would have

---

[33] For reference, CRS calculates that a new coal-fired steam generator would produce electricity for about 3.5 cents/Kwh, confirming the conventional wisdom with respect to natural gas.

significant air emissions, particularly for CO2, and, depending on the fate of various EPA rulemakings, on NOx. As SO2 emissions are currently capped by title IV of the 1990 Clean Air Act Amendments, the effects of restructuring on SO2 emissions should be negligible.

The most substantial effects of restructuring would be for carbon dioxide emissions, because they are currently uncontrolled. CO2 emissions from 23,000 Mw of coal-fired capacity would be about 200,000,000 short tons, an increase of about 11% over 1996 CO2 emissions by coal-fired electricity generation. This compares with emissions from a natural gas combined-cycle equivalent capacity of about 80,000,000 short tons, or a difference of 120,000,000 short tons.

Calculating the potential effects on NOx emissions is more difficult as existing sources could be controlled under several provisions of the Clean Air Act (see table 3). For example, the final rule for the NOx reduction program under section 407 of title IV of the Clean Air Act Amendments of 1990 was promulgated in 1996.[34] The rule will reduce the NOx emission rate of coal-fired facilities examined here to an average of 0.48 lb/mmBtu. Based on this result, emissions from 23,000 Mw would come to about 480,000 tons, an increase of about 9% over 1996 coal-fired NOx emissions. This would compare with emissions of 70,000 tons from equivalent natural gas combined-cycle technology, or a difference of 410,000 tons.[35]

As identified earlier, other control possibilities, such as implementation of EPA's Ozone Transport Rule, also could reduce these emissions substantially.[36] Under this regulation, NOx emissions across a 21-state area are "capped" at a specific level beginning September 30, 2007. That level of emissions cannot be exceeded regardless of the electric utility industry's structure.

Similarly, successful prosecution of the NSR enforcement actions could impose additional control requirements on existing coal-fired facilities.[37] Under a restructured electric generating market, increased pollution control requirements would adversely affect the economics of affected facilities, which would become more expensive to operate. Increased capital and operating costs would make coal-fired capacity less attractive in a more competitive system.

As discussed above, existing coal-fired facilities are particularly vulnerable to future regulation of several pollutants. To illustrate the sensitivity of these facilities to increased pollution-control costs, an analysis was done of a representative sample of such potential costs. The results are presented in table 5. As indicated, control costs for each of these pollutants would add about 10% or more to the total generation costs from existing coal-fired facilities. Combinations of control measures would raise these costs even more.[38] With new natural gas combined-cycle technology potentially available for 2.5 cents/Kwh, increased air pollution control represents a real threat to the continuing operation of at least some existing coal-fired capacity.

These environmental concerns are not necessarily hypothetical. For example, member states of the Ozone Transport Commission (OTC) have agreed to stringent nitrogen oxide controls on

---

[34] Environmental Protection Agency, "Acid Rain Program; Nitrogen Oxide Emission Reduction Program," 61 *Federal Register* 67111-67264 (December 19, 1996).

[35] Based on an average BACT determination of 0.1 lb/mmBtu. See Larry Parker, *Nitrogen Oxides and Electric Utilities: Revising the NSPS.* CRS Report 96-737, Updated October 13, 1998.

[36] For a discussion of the transport rule, see Larry Parker and John Blodgett, *Air Quality: EPA's Ozone Transport rule, OTAG, and Section 126 Petitions – A Hazy Situation?* CRS Report 98-236, updated July 14, 200.

[37] For an update on events surrounding EPA NSR enforcement activities, see: Larry B. Parker and John E. Blodgett, *Air Quality and Electricity: Initiatives to Increase Pollution control,* CRS Report RS20553, updated December 28, 2000.

[38] Readers are cautioned not to simply add the incremental costs of these controls measures together. There may be overlaps or efficiencies to be gained from controlling some of pollutants together that are presented in Table 5.

stationary sources, including electric generating plants, in then northeastern states. Depending on how the states and utilities choose to implement the program, selective catalytic reduction (SCR) or other control devises may have to be installed on some coal-fired power plants. This could also be the result of EPA's Ozone Transport Rule and/or a successful Section 126 petition with respect to interstate ozone pollution.

For natural gas combined-cycle facilities, the major *potential* environmentally related cost increase would be control of carbon dioxide.[39] If a new natural gas combined-cycle plant were required to offset all its potential CO_2 emissions under a future emissions cap, it could increase operating costs by about 0.2 cents/Kwh.[40] This would raise the total production costs for such facilities to 2.6-2.7 cents/Kwh, or 3.6-3.7 cents/Kwh if the high-cost gas scenarios were operative.

Table 5. Potential Pollution Control Cost for Existing Coal-fired Power Plants (500 Mw, 1995$)

Cost Factor	Nitrogen Oxides	Carbon Dioxide	Mercury	Sulfur Dioxide
Capital Costs	$49/Kw	0	$40.5/Kw	$190/Kw
Fixed O&M	$4.27/Kw	0	$6.9/Kw	$6.8/Kw
Variable O&M	0.023 cents/Kwh	0.2 cents/Kwh	0.04 cents/Kwh	0.1 cents/Kwh
Total Costs of control	0.17 cents/Kwh	0.2 cents/Kwh	0.22 cents/Kwh	0.53 cents/Kwh
Total Production Costs	2.17 cents/Kwh	2.2 cents/Kwh	2.22 cents/Kwh	2.53 cents/Kwh

Control Assumptions: For nitrogen oxides – installation of Selective Catalytic Reduction (SCR) with 70% removal; for carbon dioxide – buying carbon offsets for 50% of emissions at $5 a ton; for mercury – installation of carbon injection with spray cooling and fabric filter; for sulfur dioxide – installation of flue-gas desulfurization (FGD) with 95% removal.

Sources: U.S. EPA, Office of Air and Radiation, *Analyzing Electric Power Generation under the CAAA* (July 1996); and Larry Parker, *Coal Market Effects of CO2 Control Strategies as Embodied in H.R. 1086 and H.R. 2663*, CRS Report 91-883, December 13, 1991.

ASSESSING THE IMPACTS OF RESTRUCTURING

Emissions from electricity generation are determined by an interactive process involving a utility industry and an environmental regulatory system that are both undergoing change. The dynamic linkages between electricity generation, resulting emissions, and pollution control make it difficult to separate out one factor (in this case, electricity restructuring) for analysis. The difficulty in doing this has been illustrated by various studies attempting to estimate the impact of restructuring on the environment.

For example, an early component of electricity restructuring is the Federal Energy Regulatory Commission's (FERC) Order 888 that promotes wholesale competition through open, non-discretionary access to transmission services to all participants in the wholesale generation market. In developing the Order, FERC conducted an environmental impact statement (EIS) to examine

---

[39] The costs estimates cited above already include installation and operation of SCR. Natural gas plants emit very minor amounts of sulfur dioxide and mercury.

[40] This cost is very speculative. For a further discussion, see Larry Parker, *Coal Market Effect of CO2 Control Strategies as Embodied in H.R. 1086 and H.R. 2663*, CRS Report 91-882, December 13, 1991.

the implications of the proposed Order for emissions of pollutants by affected generating facilities. This assessments covered only a limited part of what would be affected by a comprehensive restructuring of the electricity generating industry; specifically, the Order is limited to the transmission of wholesale electricity, about 10% of total sales. Nevertheless, studies of the rule, including those critical of FERC's analysis, illustrate the difficulties in isolating the impacts of restructuring from other factors present in the system.

For example, an early component of electricity restructuring is the Federal Energy Regulatory Commission's (FERC) Order 888 that promotes wholesale competition through open, non-discretionary access to transmission services to all participants in the wholesale generation market. In developing the Order, FERC conducted an environmental impact statement (EIS) to examine the implications of the proposed Order for emissions of pollutants by affected generating facilities. This assessment covered only a limited part of what would be affected by a comprehensive restructuring of the electricity generating industry; specifically, the Order is limited to the transmission of wholesale electricity, about 10% of total sales. Nevertheless, studies of the rule, including those critical of FERC's analysis, illustrate the difficulties in isolating the impacts of restructuring from other factors present in the system.

FERC issued its findings in a draft EIS[41] in November 1995. From two baselines – projections about electricity generation without the proposed rule – FERC analyzed changes in electricity generation that might result from the proposed rule, and the consequent changes in emission that would therefore be expected. The two baselines differed in assumptions about the relative prices of gas and coal. Based on the models used by FERC and the assumptions adopted, the analyses, indicated that the proposed rule would have a small effect on emissions. In general, through 2010, assumptions that favor gas could slightly decrease overall emissions, and assumptions that favor coal could slightly increase overall emissions. A regional analysis similarly found relatively small effects. Given the modest environmental impacts, FERC concluded that there was no need to undertake mitigation – although it discussed options – and in fact concluded that it had little appropriate authority to require any mitigation.

Comments on the draft were numerous; they are summarized in the final EIS issued in April 1996.[42] Three issues received particular attention. Two sets of comments addressed two aspects of the analyses that commenters argued could have underestimated potential increases in emissions. A third set of comments focused on the issue of mitigation.

One set of thee comments concerned the possibility that restrictions built into FERC's analysis on the amount of power that could be transmitted among regions unduly limited projections of the amount of electricity generated and exported from high-emitting, coal-fired sources in the Ohio River Valley. These comments[43] suggested that the rule would increase the amount of power transported, leading to additional construction of more transmission capacity if necessary, and would thus result in more emissions than projected. In particular, it would increase

---

[41] Federal Energy Regulatory Commission, *Promoting Wholesale Competition through Open Access Non-Discriminatory Transmission Services by Public Utilities (RM95-80000)...* Draft Environmental Impact Statement (November 1995) FERC/EIS-0096D.

[42] Federal Energy Regulatory Commission, *Promoting Wholesale Competition through Open Access Non-Discriminatory Transmission Services by Public Utilities* (RM95-8-000) ... Final Environmental Impact Statement (April 1996) FERC/EIS – 0096, Appendix J.

[43] See, for example, Alliance for Affordable Energy, et al., Joint Comment on Draft Environmental Impact Statement (February 1, 1996, p. 32.

NOx emissions that could be expected to affect the Northeast. As a result, for its final EIA, FERC added further analysis of this possibility, but concluded the effects would not be significant.[44]

Another set of comments argued that the rule would have the effect of decreasing electricity prices and therefore would likely increase demand, leading to the generation of more electricity than assumed in the base cases. FERC basically said this possibility would be a second-order effect that lay outside appropriate analysis.[45] Despite FERC's response, ignoring demand seems unrealistic. As noted earlier, electricity demand is a critical component in assessing emission-related impacts. However, the model FERC used for its analysis is incapable of analyzing the price-demand effects of restructuring because its demand assumption is exogenous to the model. FERC chose to assume that the lower prices of restructuring would not result in any increase in electricity demand from baseline conditions – an unlikely outcome. To ignore the price-demand relationship reduces confidence in FERC's conclusion.

The third set of comments, on mitigation, ranged from those supported FERC's conclusion that there was nothing that needs mitigating to arguments that FERC was obligated and has the authority to require mitigation.[46]

Subsequent reports challenge the FERC analysis. In April 1997, the Natural Resources Defense Council, Public Service Electric and Gas Co., and pace University's Mid-Atlantic Energy Project jointly issued a report evaluating the contribution of utility generating companies to air pollution. Presenting data indicating that "the 'lowest cost' producers of electricity" are often "some of the highest emitters of pollutants," the authors concluded that

> In order to implement fair competition and to prevent a considerable increase in electric utility emissions due to increased use of older, higher-emitting units, the restructuring process should apply consistent environmental standards to all competitors.[47]

In January 1998, the Northeast States for Coordinated Air Use Management (NESCAUM) issued a report concluding that recent trends contradict FERC's finding in the EIS. Specifically, NESCAUM presented data challenging two assumptions that has led to the EIS conclusion that emissions growth would be negligible. Contrary to the EIS analysis, NESCAUM shows that between 1995 and 1996, coal-fired generation increased while natural gas-fired generation declined and that growth in the use of interregional power transmission had "outstripped FERC's longer-term growth assumptions."[48] According to NESCAUM, these preliminary findings suggest that increased competition is contributing to increased emissions at coal-intensive utilities, and that some form of mid-course public policy correction may be necessary. These findings underscore the need for comprehensive efforts to document the impacts of restructuring on air quality, and lend impetus to state and federal efforts to establish adequate emissions tracking and disclosure systems. Moreover, these findings suggest that equitable environmental standards must be made an integral part of ongoing competitive reforms.[49]

---

[44] FERC, Final EIS, pp. J-34 - J-39 and pp. 6-25 - 6-41.

[45] See FERC, Final EIS, pp. J-69 - J-70.

[46] Mitigation is discussed in Chapter 7 of the EIS; comments are discussed in the Final EIS at pp. J-78 - J-105.

[47] Natural Resources Defense Council, et al., Benchmarking Air Emissions of Electric Utility Generators in the Eastern United States, 2nd Edition (April 1997), p. 41.

[48] Northeast States for Coordinated Air Use Management, Air Pollution Impacts of Increased Deregulation in the Electric Power Industry: An Initial Analysis (January 15, 1998), p. 1 At [http://www.nescaum.org/about.html]

[49] Ibid., p. 2.

Thus, environmental interest groups continue to warn that FERC underestimated emissions resulting from its rule – and that restructuring portends even greater impacts; and that, therefore, mitigation of the effects of the rule and of restructuring is necessary. However, as suggested above, increased emissions may be the result of existing trends in the industry, and not strictly due to restructuring. As noted, renovating coal-fired capacity has been an increasing trend in the industry for over a decade. As the NESCAUM data reflect a time period before implementation of Order 888, ascribing emission increases solely to restructuring is debatable. This situation illustrates the difficulties in assigning cause to potential emission increases over the next 5-10 years from existing coal-fired facilities.

CONCLUSION

The relationship between restructuring electricity generation and environmental consequences is not a simple one. The environmental outcome will result from an interactive, iterative process of many changes in existing trends affecting electricity generation. The two most crucial trends are: (1) decisions with respect to meeting future electricity demand, including the renovation of existing generating capacity, choice of new generating technologies for new construction, and enhancement of transmission capacity; and, (2) decisions with respect to implementing existing environmental regulations, and the potential approval of future environmental regulations. Restructuring would influence each of these trends to varying degrees, encouraging some, such as renovating existing capacity, and challenging others, such as existing environmental regulations.

Electricity Demand

Restructuring and the other trends underway point to changes in demand and technological developments that will ultimately be reflected in environmental consequences. To the extent restructuring and the other changes lead to a more efficient generation industry, baseload prices should decline, which would be expected to lead to higher demand and greater consumption. Lower baseload prices could encourage owners of existing coal-fired facilities with low operating costs to extend and enhance electricity generation from such facilities rather than risk investing in new construction. Estimates indicate that between 23,000 and 53,000 Mw of existing coal-fired capacity is currently underutilized and could be made available if economics and transmission capacity justified such a decision. Renovating existing coal-fired capacity has been an increasing trend in the industry for over a decade. The more competitive generating market of a restructured electric utility industry could further encourage this trend.

Reduced baseload electricity prices also change the signals affecting consumer choices related to energy efficiency. Lower baseload electricity prices could diminish the incentive to invest in increased conservation, such as more efficient refrigerators or insulation. Cost-considerations may also work against power generation by renewables such as solar, wind power, and geothermal, which currently are not cost-competitive with natural gas or coal technologies. It may also work against nuclear which is a capital intensive technology, and which has contradictory environmental implications – being essentially free of air emissions, but posing waste disposal problems that some see as more hazardous and less controllable. Finally cost concerns may further encourage natural gas-generated power in new construction (the existing technology of choice), which is more environmentally friendly than coal or oil alternatives.

But at the same time, if prices reflect marginal costs, the price signal is likely to dampen peak demand, which typically is met by the most costly and inefficient generating capacity – thereby leveling the demand curve. Higher prices for peak load power could strengthen the signal for load management – conservation measures that reduce peak usage, such as automatic shutoffs of hot water heating during peak demand. Also, to the degree consumers are given the choice of electricity suppliers, they may create new markets for different types of generation by basing their decisions on factors other than economics, such as environmental ones. One such possibility is "green pricing," where some consumers choose to purchase electricity that costs more economically but costs less environmentally – such as that produced by renewables. Such a "green market" is being developed in California, but it is too early to anticipate the size that it may achieve.

How these differing effects play out will determine the potential for increased emissions from restructuring. As indicated, some, such as renovating existing coal-fired capacity, represent a furthering of an existing trend. Others, such as green pricing, represent a new trend created by restructuring. Although the overall effect on emissions is difficult to assess, involving several currently unquantifiable variables the most substantial environmental effect in the short- to mid-term is likely to come from enhanced operation of existing coal-fired capacity. Whether one can ascribe that effect to general trends in the industry or to restructuring is debatable.

Air Quality Regulations

Restructuring, combined with the outcome of the other trends, has the potential to increase emissions of some pollutants of concern; the question is whether existing (or proposed) regulatory limits on those emissions would effectively prevent adverse effects.

- For SO_2, restructuring is unlikely to have any effects on emissions. The CAA requirements statutorily "cap" the nation's utility SO_2 emissions, making industry structure essentially irrelevant. Increasing numbers of participants may make monitoring and enforcement more demanding, but the SO_2 program contains substantial penalties for non-compliance, and no compliance difficulties have emerged to date.
- For NO_x, the potential of extended and enhanced coal-fired capacity utilization encouraged by restructuring could significantly increase emissions. NO_x emissions from an additional 23,000 MW of coal-fired capacity could be in the range of 480,000 tons, compared with about 70,000 tons if that electricity was generated from natural gas. However, several EPA regulatory actions could reduce or eliminate that potential increase. For example, EPA's Ozone Transport Rule would in effect set a "cap" on emissions in 21 eastern states where they currently contribute to unacceptable ozone pollution; these 21 states are where the majority of potential coal-fired related NO_x emission increases could occur. However, the primary implementation of the process lies with the states. As a result, the NO_x control program would be administratively more complicated and could be less economically efficient than the SO_2 control program. A system of state-based programs to control NO_x emissions might dovetail with the current electricity generation system in which state regulation plays a large role; but if restructuring leads to a more regionally-based, competitive electricity generating system, then implementing a NO_x control program based on state programs could lead to industry segments being subject to inconsistent requirements in the various states. Indeed, the inconsistencies could constitute barriers - or opportunities – to the restructuring process.

But if the process works, then there would be no increase in NOx in the 21-state region, and the structure of the industry would be irrelevant. If this process is delayed, other regiments, including section 126 petitions, are available for relief.

- For CO2, the potential for extended and enhanced coal-fired capacity utilization encouraged by restructuring could significantly increase emissions. CO2 emissions from an additional 23,000 Mw of coal-fired capacity would be about 200,000,000 short tons, compared with 80,000,000 tons if that electricity was generated from natural gas. CO2 emissions are not controlled by the Clean Air Act, nor does there appear to be any readily applicable provision that used to control such emissions. If the U.S. ratifies the Kyoto Agreement, it would effectively "cap" emissions, and restructuring would become irrelevant in terms of emission increases. But how emissions would be controlled and how reductions would be allocated and implemented would remain to be determined by future domestic legislation.

- For Hg, increased utilization of coal-fired capacity would result in increased Hg emissions, although uncertainty exists as to how much that increase would be. Studies have been completed that could be the basis for regulation under existing CAA authorities, if EPA were to conclude controls are necessary.[50] How well these would mesh with a more competitive electric generating market is unclear.

Ultimately, whether future developments in electricity generation will lead to pollution increases of health and environmental concern depends on the effectiveness of CAA requirements and of EPA implementation and enforcement (or on future enactment's of new controls) – and, in the case of CO2, on whether the U.S. ratifies the Kyoto Convention and its requirements are implemented.

Responses

If one has confidence that these authorities will prove adequate to protect human health and the environment and will be effectively implemented, one may be comfortable in adopting the stance that "no action" is necessary to address any emissions implications of restructuring proposals. The result might not be as cost-effective as a regulatory regime more tied to a competitive market (such as a SO2 style "cap and trade" program), but except for CO2 (for which the need for controls is highly contentious), the CAA provides control authorities – notably for emissions of particular concern, NOx and Hg.[51]

Conversely, if one fears that existing approaches to pollution control will not be effective or not be implemented, or that controls on CO2 are requisite, then one is likely to press actions for immediate response. Those having such concerns could be expected to pursue several actions to address perceived unacceptable environmental impacts, such as:

- aggressively using the existing regulatory regimen to address environmental deteriorations;
- proposing to embed environmental protections in any restructuring programs; and

---

[50] Specifically, see: Environmental Protection Agency, Mercury Study Report to Congress, EPA-452/R-97-003 (December 1997).

[51] While Hg emissions from electric utilities are not currently regulated, the 1990 CAA Amendments provide EPA with the authority to do so based on studies mandated by the Act (section 112(n)).

- proposing revisions of appropriate environmental statutes, in particular, the CAA – and supporting prompt ratification of the Kyoto Agreement and enactment of appropriate implementation legislation.

Those seeking to assure rigorous application of existing air pollution controls could aggressively use the citizen suite or section 126 provisions of the CAA to press their case whenever they perceive inadequate or ineffective implementation. While this may be effective for controlling NOx and Hg emissions, it would not appear to be a fruitful course with respect to CO2 emissions for which any controls are only prospective.

The case for adding environmental protections to restructuring proposals depends in part on the extent to which restructuring itself is a likely cause of more pollution; or if the restructured industry were to pose implementation, enforcement, or other problems that the current regulatory structure proves ill-equipped to cope with. (For some, attaching environmental issues to restructuring may be a surrogate for debates on a comprehensive review of the CAA or for CO2 controls.) As indicated by the analysis of this paper, restructuring's role is not clear; it is quite possible that some utility emissions of concern could increase as a result of other trends underway, and in fact that may be happening. As the NESCAUM report indicates, coal-fired generation appears already to be on the rise, before restructuring efforts such as FERC's rule to promote wholesale competition through open access to transmission services could be having an effect. Likewise, monitoring shows that (unregulated) CO2 emissions have risen since 1990.[52] Thus, tying environmental protection to restructuring might fail to address actual causes for increased emissions.

Responding to any problems that arise by then revising environmental statutes may seem risky to those who already perceive significant environmental risks from changes in electricity generation. They could point to the history of acid rain legislation as an example of the risk: it took about 10 years from the time legislation was first proposed to address acid rain to enactment of a program – which required movement of a comprehensive set of CAA amendments. The lesson many draw is that consideration and enactment of environmental legislation separate from legislation that might have the potential to cause environmental problems can be delayed and difficult. From this perspective, at least, it could make sense that if Congress is to enact restructuring legislation, to attach to those bills any potentially necessary environmental responses even if the problem is not solely due to restructuring.[53]

All in all, as the preceding analysis and discussion indicates, the potential for environmental deterioration from restructuring electricity generation is difficult to project – both because various technical and economic changes are affecting the industry at the same time and because of an evolving policy context. As a result of this uncertainty, those who are focused on preventing environmental deterioration tend to take a precautionary stance, to propose immediate preventative measures, and to argue that such measures be attached to available legislative vehicles. In contrast, those who doubt that there will be significant environmental effects or who are focused on the substantial regulatory structure in place tend to take a wait-and-see position. Further complicating

---

[52] Larry Parker and John Blodgett, *Global Climate Change: Reducing Greenhouse Gases – How Much from What Baseline?* CRS Report 235, March 11, 1998.

[53] For information on legislative proposals relating restructuring to environmental controls, see Larry Parker and Amy Abel, *Electricity: The Road Toward Restructuring*, CRS Issue Brief IB10006 (updated regularly); and Larry Parker, *Electricity Restructuring: Comparison of Comprehensive Bills*, CRS Report RL 30087, (updated regularly); and, Larry Parker, *Electricity Restructuring and Air Quality: Comparison of Proposed Legislation*, CRS Report RS20326 (July 26, 2000).

this picture is that some attitudes about restructuring are related to and partly a surrogate for a more fundamental debate that is underway because of global climate change concerns – about the future direction of energy use in the United States and the federal role in affecting it.

FUEL ETHANOL:
BACKGROUND AND PUBLIC POLICY ISSUES

Brent D. Yacobucci and Jasper Womach

INTRODUCTION

Ethanol (ethyl alcohol) is an alcohol made by fermenting and distilling simple sugars. Ethyl alcohol is in alcoholic beverages and it is denatured (made unfit for human consumption) when used for fuel or industrial purposes.[1] The biggest use of fuel ethanol in the United States is as an additive in gasoline. It serves as an oxygenate (to prevent air pollution from carbon monoxide and ozone), as an octane booster (to prevent early ignition, or "engine knock"), and as an extender of gasoline. In purer forms, it can also be used as an alternative to gasoline in automobiles designed for its use. It is produced and consumed mostly in the Midwest, where corn – the main feedstock for ethanol production – is produced.

The initial stimulus to ethanol production in the mid-1970s was the drive to develop alternative and renewable supplies of energy in response to the oil embargoes of 1973 and 1979. Production of fuel ethanol has been encouraged by a partial exemption from the motor fuels excise tax. Another impetus to fuel ethanol production has come from corn producers anxious to expand the market for their crop. More recently the use of fuel ethanol has been stimulated by the Clean Air Act Amendments of 1990, which require oxygenated or reformulated gasoline to reduce emissions of carbon monoxide (CO) and volatile organic compounds (VOCs).

While oxygenates reduce CO and VOC emissions, they also lead to higher emissions of nitrogen oxides, precursors to ozone formation. While reformulated gasoline has succeeded in reducing ground-level ozone, the overall effect of oxygenates on ozone formation has been questioned. Furthermore, ethanol's main competitor in oxygenated fuels, methyl tertiary butyl ether (MTBE), has been found to contaminate groundwater. This has led to a push to ban MTBE, or eliminate the oxygenate requirements altogether. High summer gasoline prices in the Midwest, especially in Chicago and Milwaukee, where oxygenates are required, have added to the push to remove the oxygenate requirements. The trade-offs between air quality, water quality, and consumer price have sparked congressional debate on these requirements. In addition, there has been a long-running debate over the tax incentives that ethanol-blended fuels receive.

---

[1] Industrial uses include perfumes, aftershaves, and cleansers.

Fuel ethanol is used mainly as a low concentrate blend in gasoline, but can also be used in purer forms as an alternative to gasoline. In 1999, 99.8% of fuel ethanol consumed in the United States was in the form of "gasohol" or "E10" (blends of gasoline with up to 10% ethanol).[2]

Fuel ethanol is produced from the distillation of fermented simple sugars (e.g. glucose) derived primarily from corn, but also from wheat, potatoes and other vegetables, as well as from cellulosic waste such as rice straw and sugar cane (bagasse). The alcohol in fuel ethanol is identical to ethanol used for other purposes, but is treated (denatured) with gasoline to make it unfit for human consumption.

ETHANOL AND THE AGRICULTURAL ECONOMY

Corn constitutes about 90% of the feedstock for ethanol production in the United States. The other 10% is largely grain sorghum, along with some barley, wheat, cheese whey and potatoes. Corn is used because it is a relatively low cost source of starch that can be converted to simple sugars, fermented and distilled. It is estimated by the U.S. Department of Agriculture (USDA) that about 615 million bushels of corn will be used to produce about 1.5 billion gallons of fuel ethanol during the 2000/2001 corn marketing year.[3] This is 6.17% of the projected 9.755 billion bushels of corn utilization.[4]

Producers of corn, along with other major crops, receive farm income support and price support. Farms with a history of corn production will receive "production flexibility contract payments" of about $1.186 billion during the 2000/2001 corn marketing year. Emergency economic assistance (P.L. 106-224) more than double the corn contract payments. Corn producers also are guaranteed a minimum national average price of $1.89/bushel under the nonrecourse marketing assistance loan program.[5]

The added demand for corn created by fuel ethanol raises the market price for corn above what it would be otherwise. Economists estimate that when supplies are large, the use of an additional 100 million bushels of corn raises the price by about 4¢ per bushel. When supplies are low, the price impact is greater. The ethanol market is particularly welcome now, when the average price received by farmers is forecast by USDA to average about $1.80 per bushel for the 2000/01 marketing year. This price would be the lowest season average since 1986. The ethanol market of 615 million bushels of corn, assuming a price impact of about 25¢ per bushel on all corn sales, means a possible $2.4 billion in additional sales revenue to corn farmers. In the absence of the ethanol market, lower corn prices probably would stimulate increased corn utilization in other markets, but sales revenue would not be as high. The lower price and sales revenue would be likely to result in higher federal spending on corn payments to farmers, as long as corn prices wee below the price triggering federal loan deficiency subsidies.

---

[2]U.S. Department of Energy (DOE), Energy Information Administration (EIA). *Alternatives to Traditional Transportation Fuels 1998.* October 1999.

[3]One bushel of corn generates approximately 2.5 gallons of ethanol.

[4]Utilization data are used, rather than production, due tot he existence of carryover stocks. Corn utilization data address the total amount of corn used within a given period.

[5]Detailed explanations are available in CRS Report RS20271, *Grain, Cotton, and Oilseeds: Federal Commodity Support,* and CRS 98-744, *Agricultural Marketing Assistance Loans and Loan Deficiency Payments.*

Table 1. Corn Utilization, 2000/2001 Forecast

	Quantity (Million bushels)	Share of Total Use
Livestock feed & residual	5,775	59.2%
Food, seed & Industrial:	1,980	19.9%
Fuel alcohol	615	6.2%
High fructose corn syrup	550	5.5%
Glucose & dextrose	220	2.2%
Starch	225	2.6%
Cereals & other products	190	1.9%
Beverage alcohol	130	1.3%
Seed	20	0.2%
Exports	2000	20.1%
TOTAL USE	9,775	100.00%
TOTAL PRODUCTION	9,968	

Source: Basic data are from USDA, Economic Research Service, Feed Outlook, March 10, 2000.

ETHANOL REFINING AND PRODUCTION

According tot he Renewable Fuels Association, about 55% of the corn used for ethanol is process by "dry" milling plants (a grinding process) and other 45% is processed by "wet" milling plants (a chemical extraction process). The basic steps of both processes are as follows. First, the corn is processed, with various enzymes added to separate fermentable sugars. Next, yeast is added to the mixture for fermentation to make alcohol. The alcohol is then distilled to fuel-grade ethanol that is 85-95% pure.[6] Finally, for fuel and industrial purposes the ethanol is denatured with a small amount of a displeasing or noxious chemical to make it unfit for human consumption.[7] In the U.S. the denaturant for fuel ethanol is gasoline.

Ethanol is produced largely in the Midwest corn belt, with almost 90% of production occurring in five states: Illinois, Iowa, Nebraska, Minnesota and Indiana. Because it is generally less expensive to produce ethanol close to the feedstock supply, it is not surprising that the top five corn-producing states in the U.S. are also the top five ethanol-producers. Most ethanol use is in the metropolitan centers of the Midwest, where it is produced. When ethanol is used in other

---

[6]The byproduct of the dry milling process is distillers dried grains. The byproducts of wet milling are corn gluten feed, corn gluten meal, and corn oil. Distillers dried grains, corn gluten feed, and corn gluten meal are used as livestock feed.

regions, shipping costs tend to be high, since ethanol-blended gasoline cannot travel through petroleum pipelines.

This geographic concentration is an obstacle to the use of ethanol on the East and West Coasts. The potential for expanding production geographically is a motivation behind research on ethanol, since if regions could locate production facilities closer to the point of consumption, the costs of using ethanol could be lessened. Furthermore, if regions could produce fuel ethanol from local crops, there would be an increase in regional agricultural income.

Table 2. Top 10 Ethanol Producers by Capacity, 2000
(Million Gallons Per Year)

Archer Daniels Midland (ADM)	797
Minnesota Corn Processors	110
Williams Energy Services	100
Cargill	100
New Energy Corp	85
Midwest Grain Products	78
High Plains Corporation	70
Chief Ethanol	62
AGP	52
A.E. Staley	45
Chief Ethanol	40
All Others	508
U.S. Total	2007

Source: Renewable Fuels Association, Ethanol Industry Outlook 2001.

Ethanol production is also concentrated among a few large producers. The top five companies account for approximately 60% of production capacity, and the top ten companies account for approximately 75% of production capacity. (See **Table 2**.) Critics of the ethanol industry in general – and specifically of the ethanol tax incentives – argue that the tax incentives for ethanol production equate to "corporate welfare" for a few large producers.[8]

Overall, domestic ethanol production capacity is approximately 2.0 billion gallons per year. Consumption is expected to increase from 1.7 billion gallons per year in 2000 to approximately 2.6 billion gallons per year in 2005. Production will need to increase proportionally to meet the

---

[7]Renewable Fuels Association, *Ethanol Industry Outlook 2001, Clean Air, Clean Water, Clean Fuel.*

[8]James Bovard, *Archer Daniels Midland: A Case Study in Corporate Welfare.* Cato Institute. September 26, 1995.

increased demand.[9]   However, if the Clean Air Act is amended to limit or ban MTBE, ethanol production capacity may expand at a faster rate. This is especially true if MTBE is banned while maintaining the oxygenate requirements, since ethanol is the most likely substitute for MTBE.

Fuel is not the only output of an ethanol facility, however. Co-products play an important role in the profitability of a plant. In addition to the primary ethanol output, the corn wet milling generates corn gluten feed, corn gluten meal, and corn oil, and dry milling creates distillers grains. Corn oil is used as a vegetable oil and is higher priced than soybean oil. Approximately 12 million metric tons of gluten feed, gluten meal, and dried distillers grains are produced in the United States and sold as livestock feed annually. A major market for corn gluten feed and meal is the European Union, which imported nearly 5 million metric tons of gluten feed and meal during FY1998.

Revenue from the ethanol byproducts help offset the cost of corn. The net cost of corn relative tot he price of ethanol (the ethanol production margin) and the difference between ethanol and wholesale gasoline prices (the fuel blending margin) are the major determinants of the level of ethanol production. Currently, the ethanol production margin is high because of the low price of corn. At the same time, the wholesale price of gasoline is increasing against the price of ethanol, which encourages the use of ethanol as an octane enhancer.

FUEL CONSUMPTION

Approximately 1.4 billion gallons of ethanol fuel were consumed in the United States in 1999, mainly blended into E10 gasohol. While large, this figure represents only 1.2% of the approximately 125 billion gallons of gasoline consumption in the same year.[10] According to DOE, ethanol consumption is expected to grow to 2.6 billion gallons per year in 2005 and 3.3 billion gallons per year in 2020. This would increase ethanol's market share to approximately 1.5% by 2005. This 1.5% share is projected to remain constant through 2020.[11]

The most significant barrier to wider use of fuel ethanol is its cost. Even with tax incentives for ethanol producers (see the section on Economic Effects), the fuel tends to be more expensive than gasoline per gallon. Furthermore, since fuel ethanol has a somewhat lower energy content, more fuel is required to travel the same distance. This energy loss leads to an approximate 3% decrease in miles-per-gallon vehicle fuel economy with gasohol.[12]

However, ethanol's chemical properties make it very useful for some applications, especially as an additive in gasoline. Major stimuli to the use of ethanol have been the oxygenate requirements of the Reformulated Gasoline (RFG) and Oxygenated Fuels programs of the Clean Air Act.[13] Oxygenates are used to promote more complete combustion of gasoline, which reduces carbon monoxide and volatile organic compound (VOC) emissions.[14] In addition, oxygenates can replace other chemicals in gasoline, such as benzene, a toxic air pollutant (see the section on Air Quality).

---

[9]DOE, EIA, *Annual Energy Outlook 2001*. December 22, 2000. Table 18.

[10]DOE, EIA, *Alternatives to Traditional Transportation Fuels 1998*. October 1999. Table 10.

[11]DOE, EIA, *Annual Energy Outlook 2001*. December 22, 2000 Tables 2 and 18.

[12]It should be noted that the use of ethanol does not effect the efficiency of an engine. There is simply less energy in one gallon of ethanol than in one gallon of gasoline.

[13]Section 211, subsections k and m (respectively). 42 U.S.C. 7545

[14]CO, VOCs and nitrogen oxides (NOx) are the main precursors to ground-level ozone.

The two most common oxygenates are ethanol and methyl tertiary butyl either (MTBE). MTBE, primarily made from natural gas or petroleum products, is preferred to ethanol in most regions because it is generally much less expensive, is easier to transport and distribute, and is available in greater supply. Because of different distribution systems and blending processes (with gasoline), substituting one oxygenate for another can lead to significant cost increases.

Despite the cost differential, there are several possible advantages of using ethanol over MTBE. Ethanol contains 35% oxygen by weight – twice the oxygen content of MTBE. Furthermore, since ethanol is produced from agricultural products, it has the potential to be a sustainable fuel, while MTBE is produced from natural gas and petroleum, fossil fuels. In addition, ethanol is readily biodegradable, eliminating some of the potential concerns about groundwater contamination that have surrounded MTBE (see the section on MTBE).

Both ethanol and MTBE also can be blended into otherwise non-oxygenated gasoline to raise the octane rating of the fuel, and therefore improve its combustion properties. High-performance engines and older engines often require higher octane fuel to prevent early ignition, or "engine knock." Other chemicals may be used for the same purpose, but some of these alternatives are highly toxic, and some are regulated as pollutants under the Clean Air Act.[15] Furthermore, since these additives do not contain oxygen, they do not result in the same emissions reductions as oxygenated gasoline.

In purer forms, ethanol can also be used as an alternative to gasoline in vehicles specifically designed for its use, although this only represents approximately 0.2% of ethanol consumption in the U.S. The federal government and state governments, along with businesses in the alternative fuel industry, are required to purchase alternative-fueled vehicles by the Energy Policy Act of 1992.[16] In addition, under the Clean Air Act Amendments of 1990, municipal fleets can use alternative fuel vehicles to mitigate air quality problems. Blends of 85% ethanol with 15% gasoline (E85), and 95% ethanol with 5% gasoline (#95) are currently considered alternative fuels by the Department of Energy.[17] The small amount of gasoline added to the alcohol helps prevent corrosion of engine parts, and aids ignition in cold weather.

---

[15]Lead was commonly used as an octane enhancer until it was phased -out through the mid-emissions control devices, and because it is toxic to humans.

[16]P.L. 102-486.

[17]More diluted blends of ethanol, such as E10, are considered to be "extenders" of gasoline, as opposed to alternatives.

Table 3. Estimated U.S. Consumption of Fuel Ethanol, MTBE
and Gasoline
(Thousand Gasoline-Equivalent Gallons)

	1994	1996	1998	2000 (Projected)
E85	80	694	1,727	3,283
E95	140	2,699	59*	59
Ethanol in Gasohol (E10)	845,900	660,200	916,000	908,700
MTBE in Gasoline	2,108,800	2,749,700	2,915,600	3,111,500
Gasoline**	113,144,000	117,783,000	122,849,000	127,568,000

Source: Department of Energy, Alternatives to Traditional Transportation Fuels 1998.
*A major drop in E95 consumption occurred between 1997 and 1998 because of a significant decrease in the number of E95-fueled vehicles in operation (347 to 14), due to the elimination of an ethanol-fueled bus fleet in California.
**Gasoline consumption includes ethanol is gasohol and MTBE in gasoline.

Approximately 1.7 million gasoline-equivalent gallons (GEG)[18] of E85, and 59 thousand GEG of #95 were consumed in 1998, mostly in Midwestern states.[19] (See **Table 3**). One reason for the relatively low consumption of E85 and E95 is that there are relatively few vehicles on the road that operate on these fuels. In 1998, approximately 13,000 vehicles were fueled by E85 or E95,[20, 21] as compared to approximately 210 million gasoline- and diesel-fueled vehicles that were on the road in the same year.[22] One obstacle to the use of alternative fuel vehicles is that they are generally more expensive than conventional vehicles, although this margin has decreased in recent years with new technology. Another obstacle is that, as was stated above, fuel ethanol is generally more expensive than gasoline or diesel fuel. In addition, there are very few fueling sites for E85 and E95, especially outside of the Midwest.

RESEARCH AND DEVELOPMENT IN CELLULOSIC FEEDSTOCKS

For ethanol to play a more important role in U.S. fuel consumption, the fuel must become price-competitive with gasoline. Since a major part of the total production cost is the cost of feedstock, reducing feedstock costs could lead to lower wholesale ethanol costs. For this reason, there is a great deal of interest in the use of cellulosic feedstocks, which include low-value waste products, such as recycled paper, or dedicated fuel crops, such as switch grass. A dedicated fuel crop is one that would be grown and harvested solely for the purpose of fuel production.

---

[18] Since different fuels produce different amounts of energy per gallon when consumed, the unit of a gasoline-equivalent gallon (GEG) is used to compare total energy consumption.
[19] DOE, EIA, *Alternatives to Traditional Transportation Fuels* 1998.
[20] Ibid.
[21] In 1997, some manufacturers made flexible E85/gasoline fueling capability standard on some models. It is expected, however, that most of these vehicles will be fueled by gasoline.
[22] Stacy C. Davis, DOE, *Transportation Energy Data Book: Edition 20.* November 2000.

However, as the name indicates, cellulosic feedstocks are high in cellulose, and cellulose cannot be fermented. Cellulose must first be broken down into simpler carbohydrates, and this can add an expensive step to the process. Therefore, research has focused on both reducing the process costs for cellulosic ethanol, and improving the availability of cellulosic feedstocks.

On August 12, 1999, the Clinton Administration announced the Biobased Products and Bioenergy Initiative, which aims to triple the use of fuels and products derived from biomass by 2010.[23] Research and development covers all forms of biobased products, including lubricants, adhesives, building materials, and biofuels. Because federal research into cellulosic ethanol is ongoing, it is likely that funding would increase under the initiative.

COSTS AND BENEFITS OF FUEL ETHANOL

Economic Effects

Given that a major constraint on the use of ethanol as an alternative fuel, and as an oxygenate, is its high price, ethanol has not been competitive with gasoline as fuel. Wholesale ethanol prices, before incentives from the federal government and state government, are generally twice that of wholesale gasoline prices. With federal and state incentives, however, the effective price of ethanol is much lower. Furthermore, gasoline prices have risen recently making ethanol more attractive.

The primary federal incentive to support the ethanol industry is the 5.4¢ per gallon exemption that blenders of gasohol (E10) receive from the 18.4¢ federal excise tax on motor fuels.[24] Because the exemption applies to blended fuel, of which ethanol comprises only 15%, the exemption provides for an effective subsidy of 54¢ per gallon of pure ethanol. (See **Table 4.**)

Table 4. Price of Pure Ethanol Relative to Gasoline
July 1998 to June 1999

Ethanol Wholesale Price*	103¢/gallon
Alcohol Fuel Tax Incentive	54¢/gallon
Effective Price of Ethanol	49¢/gallon
Gasoline Wholesale Price**	46¢/gallon

Source: Hart's Oxy-Fuel News; Energy Information Agency, Petroleum Marketing Monthly.
* This is the average price for pure ("neat") ethanol.
**This is the average price for regular conventional gasoline (i.e. non-oxygenated, standard octane).

It is argued that the ethanol industry could not survive without the tax exemption. An economic analysis conducted in 1998 by the Food and Agriculture Policy Research Institute, in conjunction with the congressional debate over extension of the tax exemption, concluded that

---

[23]Executive Order 13134. August 12, 1999.
[24]26 U.S.C. 40.

ethanol production from corn would decline from 1.4 billion gallons per year, and stabilize at about 290 million gallons per year, if the exemption were eliminated.[25]

The tax exemption for ethanol is criticized by some as a corporate subsidy,[26] because, in this view, it encourages the inefficient use of agricultural and other resources, and deprives the Highway Trust Fund of needed revenues.[27] In 1997, the General Accounting Office estimated that the tax exemption would lead to approximately $10.4 billion in foregone Highway Trust Fund revenue over the 22 years from FY1979 to FY2000.[28] The petroleum industry opposes the incentive because it also results in reduced use of petroleum.

Proponents of the tax incentive argue that ethanol leads to better air quality, and that substantial benefits flow to the agricultural sector due tot he increased demand for corn created by ethanol. Furthermore, they argue that the increased market for ethanol leads to a stronger U.S. trade balance, since a smaller U.S. ethanol industry would lead to increased imports of MTBE to meet the demand for oxygenates.[29]

Air Quality

One of the main motivations for ethanol use is improved air quality. Ethanol is primarily used in gasoline to meet minimum oxygenate requirements of two Clean Air Act programs. Reformulated gasoline (RFG)[30] is used to reduce vehicle emissions in areas that are in severe or extreme nonattainment of National Ambient Air Quality Standards (NAAQS) for ground-level ozone.[31] Ten metropolitan areas, including New York, Los Angeles, Chicago, Philadelphia, and Houston are covered by this requirement, and many other areas with less severe ozone problems have opted into the program, as well. In these areas, RFG is used year-round. By contrast, the Oxygenated Fuels program operates only in the winter months in 20 areas[32] that are listed as carbon monoxide (CO) nonattainment areas.[33]

EPA states that RFG has led to significant improvements in air quality, including a 17% reduction in volatile organic compounds (VOCs) emissions from vehicles, and a 30% reduction in toxic emissions. Furthermore, according to EPA "ambient monitoring data from the first year of the RFG program (1995) also showed strong signs that RFG is working. For example, detection of

---

[25]Food and Agriculture Policy Research Institute. *Effects on Agriculture of Elimination of the Excise Tax Exemption for Fuel Ethanol,* Working Paper 01-97, April 8, 1997.

[26]James Bovard. P.8.

[27]U.S. General Accounting Office, *Effects of the Alcohol Fuels Tax Incentives.* March, 1997.

[28]Ibid.

[29]Katrin Olson, "USDA Shows Losses Associated with Eliminating Ethanol Incentive," *Oxy-fuel News.* May 19, 1997. P.3.

[30]Clean Air Act, Section 211, subsection k. 42 U.S.C. 7545.

[31]Ground-level ozone is an air pollutant that causes smog, adversely affects health, and injures plants. It should not be confused with stratospheric ozone, which is a natural layer some 6 to 20 miles above the earth and provides a degree of protection from harmful radiation.

[32]Only the Los Angeles and New York areas are subject to both programs.

[33]Clean Air Act, Section 211, subsection m. 42 U.S.C. 7545.

benzene (one of the air toxins controlled by FT, and a known human carcinogen) declined dramatically, with a median reduction of 38% from the previous year."[34]

However, the need for oxygenates in RFG has been questioned. Although oxygenates lead to lower emissions of VOCs, and CO, they may lead to higher emissions of nitrogen oxides (NOx). Since all three contribute to the formation of ozone, the National Research Council recently concluded that while RFG certainly leads to improved air quality, the oxygenate requirement in RFG may have little overall impact on ozone formation.[35] Furthermore, the high price of Midwest gasoline in Summer 2000 has raised further questions about the RFG program (see the section on Phase 2 Reformulated Gasoline).

Evidence that the most widely-used oxygenate, methyl tertiary butyl either (MTBE), contaminates groundwater has led to a push by some to eliminate the oxygen requirement in RFG. MTBE has been identified as an animal carcinogen, and there is concern that it is a possible human carcinogen. In California, MTBE will be banned as of December 31, 2002, and the state is lobbying Congress for a waiver to the oxygen requirement (see section on MTBE). Other states, such as states in the Northeast, are also seeking waivers.

If the oxygenate requirements were eliminated, some refiners claim that the environmental goals of the RFG program could be achieved through cleaner, although potentially more costly, gasoline that does not contain any oxygenates.[36] These claims have added tot he push to remove the oxygen requirement and allow refiners to produce RFG in the most cost-effective manner, whether or not that includes the use oxygenates. However, some environmental groups are concerned that an elimination of the oxygenate requirements would compromise air quality gains resulting from the current standards, since oxygenates also displace other harmful chemicals in gasoline. This potential for "backsliding" is a result of the fact that the current performance of RFG is substantially better than the Clean Air Act requires. If the oxygenate standard were eliminated, environmental groups fear that refiners would only meet the requirements of the law, as opposed to maintaining the current overcompliance.

While the potential ozone benefit from oxygenates in RFG has been questioned, there is little dispute that the winter Oxy-Fuels programs has led to lower emissions of CO. The Oxy-Fuels program requires oxygenated gasoline in the winter months to control CO pollution in NAAQS nonattainment areas for the CO standard. However, this program is small relative to the RFG program.[37]

The air quality benefits from purer forms of ethanol can also be substantial. Compared to gasoline, use of E85 and E95 can result in a 30%-50% reduction in ozone-forming emissions. And while the use of ethanol also leads to increased emissions of acetaldehyde, a toxic air pollutant, as defined by the Clean Air Act, these emissions can be controlled through the use of advanced catalytic converters.[38] However, as was stated above, these purer forms of ethanol have not seen wide use.

---

[34]Margo T. Oge, Director, Office of Mobile Sources, U.S. EPA, *Testimony Before the Subcommittee on Energy and Environment of the Committee on Science, U.S. House of Representatives.* September 14, 1999.

[35]National Research Council, *Ozone-Forming Potential of Reformulated Gasoline.* May 1999.

[36]Al Jessel, Senior Fuels Regulatory Specialist of Chevron Products Company, *Testimony Before the House Science Committee Subcommittee on Energy and Environment.* September 39, 1999.

[37]In 1998, an average of 90.9 million gallons per day of RFG were sold in the U.S., as opposed to 8.0 million gallons per day of Oxy-Fuel gasoline.

[38]California Energy Commission, *Ethanol-Powered Vehicles.*

Climate Change

Another potential environmental benefit from ethanol is the fact that it is a renewable fuel. Proponents of ethanol argue that over the entire fuel-cycle[39] it has the potential to reduce greenhouse gas emissions from automobiles relative to gasoline, therefore reducing the risk of possible global warming.

Because ethanol (C_2H_5OH) contains carbon, combustion of the fuel necessarily results in emissions of carbon dioxide (CO_2), the primary greenhouse gas. However, since photosynthesis (the process by which plants convert light into chemical energy) requires absorption of CO_2, the growth cycle of the feedstock crop can serve – to some extent – as a "sink" that absorbs some of these emissions. In addition to CO_2 emissions, the emissions of other greenhouse gases may increase or decrease depending on the fuel cycle.[40]

According to Argonne National Laboratory, using E10, vehicle greenhouse gas emissions (measured in grams per mile) are approximately 1% lower than with the same vehicle using gasoline. With improvements in production processes, by 2010, the reduction in greenhouse gas emissions from ethanol relative to gasoline could be as high as 8-10% for E10, while the use of E95 could lead to significantly higher reductions.[41]

While some studies have called into question the efficiency of the ethanol production process, most recent studies find a net energy gain.[42] If true, then the overall reductions in greenhouse gas emissions would be diminished due to higher fuel consumption during the production process.

Energy Security

Another frequent argument for the use of ethanol as a motor fuel is that it reduces U.S. reliance on oil imports, making the U.S. less vulnerable to a fuel embargo of the sort that occurred in the 1970s, which was the event that initially stimulated development of the ethanol industry. According to Argonne National Laboratory, with current technology the use of E10 leads to a 3% reduction in fossil energy use per vehicle mile, while use of E95 could lead to a 44% reduction in fossil energy use.[43]

However, other studies contradict the Argonne study, suggesting that the amount of energy needed to produce ethanol is roughly equal to the amount of energy obtained from its combustion, which could lead to little or not reductions in fossil energy use.[44] Thus, if the energy used in ethanol production is petroleum-based, ethanol would do nothing to contribute to energy security. Furthermore, as was stated above, fuel ethanol only displaces approximately 1.2% of gasoline consumption in the United States. This small market share led the GAO to conclude that the

---

[39]The fuel-cycle consists of all inputs and processes involved in the development, delivery and final use of the fuel.

[40]For example, nitrous oxide emissions tend to increase with ethanol use because nitrogen-based fertilizers are used extensively in agricultural production.

[41]M. Wang, C. Saricks, and D. Santini, "Effects of Fuel Ethanol on Fuel-Cycle Energy and Greenhouse Gas Emissions." Argonne National Laboratory.

[42]Hosein Shapouri, James A. Duffield, and Michael S. Graboski, USDA, Economic Research Service, *Estimating the Net Energy Balance of Corn Ethanol*. July 1995.

[43]Wang, et al. P. 1.

[44]Shapouri, et al. Table 1.

ethanol tax incentive has done little to promote energy security.[45] Furthermore, since ethanol is currently dependent on the U.S. corn supply, any threats to this supply (e.g. drought), or increases in corn prices, would negatively affect the cost and/or supply of ethanol. This happened when high corn prices caused by strong export demand in 1995 contributed to an 18% decline in ethanol production between 1995 and 1996.

POLICY CONCERNS AND CONGRESSIONAL ACTIVITY

Recent congressional interest in ethanol fuels has mainly focused on three sets of issues: 1) implementation of Phase 2 of the RFG program; 2) a possible phase-out of MTBE; and 3) the alcohol fuel tax incentives.

Phase 2 Reformulated Gasoline

Under the new Phase 2 requirements of the RFG program, which took effect in 2000, gasoline sold in the summer months (beginning June 1) must meet a tighter volatility standard.[46] Reid Vapor Pressure (RVP) is a measure of volatility, with higher numbers indicating higher volatility. Because of its physical properties, ethanol has a higher RVP than MTBE. Therefore, to make Phase 2 RFG with ethanol, the gasoline, called RBOB,[47] must have a lower RVP. This low-RVP fuel is more expensive to produce, leading to higher production costs for ethanol-blended RFG.

Before the start of Phase 2, estimates of the increased costs to produce RBOB for ethanol-blended RFG ranged from 2 to 4 cents per gallon, to as much as 5 to 8 cents per gallon.[48] In Summer 2000, RFG prices in Chicago and Milwaukee were considerably higher than RFG prices in other areas, and it has been argued that the higher production cost for RBOB was one cause. However, not all of the price difference is attributable to the new Phase 2 requirements or the use of ethanol. Conventional gasoline prices in the Midwest were also high compared with gasoline prices in other areas. High crude oil prices, low gasoline inventories, pipeline problems, and uncertainties over a patent dispute pushed up prices for all gasoline in the Midwest.

To decrease the potential for price spikes, on March 15, 2001, EPA announced that Chicago and Milwaukee will be allowed to blend slightly higher RVP reformulated gasoline during the summer months.[49] This action is not a change in regulations but a revision of EPA's enforcement guidelines. In addition to EPA's action, one possible regulatory option that has been suggested to control summer RFG prices is a more significant increase in the allowable RVP under Phase 2. Although the volatility standard is set by the Clean Air Act, the Environmental Protection Agency (EPA) is currently reviewing whether credits from ethanol's improved performance on carbon monoxide emissions are possible as an offset to its higher volatility. Legislative options have included eliminating the oxygenate standard for RFG, or suspending the program entirely. However, some in the petroleum industry suggest that additional changes to fuel requirements

[45]U.S. General Accounting Office, *Effects of the Alcohol Fuels Tax Incentives.* March, 1997.

[46]Volatility of gasoline is its tendency to evaporate.

[47]RDOB: Reformulated Gasoline Blendstock for Oxygenate Blending.

[48]Estimates from the Renewable Fuels Association and EPA, respectively.

[49]Pamela Najer, "Refiners Get Flexibility to Blend Ethanol for Summer Fuel Supply in Two Cities," *Daily Environment Report.* March 19, 2001. P. A9.

could further disrupt gasoline supplies. No bills to address the VP issue have been introduced in the 107th Congress.

MTBE

Another key issue involving ethanol is the current debate over MTBE. Since MTBE, a possible human carcinogen, has been found in groundwater in some states (especially in California), there has been a push both in California and nationally to ban MTBE.[50] IN March 1999, California's Governor Davis issued an Executive Order requiring that MTBE be phased out of gasoline in the state by December 31, 2002. Arizona, Connecticut, Iowa, Minnesota, Nebraska, New York, and South Dakota have also instituted limits or and on MTBE. In July 1999, an advisory panel to EPA recommended that MTBE use should be "reduced substantially."[51]

A possible ban on MTBE could have serious consequences for fuel markets, especially if the oxygenate requirements remain in place. Since ethanol is the second most used oxygenate, it is likely that it would be used to replace MTBE. However, there is not currently enough U.S. production capacity to meet the potential demand. Therefore, it would likely be necessary to phase out MTBE over time, as opposed to an immediate ban. Furthermore, the consumer price for oxygenated fuels would likely increase because ethanol, unlike MTBE, cannot be shipped through pipelines and must be mixed close to the point of sale, adding to delivery costs. Increased demand for oxygenates could also be met through imports form countries such as Brazil, which is a leader worldwide in fuel ethanol production, and currently has a surplus.[52]

While ban on MTBE would seem to have possible implications for ethanol producers, it could actually work against them. Because MTBE is more commonly used in RFG and high-octane gasoline, and because current ethanol production cannot currently meet total U.S. demand for oxygenates and octane, there is also a push to suspend the oxygenate requirement in RFG, which would remove a major stimulus to the use of fuel ethanol. Furthermore, environmental groups and state air quality officials, although supportive of a ban on MTBE, are concerned over the possibility of "backsliding" if the oxygenate standard is eliminated. Because current RFG formulations have a lower level of toxic substances than is required under the Clean Air Act, there are concerns that new RFG formulations without oxygenates will meet the existing standard, but not the current level of overcompliance.

On March 20, 2000, the Clinton Administration announced a plan to reduce or eliminate MTBE use, and to promote the use of ethanol. Although no legislative language was suggested, the framework included three recommendations. The first was to "provide the authority to significantly reduce or eliminate the use of MTBE." The second recommendation was that "Congress must ensure that air quality gains are not diminished." The third was that "Congress should replace the existing oxygenate requirement in the Clean Air Act with a renewable fuel standard for all gasoline." Moreover, the Clinton Administration discussed the possibility of limiting the use of MTBE through the Toxic Substances Control Act (P.L. 94-469), which gives EPA the authority to control any substance that poses unreasonable risk to health or the

---

[50]For more information, see CRS Report 98-290 ENR, *MTBE in Gasoline: Clean Air and Drinking Water Issues.*

[51]Blue Ribbon Panel on Oxygenates in Gasoline, *Achieving Clean Air* and *Clean Water: The Report of the Blue Ribbon Panel on Oxygenates in Gasoline.*

[52]Adrian Schofield, "Brazilian Ambassador Sees Opportunity in United States Ethanol Market," *New Fuels & Vehicles Report.* September 16, 1999. P. 1.

environment. However, this process could take several years.[53] MTBE producers argued that such an initiative will lower clean air standards, and raise gasoline prices, while ethanol producers and some environmental groups were generally supportive of the announcement.[54]

In the 107th Congress, six MTBE-related bills have been introduced. (See **Appendix 1**.) All have been referred to Committee. These bills address different facets of the MTBE issue, including limiting or banning the use of MTBE, granting waivers to the oxygenate requirement, and authorizing funding for MTBE cleanup.

Alcohol Fuel Tax Incentives [55]

As stated above, the exemption that ethanol-blended fuels receive from the excise tax on motor fuels is controversial. The incentive allows fuel ethanol to compete with other additives, since the wholesale price of ethanol is so high. Proponents of ethanol argue that this exemption lowers dependence on foreign imports, promotes air quality, and benefits farmers.[56] A related, albeit smaller incentive for ethanol production is the small ethanol producers tax credit. This credit provides 10 cents per gallon for up to 15 million gallons of annual production by a small producer.[57]

Opponents of the tax incentives argue that the incentives promote an industry that could not exist on its own, and reduce potential fuel tax revenue. Despite objections from opponents, Congress in 1998 extended the motor fuels tax exemption through 2007, but at slightly lower rates (P.L. 105-178). A bill in the 107th Congress, S. 312, would increase the size of a covered producer under the small producer tax credit. (See **Appendix 1**.)

CONCLUSION

As a result of the current debate over the future of MTBE in RFG, and the RFG program in general, the future of the U.S. ethanol industry is uncertain. A ban on MTBE would greatly expand the market for ethanol, while an elimination oxygenate requirement would remove a major stimulus for its use. Any changes in the demand for ethanol will have major effects on corn producers, who rely on the industry as a partial market for their products.

The current size of the ethanol industry depends significantly on federal laws and regulations that promote its use for air quality and energy security purposes, as well as tax incentives that

---

[53]U.S. Environmental Protection Agency, *Headquarters Press Release: Clinton-Gore Administration Acts to Eliminate MTBE, Boost Ethanol.* March 20, 2000.

[54]Jim Kennett, "Government Seeks to Ban Gas Additive," *Houston Chronicle.* March 21, 2000. P. A1

[55]For more information, see CRS Report 98-435 E. *Alcohol Fuels Tax Incentives.*

[56]U.S. General Accounting Office (GAO), *Effects of the Alcohol Fuels Tax Incentives.* March, 1997.

[57]Defined as having a production capacity of less than 30 million gallons per year.

lessen its cost to consumers. Without these, it is likely that the industry would shrink substantially in the near future. However, if fuel ethanol process costs can be decreased, or if gasoline prices increase, ethanol could increase its role in U.S. fuel consumption.

Appendix 1. Ethanol and Reformulated Gasoline Bills in the 107th Congress

Bill No.	Sponsor	Last Major Action	Key Provisions
H.R. 20	Greenwood	Referred to House Energy and Commerce	• Allows states to petition EPA for a waiver from the RFG oxygenate requirement • Grants EPA the authority to control or prohibit the use of any oxygenate • Limits MTBE levels tot he average of 1986 to 1991 levels, starting in 2005 • Prohibits "backsliding" on toxic air pollutant emissions
H.R. 52	Condit	Referred to House Energy and Commerce	• Allows California to apply state RFG standards in ozone nonattainment areas if they will result in equivalent or greater emissions reductions
H.R. 454	Johnson, T.	Referred to House Energy and Commerce	• Prohibits the use of MTBE effective three years from enactment of the act • Authorizes EPA to provide $10 million in grants for research on the testing and remediation of MTBE contamination • Increases the allowable Reid vapor pressure in RFG containing 3.5% oxygen by weight
H.R. 532	Capps	Referred to House Energy and Commerce	• Authorizes $200 million from the Leaking Underground Storage Trust Fund for MTBE contamination

H.R. 608	Ganske	Referred to House Energy and Commerce	• Prohibits the use of MTBE effective three years from enactment of the act • Requires EPA to give priority to MTBE contamination in issuing guidelines for state source water assessment programs • Allows refiners to meet an average oxygen standard in RFG areas, as opposed to the existing per gallon standard • Limits aromatic hydrocarbon content in RFG, and prohibits "backsliding" on ozone-forming emissions
S. 265	Fitzgerald	Referred to senate Environment and Public Works	• Prohibits the use of MTBE effective three years from enactment of the act • Authorizes EPA to provide $10 million in grants for research on the testing and remediation of MTBE contamination
S.312	Grassley	Referred to Senate Finance	• Increases the maximum production allowable for the small ethanol producer tax credit • Allows cooperatives to distribute small producer tax credit to patrons

DOMESTIC OIL AND GAS PRODUCERS:
PUBLIC POLICY WHEN OIL PRICES ARE VOLATILE

Robert Bamberger, Bernard A. Gelb, Lawrence Kumins,
Salvatore Lazzari, Vladimir Pregelj, and Jeanne J. Grimmet

This report examines the policy options that have been debated in the 106th Congress in response to declining domestic oil production and oil price volatility. A prolonged drop in crude oil prices contributed to falling domestic oil production and a contraction of industry infrastructure. Congress has debated a number of policy options to assist the domestic oil industry, a debate made more complicated because it has taken place as crude oil prices were experiencing a sharp recovery.

From 1997 to the end of 1998, refiner acquisition cost of crude oil fell from an average $23.59/barrel (bbl) to a low of $9.84/bbl.[1] The price decline into 1999 was a factor contributing to a fall in domestic production of more than 500,000 barrels per day (b/d).

Other measures of reduced activity in the sector have been reported during 1999. The American Petroleum Institute (API) found during the period from late 1997 to early 1999 that the number of active rotary rigs drilling wells dropped from 371 to 111. A survey conducted by Salomon Smith Barney showed a decline in domestic exploration and production spending from 1998 to 1999 of 23% among surveyed independents and 19% by fifteen major U.S. producers. Meanwhile, the Independent Petroleum Association of America (IPAA) reported in early February 1999 that 136,000 domestic oil wells were shut in between November 1997 and early 1999.[2]

Producers normally maintain facilities, even when crude prices decline to levels near or below the cost of production, on the expectation that prices will recover. However, if the decline is prolonged and deep enough, marginal production may be capped, maintenance may be cut back, new exploration suspended, and skilled employees eliminated. The result can be a loss of output

---

[1] The average refiner acquisition cost for domestic and imported crude was $19.04/bbl in 1997, declining to $12.57/bbl in 1998. See: U.S. Department of Energy. Energy Information Administration. *Monthly Energy Review.* August 1999: p. 111.

[2] American Petroleum Institute. Perkins, Jody M. Policy Analysis and Strategic Planning Department. *Economic State of the US Oil and Natural Gas Exploration and Production Industry: Long-Term Events and Recent Events.* April 30, 1999: p. 7-11. See also: "Comments on National Security Investigation of Imports of Crude Oil and Petroleum Products [Docket No. 990427107-9107-01] on behalf of the Independent Petroleum Association of America and the National Stripper Well Association."

and output capacity that may not be reconstituted when prices recover. Independent producers may be especially vulnerable during this sort of downturn because, more often than larger firms, they have onshore properties with relatively low output.

By late 1998, there were calls on Congress and federal agencies to assist the domestic oil and gas industry to weather the slump in prices that seemed to have little prospect of ending soon. While low oil prices benefit the nation's economy, some producers argued that they were beginning to have adverse impacts on the industry infrastructure from which there would be no quick recovery when and if prices recovered. In the meantime, some producers contended, the United States would become even more dependent upon imported oil.

A number of possible responses were debated during the first session of the 106th Congress. These included:

- an oil and gas guaranteed loan program for small independent domestic producers, approved by Congress in late July 1999 and signed by the President (P.L. 106-51, H.R. 1664);
- proposals to expand or create new tax incentives or tax policies to benefit producers, included in the Taxpayer Refund and Relief Act of 1999 (TRRA, H.R. 2488), which, for reasons unrelated to the producer incentive provisions, was vetoed by the President on September 23, 1999;
- delivery to the Strategic Petroleum Reserve (SPR) of royalty-in-kind (RIK)[3] oil produced from offshore federal leases in the Gulf of Mexico.

Low prices also revived discussion of oil import fees, tariffs and quotas. A petition was filed in June 1999 by a coalition of independent producers alleging that four major exporting countries – Saudi Arabia, Venezuela, Mexico, and Iraq – had dumped crude into U.S. markets at below-market prices. Thought the Department of Commerce rejected the petition on August 9, 1999, the matter heightened attention to the oil and gas sector while also having some repercussions on U.S. trade relations and policy while the petition was pending. The decision is being appealed.

After the Organization of Petroleum Exporting Countries (OPEC) announced a production cutback in the late spring of 1999, prices rose sharply. But interest in policy measures to help the domestic oil industry continued. A program to provide RIK oil to the SPR was not expected to have much bearing on price, but it was, from the industry perspective, a welcome and long-sought demonstration of the possibilities for RIK payment. The guaranteed loan program had a momentum not altogether tied to current oil prices because it was part of legislation (H.R. 1644) that also included a guaranteed loan program for the U.S. steel industry.[4] In addition, some have argued that having policies and programs in place would make it possible to respond more quickly to possible future extended slumps in the volatile oil market.

The increase in crude prices also became a theme in Congress. It was referenced in the Senate in late September in the face of a filibuster over a controversial amendment to the FY2000 Interior Appropriations bill that would have delayed, for another fiscal year, a rule from the Minerals Management Service (MMS) that would revise the method for valuing oil for royalty purposes. Opponents of the delay cited losses to date to the Treasury of $88 million and prospectively, an additional $66 million. Supporters of the amendment suggested that a boost in

---

[3] Royalties on production from federal leases are typically paid to the U.S. Treasury in cash. Royalty-in-kind means the royalty share is paid in physical barrels. For example, if a 12% royalty were due, the government would receive 12 of every 100 barrels produced on leases subject to that royalty.

[4] As is noted elsewhere, this legislation became public law, P.L. 106-51 on August 17, 1999.

the royalty valuation could raise the price of gasoline further. The amendment was passed, but the conferees agreed to delay the rule for 6 months, pending study and analysis by the General Accounting Office (GAO). It is not clear to what extent the price environment affected the outcome.[5]

When OPEC reconvened in Vienna on September 22, 1999 to review its production quotas, crude was approaching \$25/bbl. As was generally anticipated, the ministers agreed to maintain output quotas at current levels until March 2000. OPEC argued that worldwide stocks had not declined sufficiently to merit a production increase and that the OPEC nations still had the considerable revenues they needed to recoup from the sustained price collapse.

A few days earlier, anticipating the OPEC ministers' decision, and expecting that retention of the OPEC production ceiling would put additional pressure on prices when the weather turned colder, Senator Schumer wrote the Clinton Administration to request that the President authorize a sale of SPR oil to blunt a further rise in oil prices. Home heating oil price and supply are an historic concern in the Northeast part of the nation, where its use is more common. The Administration sent varying signals on the matter initially, but has generally distanced itself since from any sale at this time.

OIL PRICES AND U.S. OUTPUT

Worldwide, falling petroleum demand and essentially stable output resulted in depressed prices on world crude markets during 1998. U.S. oil output fell along with prices, and stood in late summer 1999 at 5.9 million barrels per day (mbd), a level last seen in 1946. As domestic output has fallen, demand has increased. Oil imports have risen from 1985's unusually low level of 3.2 mbd to 9.7 mbd in 1999 Net imports now comprise 51% of all petroleum used in the nation. The year 1998 marked the first in which *net* imports exceeded half of U.S. consumption, averaged over the entire year.[6] Onshore production in the lower-48 states, the operating locale for many independent producers, has fallen by 40% since 1980; these producers' current-dollar revenues are only one-fourth of 1980 levels when crude prices were at their height.

---

[5] A more detailed discussion of this particular issue appears later. See also: U.S. congressional Record. Vol. 145, No. 125, S 11277-S11347.

[6] U.S. Department of Energy. Energy Information Administration. *Monthly Energy Review, September 1999*, p. 15.

**Figure 1. U.S. Crude Producer Prices, 1980-1998
(Current Dollars)**

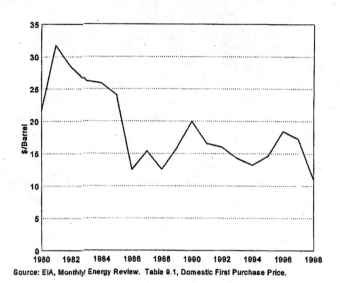

Source: EIA, Monthly Energy Review. Table 9.1, Domestic First Purchase Price.

Figure 1 shows the average price received by domestic producers from refiners since 1980. It traces a reasonably consistent decline from over $30 per barrel to the end of 1998. Prices firmed during the 1994-1996 period, and rose into the high teens because growing world demand – led by Asian growth – pressed the supply available to the world market. But changing market conditions, and oil exporters' inability to adjust to them, resulted in resumption of a downward price trend until OPEC convened in the late spring of 1999.

The turn in petroleum prices beginning in the spring of 1999 has been dramatic. Figure 2 outlines price developments during the past 14 months. It includes gasoline prices as a point of reference because prices at the gas pump have such high public visibility. Together, these two figures illustrate the recent volatility and dramatic recovery of oil prices. From September 1998 to September 1999, crude oil prices increased by 65; gasoline prices increased by 23%.[7]

---

[7] U.S. Department of Energy. Energy Information Administration. Weekly Petroleum Status Report.

Figure 2
Crude Oil and Gasoline Prices, July 1998-September 1999

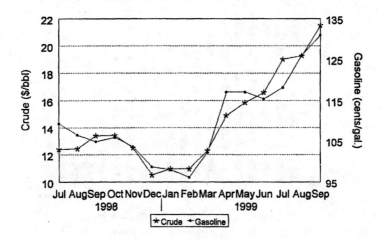

Source: Weekly Petroleum Status Report, Tables 18-19.

Figure 3 shows domestic crude output by producing region since 1980. Total production including Alaska, the Outer Continental Shelf (OCS), and the lower-48 states has fallen 30% from a recent high in 1985 of 9.0 million barrels per day (mbd) to a 1998 average of 6.3 mbd (the mid-1999 figure declined to 5.9 mbd). But on-shore lower 48-state output – the operating base of most small producers – has suffered the largest percentage production drop, with a 40% fall between 1985 and 1998. Gross on-shore producer receipts for the lower-48 have declined in current dollars from an estimated high in 1981 of $67 billion to an estimated $15 billion during 1998. This revenue drop stems from both falling prices and declining output (which may relate both to price as well as to the geology of a mature field), jeopardizing the viability of some U.S. production and the well-being of some domestic producers, especially smaller ones. Given the dramatic shrinkage in on-shore revenues, consolidation among firms producing oil can be expected to continue.

Figure 3. U.S. Crude Oil Production by Area, 1980-1998

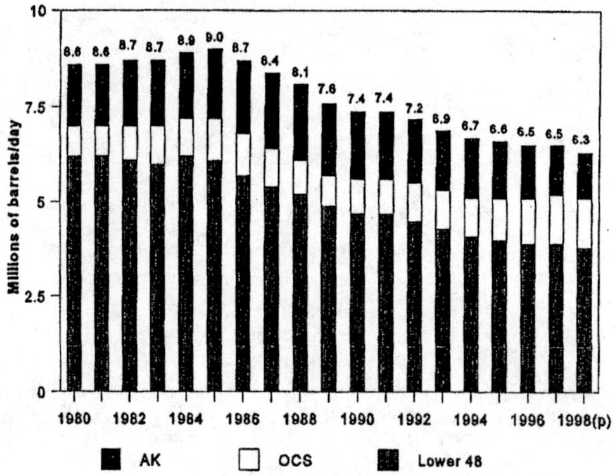

Source: EIA, Monthly Energy Review; Minerals Management Service, Mineral Revenues, Federal Offshore Statistics.

OPEC Acts to Reduce Production

OPEC was founded in 1960 to maintain crude oil prices on behalf of its members. Eleven countries presently make up the Organization of Petroleum Exporting Countries (OPEC). They produce 40% of the world's oil, hold 77% of proved oil reserves, and control most of the unused capacity capable of producing more oil.

Despite presenting a seemingly powerful market force, OPEC has an uneven record of establishing and maintaining prices, holding its members to individual production quotas, and dealing with price declines. When, for example, prices collapsed in early 1986, OPEC's members failed to adhere to the production quotas which were necessary to keep control – or maintain substantial influence – over prices. With a few short-lived exceptions, OPEC was unable to stabilize prices for a significant period until late 1996. By then, growing demand from a strong world economy, producer self-interest, and the absence of Iraq from the world marketplace enabled the cartel to balance supply with demand. In 1997, when declining global economic activity reduced demand, OPEC members reacted by exceeding production quotas in order to make up for the fall in revenues as prices declined.

With prices dropping and production increasing, the OPEC "basket" of eight kinds of crude oil averaged only $12.28 per barrel during 1998, the lowest annual average since OPEC began calculating. This was nearly $9/bbl below $21.00/bbl, the publicly stated target that OPEC was attempting to hold and maintain by adjusting member nation quotas.

To remedy the price situation and restore member nation oil revenues, OPEC, joined by key non-OPEC producers – Mexico, Norway, Russia and Oman – met in March 1999 and negotiated production cuts for the group. The quotas they agreed upon were intended to raise prices to an average of $21.00/bbl for the full calendar year. Some producers responded to the quotas tentatively, but the initial success encouraged wider compliance. By the time OPEC reconvened in Vienna in September 1999, production cuts totaled 4.1 mbd. Higher export revenues had reinforced the resolve of the participating OPEC countries, and they agreed to maintain current output levels until March 2000.

Prices reached $25/bbl shortly after the September meeting. However, the average price for the "basket" was only $15 through mid-September 1999. Given OPEC's objective to achieve an average per barrel price of $21 for calendar 1999, the implication was for prices higher than $21/bbl during the fall of 1999 to offset the lower prices that prevailed earlier in the year. It may well be that prices will remain above the $21 target for all or part of the 1999-2000 heating season, but it is difficult to venture any predictions. Winter weather and other factors will influence prices before OPEC meetings next in March 2000. The winter of 1998-99 was abnormally warm in both North America and Europe; a heating season closer to normal should quickly eliminate any overhanging inventory.[8]

At an average of $21/bbl, and current production levels set at about 23 million barrels per day, the ten participating OPEC members (Iraq, whose crude receipts are paid to the U.N., is excluded) would realize about $175 billion at an annual rate. During 1998, these ten OPEC producers produced about 25.7 mbd valued at $115 billion. Under these assumptions, the ten could realize $60 billion greater revenue by producing 2.7 mbd less oil, illustrating the incentive for sticking with assigned production caps. Non-member quota participants reap similar rewards.

Many foreign producers that have been adversely affected by low oil prices had petro-dollar fueled budget surpluses during the 1970s and 1980s and can regain former prosperity by adherence to OPEC production discipline. In the case of Venezuela, an OPEC founding member that over-produced greatly during 1998-99 and experienced economic adversity as a result, recently-elected President Hugo Chavez announced a year 2000 budget based on his nation's September quota of 2.72 mbd. He pledged that impoverished Venezuelans would see some of the extra petro-dollars in the form of salary hikes and social program spending. President Chevez predicted 2.2% real growth in year 2000 as a result of enlarged oil receipts, in contrast to a 6.6% contraction in 1999.[9]

Issues for Public Policy

Whether the recent recovery in oil prices will be a long term development or a transitory market fluctuation is not yet clear. OPEC's cohesion on limiting supply in order to maintain prices appeared to be holding into the fall of 1999 But, is it not readily apparent that OPEC will be able to adjust to changing market conditions and hold a target price over time. Thus, the future path of oil prices is always a matter of some speculation, and predicting that path is extremely difficult.

The especially low oil prices that prevailed during 1998 and early 1999 have been cited as the chief cause of impacts on domestic crude output and producers. Even the historically robust supply from Alaska is likely to continue to decline. Many of the policy options discussed here aim to stem the losses in U.S. production capacity and infrastructure. These policy options have the potential or the direct goal of raising prices or lowering producer costs, with the volatility of oil prices underscoring the complexity of the issue. A number of questions might be considered, beginning with whether policymakers should take action during periods of sustained low prices. How long would low oil prices persist before a response is activated? How much price support would be required, and how much lost production might be protected or regained?

On the other hand, low oil prices benefit consumers and the overall U.S. economy. In early 1999, consumers enjoyed the lowest real-dollar pump prices in history (even after steadily

---

[8] The *1999-2000 Winter fuels Outlook*, released by the Energy Information Administration of DOE on October 8, 1999, suggests that while supplies of winter fuels are expected to be "more than adequate," consumer prices "could be much higher than those of a normal winter season."

[9] *Platt's Oilgram News*, Sept. 29, 1999. Page 4.

increasing federal, state and sometimes local taxes are considered). The performance of the economy has been enhanced by years of declining commodity prices, including those based on petroleum. Any policy debate would include consideration of how higher oil prices resulting from intervention in markets would affect economic conditions, especially in the current situation of declining commodity prices and extremely low inflation. There are macroeconomic consequences as well as impacts upon consumers when the price of oil rises.[10]

Through much of this debate, the Administration has acknowledged that the plight of the producers is very real, but has been guarded about possible actions. In late February 1999, testifying before a House appropriations subcommittee, Secretary of Energy Richardson indicated that his Department wanted to help the oil industry, but did not "want to tamper with the markets," or to do anything "that affects oil prices." He indicated that tax policy and emergency loans were under discussion but were not at that time "administration policy."[11] Advocates of assistance for the domestic oil industry might argue that neither the loan guarantee program subsequently passed by Congress and enacted into law, nor the scale of the tax provisions included in tax relief legislation sent to the President, constitute direct interference with prices or a significant bailout to the industry. However, others would argue that policies favoring the oil and gas industry are at cross-purposes with environmental policy objectives, calling for an even more sensitive balancing of policy objectives.[12]

Given the volatility in oil prices, proponents of government action might suggest a broader debate to include policies that can address not just persistently low petroleum prices, but which can be sufficiently flexible and responsive in the face of volatility in prices. There are others, however, who believe that the best economic course is to allow the market to function without further government intervention.

THE CONTROVERSY OVER REVISING ROYALTY VALUATIONS

One of the most contentious issues addressed in conference on the FY2000 Department of Interior Appropriations bill (H.R. 2466) was a rider affecting promulgation of a rule by the Minerals Management Service (MMS) that would affect the valuation of oil produced from federal lands for determining the royalty the producer owes to the government. Royalty payments are computed as a percentage of the value of the commodity as it is removed from the lease. Establishing that value in situations other than those where the hydrocarbons are sold in arm's length, third-party transactions has been a source of controversy. Current regulations provide for a 5-step valuation process which ultimately imputes a price providing a best approximation of a market price.[13] This process may be applied to transactions which are intra-corporate (e.g., a

---

[10] For some discussions of the potential economic costs of rapid fluctuations in energy prices, see: *Oil Imports: An Overview and Update of Economic and Security Effects.* CRS Report for Congress. December 12, 1997. 98-1-ENR, p. 6-7. Proposals in the past typically suggested an oil import fee of $.10/gallon as a starting point to achieve policy objectives. It is worth noting that the price increase during the spring and summer of 1999 has been in the range of nearly $10.00 per barrel, the rough equivalent of $.24 cents per gallon, and that this was altogether independent of public policy.

[11] Secretary Says Disaster Relief Money Not in the Cards for the Oil Industry." Appearing in *Inside Energy/with Federal Lands*, March 1, 1999: p. 7-8.

[12] Last-Minute Legislative Efforts to Help Oil and Other Companies..." appearing in *Inside Energy/with Federal Lands*, August 9, 1999; p. 20.

[13] See 30 CFR Part 206.

producer transferring the oil to its refining arm). Here, the hydrocarbon has not actually been sold, but a market value must be ascribed in order to compute a royalty payment. In situations where transport costs from lese-to-market are a factor, value for royalty computation may be adjusted to reflect the cost of transporting the oil to market.

Royalty payments are generally computed as a percentage of the value of oil appraised at posted prices, prices that are established by oil producers in the field. The fact that producers set this price themselves has led to a number of lawsuits disputing the fairness of posted prices as measures of the value of the oil. Many of the disputes involved states suing for their share of royalties from production on state as well as federal lands. In recent years, a number of lawsuits were settled for amounts totaling $5 billion,[14] including a $3.7 billion settlement in Alaska.

Critics of the current valuation system contend that the settlements themselves are evidence that oil is being regularly undervalued in computation of royalty payments. They are especially concerned about situations where the crude is used in refineries owned by the producing firm, but the value of the oil is determined by the producer alone. Producers fear that the new rule may value the crude at some point away from the wellhead and not allow companies to deduct marketing and transportation costs.[15]

For nearly 3 years, MMS has been working on a new valuation rule. MMS proposed issuing final valuation regulations in 1998 that base value on a series of benchmarks for each field. The benchmarks would be computed from oil traded on public markets, with transportation, location and quality differentials factored in the new rules would likely result in higher royalty collections. Promulgation of the rule during FY 1999 was blocked in that year's Interior Appropriations and for the two years preceding.

Producer opposition to the new rules has been strong. Senator Hutchison introduced an amendment to the FY 2000 Interior appropriations bill (H.R. 2466) extending the appropriation ban for another year. In debate, the proposed regulations were characterized as a tax increase imposed on producers. Senator Murkowski, for example, described the regulations as "another tax, a value-added tax, on oil produced in the United States on Federal leases."[16]

Senators who believe that royalty collections should be higher mounted a filibuster led by Senator Boxer. Cloture was voted (60-39) on September 23. Senator Hutchison's amendment banning final regulation implementation was then passed by a 51-47 vote. The conferees agreed to postpone release of a final rule pending a six-month study by GAO. Representative Carolyn Maloney criticized the conferees' decision, pointing out that she and Senator Boxer had previously requested a GAO report, which was released in August 1998 and concluded that MMS had been thorough.[17] Some revision to the proposed rule is expected in any case.

GUARANTEED LOANS FOR OIL AND GAS PRODUCERS

In late March 1999, Senator Domenici introduced a proposal for an oil and gas loan guarantee program that was added as a rider to the Emergency Supplemental Appropriations Act (H.R. 1411), but the language was stripped from the bill for separate consideration. The proposal was included in H.R. 1664, an emergency supplemental appropriations bill for military purposes. A

---

[14] See Senator Boxer at page S11323 of the *Congressional Record*, September 23, 1999.

[15] See: *Inside Energy/with Federal Lands.* Interior Spending Bill Conferees Cut Royalty Rule Delay to 180 Days. October 18, 1999: p. 15-6.

[16] Congressional Record, September 23, 1999 page S11324.

[17] *Inside Energy/w Federal Lands*, op cit.

larger loan guarantee program proposed for the steel industry was included in the same measure. Opponents of the loan guarantee programs sought to block consideration of the bill, but on June 15, 1999, the Senate invoked cloture (71-28), clearing the way for debate to proceed on H.R. 1664 The Senate amended the proposal on June 17, 1999, and passed the bill the following morning (63-34). On August 4, 1999, the House agreed to the Senate amendments (246-176) and the President signed the measure into public law (P.L. 106-51) on August 17, 1999.

The Details and Debate in Congress

The stated purpose of the loan guarantee program is to stem further losses in jobs and capacity in domestic oil and gas production. The loans will support small domestic independent oil and gas companies adversely affected by prolonged depression in oil and gas prices. To be eligible, a firm must be (1) an independent oil and gas company as defined by the Internal Revenue Code[18] or an oil field service company that qualifies as a small business concern under the Small Business Act[19] and (2) "have experienced layoffs, production losses, or financial losses since the beginning of the oil import crisis, after January 1, 1997."

Under the program, a total of $500 million in loans can be outstanding at any one time. (The program for the steel industry is $1 billion.) The maximum loan would be $10 million; a minimum threshold loan level of $250,000 was dropped by the Senate as likely to exclude any smaller firms the program was intended to help that want to borrow less. The borrowers pay a service fee of 0.5% of the outstanding principal to the Treasury. A reviewing board will approve or deny the applications for loan guarantees.

These guarantees will be issued by a Loan Guarantee Board on loans to qualifying companies for which "credit is not otherwise available to the company under reasonable terms or conditions sufficient to meet its financing needs." However, the board must believe that the company's "prospective earning power" and collateral provides "reasonable assurance" of repayment. The rate of interest must be reasonable and the company must agree to submit to General Accounting Office (GAO) audit. Loans guaranteed under the program would have to be repaid by the end of calendar 2010.

The original proposal provided that the board would be chaired by the Secretary of Commerce and include the Secretaries of Labor and the Treasury. As amended by the Senate on June 17, 1999, the chairs of the Federal Reserve System and the Securities and Exchange Commission would serve in place of the Secretaries of Labor and Treasury. The Chairman of the Federal Reserve was designated to be the chair of the Loan Guarantee Board.

The Senate made two other significant changes. Some opponents of the program argued during debate on the cloture motion that loan guarantee programs have not been effective in the past and that the government has had no absorb significant defaults. In particular, a 77% failure rate was frequently cited for a steel industry loan guarantee program instituted in the late 1970s.[20] An amendment to the proposal offered by Senator Stevens reduced the loan guarantee from 100%

---

[18] With some minor qualifications, an independent producer is one with average daily production of no more than 1,000 barrels of crude oil and /or 6,000,000 cubic feet of natural gas, and does not have any refinery operations.

[19] Oil and gas well drillers must have not more than 500 employees; oil and gas exploration and/or other services must have no more than $5 million in annual sales.

[20] See, for example, the remarks of Senator Nickles in the debate on H.R. 1664, *Congressional Record*, June 17, 1999: p. S7183.

to 85%, the argument being that there was no incentive for a lender to press for collection of a loan that was guaranteed at 100% by the federal government.

The other major argument against the program focused upon the budgetary scoring of the program's expense. Though the legislation included a spending offset, it also lent an emergency designation to expenditure of the funds. Opponents argued that this would mean that expenditures would not be counted against spending caps. Consequently, critics argued, any offset savings achieved would be spent anyway and come out of the Social Security surplus.[21] The Senate struck the "emergency" designation.

Senator McCain, opposing the program, argued that it was inappropriate for the Senate to approve the proposal before it had been reviewed by an authorizing committee. He offered an amendment that would have precluded the expenditure of any funds for the program until such spending had been authorized by the appropriate committee. The amendment was tabled. The bill as passed by the Senate appropriates $122.5 million to cover anticipated losses on guaranteed loans to the oil and gas industry during the life of the program.[22]

Some of the support for H.R. 1664 may have been related to another proposal (S. 395), which would have protected the domestic steel industry by imposing import quotas. Some argued that existing quotas have already boosted the price of steel alloys and drill pipe, on which the oil and gas industry is dependent, and that any stiffening of the quotas to further protect steel would worsen the effects on the oil and gas sector.[23]

A loan guarantee program may be less of an intrusion into the marketplace than are import quotas, price controls, or import fees. However, many opponents believe that the most economically efficient policy response would be to take no action at all and allow the market to determine the allocation of resources without intervention. Proponents of the program argued that it could serve as an effective financial bridge for small oil and gas producers and field service companies through a difficult period. The loans that might not be obtained without federal guarantee could be used as capital to pay for well makeovers, well reopening, and meeting payroll – applications that would tend to preserve both industry capital and labor – and for meeting and/or restructuring interest payments.

Efficacy Issues

As enacted, the program may still present practical questions as to how it will achieve its stated purpose. These include [1] whether the stated qualifying conditions are workable; [2] whether the program will keep marginal wells producing, and maintain the oil and gas service industry infrastructure; and [3] whether there are equally or more effective and efficient measures that would achieve the same purpose. Independent of these questions, opponents of the program might argue that economic interests and efficiencies would be best served by doing nothing and allowing the market to operate without granting loan guarantees.

Examining the three issues in turn[24]:

---

[21] Ibid, p. 7003.

[22] See: *Oil Daily.* House Seen Likely to Support Oil-Loan Bill. June 21, 1999: p. 5. For mention of DBO estimates of the legislation's cost earlier in the debate, see: U.S. Congress. *Congressional Record.* June 15, 1999: p S7002-S7003.

[23] See: *Oil Daily.* Oil producers To Benefit As Senate Tipped To Pass Guaranteed Loan Program. June 15, 1999: p. 5.

[24] The section that immediately follows, "Economic Questions," discusses broader economic issues.

- The language requiring companies to have "experienced layoffs, production losses, or financial losses" does not explain how these negative outcomes will be specifically demonstrated or measured, nor does it explicitly require that these difficulties be a consequence of the decline in oil prices. The latter might be easily remedied, but the first is more problematical. Questions might be raised as to what extent potential loan requesters had made use of financial instruments to minimize the effects of price volatility, such as long term contracts, futures, and options. However, by their nature, the relatively small firms that this program is intended to help probably may not be users of such instruments.

- Regarding whether the loan proceeds are used in a manner to further the goals of the program, the legislative language does not set specific parameters on how the loan money is to be used. However, it may be impractical to do so. If a loan approved under such a program keeps an operation in business that would have otherwise foundered before market conditions improved, it matters little whether loan recipients invested the borrowed funds to maintain production capacity, or whether the loan funds may have been used to simply maintain operations until the market improved or other economies were put into place.

- Lastly, while there may be more effective and less complicated approaches than a loan guarantee program, they probably would require more direct intervention in the marketplace to affect price and would likely be highly controversial. Though both guaranteed loans and price intervention policies could be embraced were it decided that some action to provide assistance to smaller players was appropriate, some would prefer loan guarantees as less intrusive than policies that would bear directly on prices.

There are other considerations. Oil prices have increased sharply since introduction of the program, likely reducing the potential call on guaranteed loans as provided by the proposed program. While some may argue that there would be advantages in having in place a loan guarantee program in the event that the need materializes,[25] opponents argue that a board composed of government officials has no special qualification to second-guess the financial sector's assessment of capital to be placed at risk.[26] In any event, in the case of this government credit assistance program, the ability of borrowers to repay may well be more dependent upon a commodity price that is determined in a world market than upon the managerial abilities of its owners and/or managers.

Economic and National Security Questions

Among the broader economic considerations are whether there are market failures or national security issues that justify government intervention. The questions are whether output losses, layoffs, financial losses, and oil industry contraction are a normal market response to recently low

---

[25] The proposed specifically authorizes loans through the end of calendar year 2001. Congress could, of course, extend this date.

[26] See remarks of Senator Nickles, appearing in congressional Record, June 15, 1999: p. S7002: "We are saying the Secretaries of Labor and commerce and Treasury have better wisdom on whether or not to be making loans than bankers throughout the country."

oil prices, and whether dependence upon imported oil poses a risk serious enough to warrant government intervention.

Market Failures

The sort of failures that in theory may be cited to justify government intervention in markets include failures of competition that create barriers to entry into markets. Intervention may also be justified by "externalities" or spillovers; these are benefits or costs to society experienced by firms or individuals that are not parties to the particular transaction or activity, and are not reflected in the prices buyers and sellers pay. In these cases, buyers and/or sellers do not pay the full cost to society of their transaction, or do not receive full return. It does not appear that crude oil markets are operating imperfectly and therefore justify on grounds of economic efficiency alone loan guarantees to small oil and gas producers.

Whether loan guarantees are an appropriate instrument also depends upon how the unimpeded operation of capital markets is perceived. Oil and gas producers face unusually large risks (compared with other industries) from sudden and sharp oil price fluctuations. Producers have access to capital generally but may have to pay a higher interest rate on loans and face more restrictive terms than less risky industries, particularly during an industry downturn due to low oil prices. This is not discrimination, but a reflection of the way in which financial markets allocate capital to its most valued use. When crude oil prices and industry profitability decline, capital markets interpret this as a signal to allocate less capital to crude oil production.

National Security

National security is one type of social cost that may justify government intervention in the oil markets. Many agree with the argument that substantial oil imports and dependence on foreign oil may pose both energy security and national security risks if such imports significantly increase the probability of supply disruptions and sharp price spikes.[27] However, this does not justify loan guarantees on *economic* grounds alone. Low oil prices lead to reduced U.S. production and greater overall demand. This tends to increase dependent, but the risk to national and energy security also depends upon (1) the level of imports related to total oil demand, and (2) more importantly, the level of imports from unreliable or unfriendly foreign suppliers, as a share of total demand. Some argue that the United States is not necessarily more secure if it produces more oil domestically and imports less, but depletes its domestic resources faster.

Experience during the 1970s and 1980s suggests that the greatest and most direct social cost of import dependence may be the sharp price spikes that accompany a supply disruption. However, as long as U.S. oil markets are open, they will be subject to world market price pressures unrelated to the degree of import dependence. Considerable adverse macroeconomic effects can result. On the other hand, the world market is much more competitive today than it was during the disruptions and oil price shocks of the 1970s. The likelihood of such disruptions

---

[27] Energy security refers to the availability of "adequate" energy supplies, particularly petroleum products (and therefore crude oil), so as to maintain economic performance and standards of living. Basically this means that demand and supply, including imported supplies, are roughly in balance. National security, as it relates to the energy industry, refers to the availability of energy supplies for the military to maintain or improve national defense and for the government to execute foreign policy.

may have decreased. The increment of security or price protection that loan guarantees may provide in the current geopolitical climate (and were it to continue) could well be too small to measure with any confidence.

TAX INCENTIVES AND OTHER TAX POLICY OPTIONS

Tax policy options suggested to help domestic oil and gas producers can be divided into four general categories: 1) expanding existing oil and gas industry tax incentives; 2) creating exceptions for the oil industry from provisions of the general income tax laws that apply to other industries; 3) offering new oil and gas tax incentives; and 4) reducing existing tax penalties, fees, and other cots. The Taxpayer Refund and Relief Act of 1999 (TRRA, H.R. 2488), which was approved by the Congress on August 5, 1999, includes provisions from the first two categories. However, on September 23, 1999, the President vetoed the measure.

Whether the provisions in TRRA would be included in a compromise measure, or whether a free-standing measure of tax policy options not necessarily confined to those already in the TRRA might be enacted is a matter of much speculation in tax policy circles. For this reason, other policy options that have been introduced or debated by Congress are described below in addition to the proposals included in the TRRA.[28]

While intended to benefit domestic producers, tax policies (particularly additional federal tax incentives) that reduce production costs of marginal wells and ostensibly increase profitability also create incentives to produce more oil. This could put downward pressure on petroleum prices. This would exacerbate the industry's problems, or at least reduce the extent of the benefits. On the other hand, demand for imported petroleum would be reduced.

Expanding Existing Tax Incentives

Three major existing tax incentives that subsidize the domestic oil industry might be liberalized or broadened as a way of reducing production costs and enhancing profitability. They are: expensing of intangible drilling costs (IDCs), the percentage depletion allowance, and the tax credit for enhanced oil recovery costs.[29]

Expensing

Expensing allows firms engaged in the production of domestic oil and gas to deduct in the year paid or incurred certain intangible costs of drilling and development, such as amounts paid for fuel, labor, supplies and repairs associated with a site. This is an exception to general tax rules,

---

[28] Many bills have been introduced in the 106th Congress to provide tax relief to the domestic oil industry (e.g., S. 162, S. 325, S. 595, S. 1042, S. 1050, H.R. 43. H.R. 423, H.R. 497, H.R. 1116, H.R. 1971). Some of provisions in these bills were consolidated and incorporated into H.R. 2488, the Taxpayer Refund and Relief Act of 1999 (TRRA).

[29] These and other energy-related tax expenditures (other than those for oil and gas) are discussed in greater detail in: U.S. Congress. Committee on Budget. *Tax Expenditures: Compendium of Background Material on Individual Provisions.* Committee Print. December 1998. Prepared by the Congressional Research Service. U.S. Govt. Print. Off. Washington, 1998.

which require capitalization of such costs. Integrated oil companies can only expense 70% of IDCs, and the excess of the expensed over the capitalized value is a tax preference item to the extent that it exceeds 65% of the net income from the property. Independent producers can expense 100% of their IDCs and do not have to report them as tax preference items.

Thus, one option for assisting the oil industry would be to remove any one or more of the restrictions on the claiming of the deduction. However, expensing of oil and gas investments – which is basically an incentive to drill more wells – is largely claimed by integrated oil and gas companies, rather than independents. For example, the 70% limitation for integrated oil companies might be removed, but this would do little to help the small domestic oil producer.

Another type of liberalization, which is included in the TRRA, would extend expensing treatment to geophysical and geologic costs and to "delay rentals," which now must be capitalized. Delay rentals are payments made by a producer to a landowner, under a lease agreement, in the absence of a producible well.

Percentage Depletion Allowance and Enhanced Recovery

The percentage depletion allowance, unlike expensing, is largely claimed by the small independent producer. This tax subsidy permits independent producers to subtract 15% of sales from a property as a deduction for the depletion or depreciation of the capital investment in the mineral reserve. The deduction for stripper oil wells and for heavy oil – which account for about 20% of total oil output – is the basic 15% plus an additional 1% for each $1 that the benchmark price of oil (the average wellhead price of crude oil in the preceding calendar year) falls below $20 per barrel. Thus, with 1998 oil prices at about $12 per barrel -- $8 below the $20 threshold – the percentage depletion allowance for stripper wells was about 23% (15% + 8%).

Thus, one way to assist large and small domestic oil and gas producers would be to raise the percentage depletion rate above 15% and to broaden it to a larger share of domestic oil output. Before the repeal of the percentage depletion allowance for major oil companies in 1975, the basic percentage depletion rate was 27.5%, and all oil producers, including major integrated oil companies, qualified for it.

Another way of liberalizing the percentage depletion allowance would be to remove one or more of its restrictions. For example, currently the percentage depletion allowance is available only to independent producers and royalty owners, and it applies only to an average daily production of up to 1,000 barrels of oil, or the equivalent amount of gas (6 million cubic feet). An independent producer is one that does not have retail or refinery operations, unless the revenue from the retail operations do not exceed $5 million per year, and refinery runs do not exceed 50,000 barrels of oil per day on any given day. The TRRA would define excluded refiners as those that on average, during the taxable year, refine more than 50,000 barrels of oil per day, thus expanding the number of oil producers that qualify for the depletion subsidy. Current law also limits the percentage depletion allowance to 100% of the net income from that property in any year (this is the net-income limitation), and to 65% of the taxpayer's overall income.[30] The TRRA suspends the 65% taxable income limitation for six years.

A third tax incentive – in current tax law but not altered by the TRRA – is the 15% income tax credit for the costs of recovering oil through one of several enhanced oil recovery methods.

---

[30] However, these limitations do not apply to marginal properties, i.e., oil produced from stripper wells, and heavy oil.

This tax incentive could also be expanded, although the impact would still be relatively limited within the domestic oil industry.

Industry Exceptions to General Tax Laws

Some proposals would assist oil producers by creating exceptions to specific provisions of the general income tax laws, which apply to all businesses generally. Focusing particularly on oil producers that were hit hard by the 1997-99 price collapse, one proposal would broaden the net operating loss carryback and carryforward provisions of the income tax laws. For example, the TRRA proposes to allow net operating losses in the case of oil and gas properties to be carried back five years, instead of the current two years.[31]

Other Policy Options and Legislative Proposals

Reducing Existing Taxes, Fees, and Other Costs

A third policy approach would attempt to reduce industry costs, not by expanding existing tax incentives or subsidies, but by lowering existing tax penalties, fees, and various other types of government-imposed costs.

The domestic oil industry currently makes a variety of payments to governments – excise taxes, severance taxes, fees, royalties, and customs duties. Some of those payments, such as the severance tax, are state and local taxes outside the direct control of the federal government. Others, such as excise taxes and royalty payments on federal lands, are under the control of the federal government. A variety of excise taxes, for example, are imposed on crude oil and petroleum products. These include various motor fuel excise taxes that fund the Highway Trust Fund and the Leaking Underground Storage Tank (LUST) Trust Fund, a petroleum tax that funds the Oil Spill Liability Trust Fund, and the petroleum tax that funds the Superfund is reauthorized . They are, however, relatively small and are assessed only on refiners and importers.

Producers that extract oil and gas from federal land pay royalties to the federal government. Royalties – although not a tax but a type of factor payment – could also be lowered to assist the oil industry, as we discussed in the previous section. The domestic oil industry is also subject to many types of regulations that, in theory, could also be reduced or loosened as a way of reducing production costs and enhancing industry profitability. Because such regulations support objectives in other policy areas, a vigorous debate might be engendered.

New Tax Incentives

Still another approach in assisting the domestic oil industry would introduce new tax incentives. Several new tax incentives have been suggested recently, though none were incorporated into the TRRA. Some of these date back to the mid 1980s, in the aftermath of the 1986 oil price collapse. For example:

---

[31] The carryforward period would remain 20 years.

- H.R. 53 proposes a production tax credit of $3 per barrel of oil and 50 cents per thousand cubic feet of natural gas from marginal wells as a way of subsidizing small, independent, high-cost oil producers;
- H.R. 497 proposes an income exclusion for output from inactive wells that resume production. S. 325 and S. 595 propose both a production tax credit for marginal oil and an income exclusion for oil produced from inactive wells.[32]

In addition, some have proposed a new tax credit for exploration and development, which would be in addition to the present deduction for intangible drilling costs.[33]

FILLING THE STRATEGIC PETROLEUM RESERVE TO REDUCE DOMESTIC SUPPLY

Royalty-in-kind (RIK) payments for the government's share of production from federal lands have been a goal of some producer groups for several years. Royalty rates vary from 12.5% to 16.67%, and are typically paid in cash. A number of disputes have arisen over the cash value of oil upon which the percentage royalty due the federal government is based. Some producers have contended that crude valuations have appraised crude too high, resulting in cash payments to the government that are too large. One remedy, these producers contend, is to pay the royalty in physical barrels of crude, rather than trying to attach a dollar value to the crude.

The Strategic Petroleum Reserve (SPR) in 1998 began receiving RIK oil from federal leases in the Gulf of Mexico to replace oil that was sold during FY 1996-1997. While the volumes involved are probably not having any appreciable effect on domestic oil prices, the industry has been pleased by the decision to use a royalty-in-kind program to acquire oil for the SPR. The intention is to acquire 28 million barrels though this program. More than 13 million barrels had been contracted for through June 1999, with additional solicitations planned for deliveries in 2000.

The SPR was authorized in late 1975 to protect the nation against a repetition of the economic dislocation caused by the 1973-74 oil embargo. Its intent was to store a volume of crude oil in salt caverns that could be drawn down and introduced into the market place to blunt the sorts of sharp price increases that had accompanied interruptions of oil imports in the 1970s and early 1980s.

Three issues dominated SPR policy for years: when to use it, how fast to fill it, and in later years, whether the volume of oil stored in the SPR would be an adequate buffer against the sorts of interruptions in supply or spikes in oil prices that might occur. A combination of the need to cut federal spending, the perceived declining likelihood of prolonged and crippling oil supply interruptions, and unregulated oil markets that appeared to operated efficiently in allocating and

---

[32] S. 595 (HR. 1116 in the House) is a very broad bill that basically uses all the tax options to provide tax relief to the oil industry discussed earlier in the text: 1) tax relief by liberalizing current provisions; 2) reduction in some of the existing tax penalties, 3) introduction of new tax incentives, and 4) exemptions from general income tax provisions. In addition, this bill proposes a variety of ways to keep imports from exceeding a specified fraction of consumption (the ceiling cannot exceed 60%). Two other broad oil industry tax relief bills are H.R. 1971 (S. 1042) and S. 1050.

[33] Several state governments, in states where the oil industry has a sizeable presence, have enacted or are considering enacting tax breaks for their oil industries. In April 1999, the Governor of New Mexico approved a tax credit for the drilling of a new oil or gas well. In May 1999, the Kansas legislature approved a bill signed by the Governor that would provide Kansas oil producers with a refundable tax credit for 75% of the property taxes paid on marginal wells.

pricing oil led Congress to agree with the Administration proposal in 1994 to suspend further purchases for the Reserve. It then held 592 million barrels. It now holds 574.9 million barrels and has unutilized capacity of roughly 115 million barrels.

Although doubtful that any appropriation for direct purchase would have supported a daily volume sufficient to boost prices significantly, the domestic industry argued that removing some domestic oil from the marketplace could at least be part of a broader package of relief measures for producers. Quite apart from whether or not the plan would boost producer prices, the SPR fill proposal may benefit producers because it is a step toward in-kind payments that many believe are more fair.

The proposal to accept crude for the SPR as royalty-in-kind in lieu of the customary cash payment collected by the Minerals Management Service (MMS) surfaced in late 1998. On February 11, 1999, Secretary of Energy Richardson announced such a plan. Final details were worked out during early 1999. DOE negotiated for an initial arrangement that would secure the greatest volume of oil as soon as possible. On April 1, 1999, DOE announced that it had signed three-month contracts with Texaco, Shell, and BP to accept a total of 3.5 million barrels, or 38,600 b/d. Adjustments were made allowing for the quality of the oil to be delivered and the expense of transportation.

While the SPR plan was praised by segments of the oil industry and by some Members of Congress who cited the benefits to nation's energy security by replenishing the SPR, the budgetary consequences of the proposed drew less explicit attention. Payment of a royalty-in-kind constitutes a barter transaction. In this deal, producers are to physically deliver oil to the SPR instead of making cash payments based on the oil's estimated value. The producers would not have to be paid for royalty oil sent to the SPR, but MMS (and ultimately the Treasury) would lose the cash royalty payments that it otherwise would have received for that oil. Theoretically, royalties paid in cash should be equivalent to royalties paid in kind. However, it is uncertain whether the value of oil received would be greater or less than the value of cash royalties foregoing. Oil prices have recovered since the RIK plan was first proposed, and it is unlikely that taking the volumes involved off of the market had a measurable effect in price. Nonetheless, producers believe they benefit form regular collection of in-kind royalties, and greeted the RIK plan as a well-intended and helpful first step.

At the same time that the SPR is being replenished, the sharp increase in oil product prices led to at least one call in late September to sell oil from the Reserve. On September 21, 1999, Senator Charles Schumer urged DOE to consider a sale of SPR oil to blunt further increases in the price of petroleum products, especially home heating oil, as winter approached.[34] Initial indications from Secretary Richardson that the idea would be given serious consideration took some by surprise, and a few days later, DOE distanced itself from this interpretation, suggesting that inventories appeared adequate for the moment.[35] The prospect of taking in oil, on the one hand, and selling it on the other, reflects the policy complexities arising out of an extremely sharp rise in prices following closely upon a period of low prices. At the same time that a sale of SPR was being proposed, the Senate Committee on Energy and Natural Resources, in its reporting of legislation

---

[34] *Schumer Seeks SPR withdrawal to Ease Price*, appearing in: The Oil Daily, Vol. 49, No. 1982, Wednesday, September 22, 1999: p. 1.

[35] *Administration Downplays Idea of SPR Sale,* appearing in: The Oil Daily, Vol. 49, No. 185, p. 1-2, An administration official remarked that the Secretary's remarks had been "taken out of context."

to reauthorize the SPR, urged DOE and DOI to consider continuing to fill the unutilized capacity of the Reserve with RIK oil.[36]

ANTIDUMPING AND COUNTERVAILING DUTY ACTIONS

A coalition of independent oil producers, Save Domestic Oil Inc. (SDO), filed antidumping and countervailing duty petitions with the U.S. Department of Commerce on June 29, 1999 alleging that Saudi Arabia, Mexico, Venezuela and Iraq have sold oil in the United States at prices below its fair market value, and that producers or exporters from these countries receive counteravailable subsidies. The Department's International Trade Administration rejected the petitions on August 9, 1999 on the ground that there was insufficient support from others within the industry to warrant an investigation.[37] While the petitions were dismissed, their very submission caused some ripples of concern.[38] Some hoped initially that some sort of resolution would be negotiated, but these attempts were not successful.[39] SDO has since filed a complaint with the U.S. Court of International Trade requesting review of the decision, arguing that the Department improperly measured industry support.[40]

While the expression "dumping" may connote in everyday language simply a large volume of imports of a product at law prices, its operative definition in international and U.S. trade law is more specific. A produce is "dumped" when it is sold by the exporter in the importing country at "less than fair value," that is, at a price which is lower than that charged to buyers in the exporter's domestic market or in sales to third countries. In addition, under World Trade Organization (WTO) agreements and U.S. law, an antidumping remedy in the form of an antidumping duty, equivalent to the unfair pricing margin, cannot be applied unless it is determined that such imports also materially injure, or threaten material injury to, an industry in the importing country, or

---

[36] U.S. Congress. Senate Committee on Energy and Natural Resources. Energy Policy and Conservation Act Amendments. Report to accompany S. 1051. S. Rept. No. 106-163, September 27, 1999, p. 3.

[37] Dismissal of Antidumping and Countervailing Duty Petitions: Certain Crude Petroleum Oil Products From Iraq, Mexico, Saudi Arabia, and Venezuela, 64 Fed. Reg. 44480 (1999). When a petition is filed requesting the imposition of antidumping or countervailing duties, U.S. law requires that the petition be filed "by or on behalf of" the domestic industry involved. The Commerce Department applies a 25%/50% test to determine if this industry support requirement is met. 19 U.S.C. §§ 1671a(c)(4), 1673a(c)(4). The test requires that: (1) the domestic producers or workers who support the petition account for at least 25% of the total production of the domestic like product and (2) the domestic producers or workers who support the petition account for more than 50% of the production of the domestic like product produced by that portion of the industry expressing support for or opposition to the petition. Otherwise stated, "of those producers expressing a view, more producers [must] support than oppose the petition." S.Rept. 103-412, at 35. With regard to the SDO petition, the Commerce Department determined that the 50% requirement was not met; because of this, it did not address the second prong of the test.

[38] "Commerce Dismisses Controversial Dumping, Subsidy Cases on Crude Oil," International Trade Reporter (BNA), August 11, 1999: p. 1330. "U.S. Agency Rejects Oil Dumping Complaint," *The Washington Post,* August 10, 1999: p. E4. See also: "Dumping Motion Filed; Mexico Eyes Retaliation," *The Oil Daily,* vol. 49, No. 124, Wednesday, June 30, 1999: p. 1,3.

[39] "How U.S. May Avoid Massive Oil Import Duties," *Petroleum Intelligence Weekly,* Vol. XXXVIII, No. 27, July 5, 1999: p. 1, 4.

[40] "Oil Group Files CIT Complaint Against Commerce for Dumping Petition," *Inside US. Trade,* September 10, 1999. The standard of review to be applied by the court is whether the Department's action was "arbitrary or capricious, an abuse of discretion, or otherwise not in accordance with law." 19 U.S.C. § 1516a(b).

materially retard the establishment of a domestic industry. Similarly, WTO agreements and U.S. law allow for the position of a countervailing duty in the event an imported product is found to be subsidized and to cause the material injury described above.[41]

The petitions sought imposition of anti-dumping duties on imports from these countries, ranging from more than 33.4% on Mexican imports to nearly 178% on Venezuelan crude imports. Additionally, SDO sought a countervailing duty of more than $6/bbl to offset alleged government subsidy of production in these nations. Some argued that imposition of duties would only redirect world oil supplies. Crude oil that would be subject to a duty in the United States would simply be sold elsewhere at market prices; price would not be appreciably higher and domestic producers would derive no benefit. Others suggested that there would be dislocation while the reallocation took place, and that refiners would have to purchase higher-quality crudes in some instances.

The petitions created problems for the Administration because the charges were lodged at certain important allies. Some suggested that it would complicate Administration free trade policy objectives, especially if there were antidumping and countervailing investigations in progress when the WTO met in Seattle in the fall. Additionally, immediately after the petition was filed, Mexico postponed its previously announced plan to lift tariffs on natural gas imported from the United States. With the announcement on August 9, 1999, that the petition had been rejected, Mexico indicated it would move forward with removing the tariff.

It is possible that an investigation of low-price petroleum imports into the United States would have found the existence of actual or threatened injury to at least one segment of the U.S. petroleum industry (small producers). It is, however, highly unlikely that such investigation would also have found the existence of sales at less than fair value, primarily because the nature and structure of the international petroleum market is such that crude oil prices essentially are set in the world market rather than by individual produces. These prices are more or less uniform, allowing for differences in quality and distance from markets.

OIL IMPORT FEES, TARIFFS AND QUOTAS

The concept of limiting petroleum imports to support domestic producer prices has been a subject of national debate dating back to the Great Depression. Efforts to support domestic prices by establishing quotas for petroleum imports began after World War II, when substantial amounts of low-priced Persian Gulf crude oil began to arrive on world markets. At the time, U.S. prices were in the $3.00 per barrel range; Persian Gulf crudes sold for as low as $1.00.

History of Oil Import Restrictions

National security provisions aimed at protecting domestic producers of key commodities – to be utilized by the President at his discretion – were include din the 1958 Trade Agreements Extension Act. These provisions are now contained in even greater detail in §232(b) gives the President authority to limit the imports of a commodity if they threaten to impair the national security.

With oil, demands for protection had grown to the point that President Eisenhower responded by establishing a voluntary import restraint program. This program was coordinated by the Oil

---

[41] An exporting country is not entitled to a material injury test in a countervailing duty case if it is not a WTO Member, it has not assumed subsidy obligations that are substantially equivalent to those imposed in the WTO Subsidies Agreement, or it is not a party to certain other trade agreements. 19 U.S.C. § 1671.

Policy Committee, a group of oil industry and government officials who advised the President. Voluntary quotas were adopted in 1957, relying on the cooperation of oil importers, and proved ineffective. On May 10, 1959, the President issued Proclamation 3279 under authority in the 1958 act. This instituted a mandatory protection program, which set quotas on imports to balance supply and demand at an acceptable target price in the $3.00 range. Mexico and Canada were exempted from the quota program, since transport was overland and considered safe from a security view. Under the Eisenhower quota, imports were not to exceed 9% of domestic demand.

This quota system became known as the Mandatory Oil Import Program (MOIP). Under the system, import "tickets" – allowing the holder to import a barrel of oil – were issued to all refiners in proportion to the amount of crude they refined. Refiners received tickets regardless of whether they imported oil or not. A "white market" for tickets quickly developed, where unneeded tickets could be bought by import-dependent refiners. The white market functioned as an auction-type market, which priced the tickets to reflect the domestic/foreign price difference. Since all refiners were given – at least during the program's initial days – equal proportions of tickets (relative to crude use), and the market priced the tickets accurately, refiners' crude costs (relative to one another) were not affected.

Later modifications were designed to benefit small refiners, among others. But initially, no refiner received an advantage or was ut at a disadvantage because of the type of oil refined, U.S. crude prices for both imported and domestic oil were held above world market levels by the quota, and U.S. producers received the highest prices in the world. Refiners importing large amounts of cheap foreign crude paid for it in part by having to buy tickets (from refiners not importing oil) in excess of their allocation. And refiners paying higher domestic prices because of the import restriction received offsets by selling their excess tickets to importing refiners.

The MOIP continued with adjustments for over 14 years. By 1969, rising oil prices – combined with a growing number of quota loopholes – made the tickets valueless. President Nixon established a Cabinet Task Force on Oil Import Control, headed by Labor Secretary George Shultz, to review the program.[42] Shultz recommended that the quota program be scrapped and replaced by an import fee system.

On June 25, 1974, the import fee system was imposed by President Nixon in Executive Order 11790. As implemented in the aftermath of the Arab oil embargo, the new fee system essentially provided for unrestricted access to imports, imposing only an import fee of a few cents per barrel.

Subsequent policy interest in oil import fees and quotas centered on periodic efforts to raise U.S. oil prices in order to achieve price-induced conservation and import reduction, as well as increase domestic output. A number of proposals were brought forward during the decade after the Arab oil embargo. Basically, they centered on an import quota or import tax, but variations aimed broadly at price-induced conservation and increasing Treasury revenue would have taxed all oil consumption. The latter variation offered no benefits to domestic producers.

Oil Import Programs – Policy Outcomes and Impacts

The oil import quotas, tariffs and fees that have been considered for the past four decades all would tend to increase the price of imported oil within the United States This would, in turn, have the effect of raising the price for domestic crude as well; with import prices increased, a target price umbrella is created, providing a domestic price floor predetermined by policymakers.

---

[42] Yergin, Daniel, *The Prize,* p. 589.

Quotas operate by limited supply so that a given price level is maintained. In order to hold a certain price point, constant quota adjustment is called for so that variations in demand are met without price instability. Sticking with one fixed quota amount would likely result in wide price swings and could cause spot shortages. Higher petroleum prices resulting from a quota would benefit domestic producers of all types.

But businesses and consumers would pay higher fuel prices. At present consumption levels, every $1.00 per barrel of price support totals nearly $7 billion annually. If passed on to consumers on a penny-for-penny basis, this would amount to about 2.4 cents per gallon of gasoline at the pump.

The imposition of a fixed fee on crude and refined product imports could achieve a more direct effect on crude oil prices without the volatility of a quota; additionally, it might offer a more easily implemented policy tool under §232(b). Tariffs or import fees would lead to higher prices for domestic oil producers, reaching the price level targeted by policy with much less chance of a supply imbalance and related price volatility in the oil patch and at the gas pump. A fee would result in a reasonably predictable amount of producer protection, a better delineated pump price increase and economic effects that would be more predictable. And the import levy would presumably accrue to the Treasury, generating revenue under current market conditions at a rate of about $3.5 billion annually for each tax increment of $1.00 per barrel.

Higher oil prices would, in turn, reduce energy consumption and related environmental damage. However, price increases would also be likely to harm the economy as a whole and create adverse effects in specific regions of the United States. Such problems would have to be balanced against the positive effect on the domestic oil industry and other benefits of reduced demand for imported petroleum.

OIL PRICES AND MERGERS

The steep decline in crude petroleum prices during 1998 put pressure on oil companies ranging in size and scope from the smallest independent producers to the largest integrated "majors," and on oil field service firms as well as producers. Merging with and/or acquiring other firms is one way that oil companies try to increases reserve-finding efficiency and reduce costs, hoping to thereby improve financial performance. Factors in addition to lower oil prices however, probably are contributing to, or have set the stage for, the recent surge in mergers and acquisitions; and mergers themselves put pressure on non-merged first to find partners. Despite the revival in oil prices in 1999, mergers continue to be announced.

Among recent completed and/or announced mergers and acquisitions involving U.S.-based companies are the British Petroleum Company PLC (BP) takeover of the Amoco Corporation, Exxon Corporation's planned merger with Mobil Corporation, and BP/Amoco's planned takeover of Atlantic Richfield. Abroad, Total S.A. (France) merged with Petrofina S.A. (Belgium); Repsol (Spain) acquired YPF SA (Argentina); and Elf Aquitaine S.A. (France) has agreed to be acquired by TotalFina.

Perhaps equally significant, the fallout of consolidations of giant firms such as the above has included the growth and the strengthening of competitive positions by a number of large domestic independent firms through acquiring assets from the major integrated companies, but also from second-tier majors and from other independents.

Non-price developments in the last 15 years are highly relevant to the boom in mergers. Since the mid-1980s, large companies have been de-emphasizing oil production activities onshore in the United States (shifting to offshore U.S. and foreign activities), focusing on their core competencies and core geographic markets, and consolidating organizationally (partly through previous mergers). At the same time, improvements in exploration and development technologies have substantially reduced finding costs.[43] (Such costs in the early to middle 1980s were driven up by the willingness of hopeful producers to spend in the context of high and rising oil prices.) As a result of these developments, cost-reduction and efficiency-improving options available to oil companies in the middle to late 1990s were diminished, leaving consolidation as one of the few remaining options.

Thus, when finding costs rose between 1995 and 1997[44] and oil prices fell in 1998, companies tended to look to mergers again (referring to the merger surge of the mid-1980s) as a performance-improving option. A merger can offer the prospect of a larger capital base, or better access to capital markets, to finance large up-front exploration and development costs of hopefully large finds, a larger number of "richer" prospects from which to chose (by virtue of a bigger menu), a dovetailing of operations in different phases of the oil business, and a reduction in overhead costs (by eliminating the duplication of staff and facilities). A larger capital base and greater diversity of operations also enable companies to better ride out periods of low oil prices. In addition, efficiencies may be gained in combining chemical operations, which constitute a not insignificant portion of most large "oil companies." Joint ventures (in any aspect of the business) may not always be workable alternatives to mergers, since criteria for business decisions may differ between firms.

Mergers, however, may have negative aspects. Sometimes they do not achieve the anticipated gains, and may even disrupt adequately functioning operations. Combining large oil companies (such as Exxon and Mobil) raises the issue of excessive concentration in production, refining, and/or marketing. However, it could be argued that concentration resulting from announced mergers does not appreciably reduce the number of crude oil suppliers to the United States inasmuch as numerous foreign domestic corporate entities supply crude markets, with more than half of U.S. crude supplies coming from abroad. Also, due to antitrust or corporate efficiency considerations, many mergers have resulted in the sale of crude oil production assets to independent producers.

Notwithstanding, or even due to, the shifting of crude oil production assets described above, mergers might increase concentrations in exploration and development. Larger companies tend to be attracted to larger fields (with potentially larger payoffs). And, with crude oil prices being set in a world market, the greater proficiency of merged companies in selecting and developing oil and natural gas prospect and the strengthening of large independents could displace some production by small U.S. producers. This, of course, would tend to counteract policy measures designed to sustain such producers.

Some are concerned about increasing concentration in the market for refined products, especially in geographic areas that are not well served by local refineries or long-haul pipelines. In such cases, U.S. regulators frequently require divestitures of some refining and marketing assets; and many mergers (past and recent) have resulted in the spinoff of refining and marketing operations. Many of these operations have been purchased by new, independent firms, and there has been an entry of foreign firms as well. However, at least for now, these remain geographic

---

[43] Finding costs are the per-barrel costs of adding new oil and gas reserves (or replacing reserves removed through production) by exploration and development activity. Such costs fell roughly 80% between 1981 and 1995 for large U.S. energy companies reporting to the Energy Information Administration (EIA). U.S. Department of Energy, EIA. *Performance Profiles of Major Energy Producers 1997.* Washington, January 1999. P. 69-70.

[44] EIA. *Performance Profiles 1997.* P. 69-71

areas with relatively few suppliers; and mergers, divestitures, etc., often disrupt existing supply arrangements, affecting numerous independent distributors, retailers, and other marketers.

It is also argued that, if the potential efficiencies of mergers are achieved to at least some extent, economic benefits would tend to accrue to the U.S. economy and the oil industry. From this perspective, mergers should not be discouraged as long as undue concentration and displacement in one or more phases of the industry do not result. It should be noted, however, that small companies (producers and many service firms) may not have the size or scope of operations to capture the types of benefits from mergers like those cited above.

Mergers are one of the consequences of the decline in oil output and the total revenues of oil producers. With much lower output and less revenues, a smaller oil industry in the United States is a given, and the smaller oil industry need not be composed of the same number of firms doing business as when the U.S. oil industry produced twice as much crude. Firms tend to have a minimum size for survival, and the need to be large enough to operate profitably remains.

ENERGY INDEPENDENCE: WOULD IT FREE THE UNITED STATES FROM OIL PRICE SHOCKS?

Marc Labonte and Gail Makinen

Over the past 25 years, the United States (and the rest of the world) has been subjected to four major oil price shocks (1973-74, 1979-80, 1990-91, and 1999-2000). While the shocks have varied in magnitude, as shown in Figure 1, each has been a catalyst for national debate over the essentials of a proper energy policy. The most recent price rise has been no exception. As the presidential campaign occurred during the price rise, the two major party candidates for that office expressed similar views on this issue. Both candidates emphasized a need for greater American energy independence and less dependence on foreign oil as an important part of a national program. Vice President Gore argued for giving new incentives for the development of domestic resources like deep gas in the Western Gulf of Mexico, stripper wells for oil, and renewable sources of energy. Governor Bush emphasized an active exploration program for oil in America and the development of our own natural gas and coal resources. In fact, an argument for energy independence has been an integral part of recommendations for a national energy policy at least since the time of the first oil price shock, 1973-74. Yet the petroleum market is not national. Rather, the market is international and the price is set internationally, even though what we do here in the United States can have an important effect on that price.

Figure 1
(Source: Energy Information Administration)

The analysis in this report suggests that the United States, short of completely isolating itself from the world market, cannot avoid the consequences of price shocks through a policy of energy independence even if that policy could lead to the U.S. again being a net exporter of oil. While a policy that encouraged alternative energy sources might moderate the effects of the shock, it may also be useful to encourage greater efficiency in the use of energy. Greater energy efficiency, by lessening the energy input to produce a unit of output, could moderate the effect of future shocks on the economy. American economic activity, as measured by gross domestic product (GDP) has become less dependent on energy since the first oil price shock, as shown in Figure 2. And this is on reason why the run-up in oil prices during 1999-2000 has not affected the economy as greatly as the three previous shocks.

AMERICAN ENERGY POLICY

Since price and other controls imposed in the 1970s were removed, U.S. energy policy has primarily relied on the market. The relatively unhindered forces of supply and demand are allowed to determine the prices of different energy sources and the public has been allowed to access any energy source for consumption. The rationale for this policy is that market prices best reflect the relative scarcity to society of the energy source in question. Reliance on the market as an energy policy is justified because it results in economically efficient decision-making.

This overall reliance on the market has not prevented the federal government from playing an active role. The government has sought to increase the supply of alternative fuels by promoting such petroleum substitutes as gasohol. It has also sought to reduce the demand for energy by mandating fuel efficiency standards for motor vehicles and appliances, and by providing subsidies to individuals to better insulate homes, among other things.

Figure 2
(Source: Energy Information Administration)

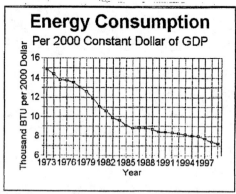

Moreover, there are conceptual objections to a totally market-based national energy policy. They rest on the argument that while market prices may incorporate all the relevant costs to the individual, they may fail to incorporate those that are relevant to the nation. There may be environmental concerns that the market price does not capture. Market prices may also fail to incorporate a premium to help counteract any unacceptable foreign influence on U.S. foreign and domestic policies. For example, this reliance could affect national security in event of an armed conflict. Considerations such as these explain the existence, and have conditioned the recent use, of the Strategic Petroleum Reserve.

Finally, since oil supply shocks are seldom anticipated, market prices can rise dramatically when they occur. When prices do rise suddenly and sharply in the short run, they can be disruptive and, in the past, have had a measurable effect on GDP, employment, and inflation. (The effects thus far from the run up of oil prices during 1999-2000 seem confined to a small boost in the rate of inflation). Since oil is an important input in the production and transport of most goods, a rise in the price of oil raises the cost of production for producers. This effect will be felt by producers using alternate energy sources as well, if those prices also rise. What makes a supply shock so difficult for policymakers to respond to is the fact that it *reduces economic output and raises the price level in the short run,* holding all else equal. If prices were perfectly flexible, producers could lower their other input prices (such as wages) leaving aggregate output and the aggregate price level the same. There would be no reduction in output or increase in the price level in the short run.

But if we live in a world of sticky prices,[1] as common observation suggests we do, then producers cannot lower their other input prices quickly, and so must pass part of the price rise on o customers. As a result, output falls as people are willing to buy fewer goods at the now higher prices. Since the price of labor is now too (relatively) high to be compatible with the higher oil price, some employers may need to lay off some of their compatible workers. With fewer workers employed, less output can be produced. In effect, the rise in the price of oil and the inability of other prices to adjust temporarily reduce the rate of growth of output that the economy can produce. Since producers have to pass part of the oil price rise on to consumers by raising the price of their goods, the general price level temporarily rises as well. When prices adjust in the long run, as economists argue that they will, the decline in output will end: the supply shock causes no real long-run change in the economy's overall productive capabilities, merely a reallocation of resources[2] that makes some individuals, such as oil producers, better off and some, such as consumers, worse off.[3] But until overall prices have fully adjusted, the economy will suffer from a lower rate of growth in output. Since a majority of our oil is purchased abroad, the adjustment process is likely to take longer than usual.

Thus an argument exists, even in the context of a policy that places primary reliance on the market, for an energy strategy that may not be strictly market driven, even if such a policy implies a reduction in economic welfare. A tradeoff can be made between market efficiency, on one hand, and enhanced security and economic stability, on the other hand. The essential question remains: if the tradeoff is desirable, is energy independence a policy that could successfully render the United States either immune or less vulnerable to oil price shocks?

---

[1] Wage contracts, publication subscriptions, and items from catalogs are three examples of prices that are believed to be particularly sticky, or relatively difficult to adjust in the short run.

[2] Some economists have theorized that the costliness of this reallocation of resources is the characteristic of an oil shock that has the greatest impact on the economy, rather than the price adjustment problem.

[3] What is not captured in this simple model is the role that overreaction played in the first two oil shocks caused by shortages and political uncertainty prevalent in the first two shocks. First, since consumer confidence is an important determinant of aggregate demand, an overreaction may have reduced aggregate demand in the short run, thereby aggravating the decline in output caused by the supply shock. Second, overreaction may have led to individuals and businesses using resources in inefficient activities such as hoarding and queuing, which could reduce their productivity, and thus aggregate output.

WOULD ENERGY INDEPENDENCE ISOLATE THE U.S. ECONOMY FROM ENERGY PRICE SHOCKS?

To answer this question, let us use counter-facial reasoning. We will suppose that during the three major oil shocks, oil prices rose exactly as they did. The only factual change will be to suppose that the United States was energy independent in the sense that it imported no oil from any foreign country. Under these altered circumstances, would the U.s. economy have been immune from the rise in world oil prices?

The answer is quite simply no. To see why, consider what would happen when oil prices outside the U.S. rose. With world oil prices rising above the U.S. price, U.S. producers would have an incentive to sell their oil in foreign markets. As U.S. supplies were diverted from domestic to foreign markets, a situation would be created in the United States in which demand exceeded supply. This "excess demand" would then cause the US. price of oil to rise to restore balance or equilibrium between U.S. demand and supply. The end result of the oil supply shock, whose origin may have been the behavior of OPEC, would be a higher domestic price of oil just as it would if the U.S. had been an oil importer. The major difference would be that in the counter factual case in which the United States was assumed to be self-sufficient in oil, it would now be an oil *exporter*.[4]

The only way to isolate the U.S. economy from supply disruptions abroad under the counter factual situation posited above would be to forbid the exportation of oil (i.e., its diversion from domestic to foreign markets) and to prohibit domestic oil companies from raising prices.[5] But we do not live in the counter factual world. Since net oil imports have accounted for about 50% of U.S. consumption in recent years, such a policy, were it to be implemented, would lead to shortages unless domestic oil prices were allowed to rise much higher than at present. This is because oil extraction in the United States on a large enough scale to meet out energy needs is much too costly to compete with foreign producers for this reason, energy independence in the long run would likely imply a price that was less volatile, but even higher than prices at their recent peak.

Even if the United States could implement such a drastic policy, a part of the oil price shock could still affect the U.S. economy.[6] Indeed, even if the U.S. were able to use only alternative energy sources, the shock could have some effect on the economy. This would occur as foreign nations adversely affected by the shock shifted to substitute energy sources. The demand for these sources of energy would rise, raising their prices, and, to the extent possible, U.S. suppliers would divert their output to the world market, possibly creating a situation in which domestic demand exceeded domestic supply. The resulting "excess demand" in the United States would then force up the domestic price of any substitutes for oil. Thus ultimately, to some degree, the original oil

---

[4] Recent history has provided another interesting example in which national behavior, motivated by a common phenomenon, is similar and unrelated to the status of energy independence. In July and August 2000, French citizens demonstrated in protest to the run up in gasoline prices. France is an oil importing country. Shortly thereafter, in September 2000, similar agitation swept the United States and the United Kingdom. It is worth noting that the United Kingdom is not only self-sufficient in oil, but is an oil exporting nation.

[5] The only other theoretical alternative to banning exports would be for U.S. producers to meet not only domestic consumption needs, but enough of world consumption to break OPEC's market power, which wold imply domestic production on an even greater scale.

[6] This presumes that the rise in oil prices is permanent or long-run in nature. If it were only temporary or short run in nature, the type of substitutions described in the following sentence would probably not occur.

price shock would reach the United States. Its magnitude would depend on the extent to which alternative energy sources were substitutes for oil and are exportable from the United States.

THE 1999-2000 OIL PRICE SHOCK

The recent run-up of oil prices has so far not produced serious consequences for the U.S. economy, for several reasons. First, the run-up measured in constant year-2000 prices is small. And it is even smaller if viewed from the perspective of 1998. Following the serious economic contraction of several Asian countries during 1997-1998, world oil prices plummeted. They declined from an average constant dollar barrel price of $25 in January 1997, this is an increase of about 36%. Contrast this with the 1973-74 shock in which per-barrel prices rose from about $8 in November 1973 to about $27 in February 1975, the 1979-80 shock in which prices rose from an average of about $29 in march 1979 to $65 in March 1981, and the 1990-91 shock in which prices rose from an average of about $19 in June 1990 to $40 that September (all prices measured in constant year 2000 dollars).

Second, this oil price shock has not been with the economy for long (yet). At first American companies were probably able to use stop-gap measures to avoid the oil price shock, but this becomes more difficult as time goes by. Not only was the 1973-74 shock large, but high real oil prices, as shown in figure 1, persisted until 1979. The 1979-80 shock was large, and although prices fell continuously from 1980, they did not reach their 1978 level until 1985. In the third shock, by contrast, prices began to fall as soon as the Gulf War was concluded, and had returned to their pre-shock level in a year and a half. The coinciding recession lasted only eight months. It is too early to assess the staying power of the current increase.

Third, the U .S. economy is far more energy efficient than it was in 1973-74. The increase in the real price of oil in particular and energy in general led to moves that increased the energy efficiency of the economy. While many of these changes resulted from the way an economy would respond to an increase in real energy prices, others, such as mandated federal gasoline mileage standards for automobiles, resulted from legislation. Energy efficiency is often touted on environmental grounds, but there is a purely macroeconomic argument for greater efficiency: the more energy-efficient an economy, the smaller the likely effect from a given oil price or energy shock. Oil shocks reduce economic output and increase prices by raising the cost of one portion of a producer's inputs. When a producer becomes more energy efficient, a fewer of his inputs are affected by an oil shock. Therefore, less economic adjustment needs to take place.[7]

Thus, policies to make the economy more energy efficient are likely to pay dividends in terms of freeing the economy from the effects of these price shocks. Whether the United States imported none or all of its oil, greater energy efficiency still implies that a sudden increase in oil prices will cause a proportionately smaller disruption to output.

---

[7] For a more comprehensive discussion of the effects of a petroleum price increase on the U.s. economy, see Library of congress, CRS *Rising Oil Prices: What Dangers Do They Pose for the Economy* by Marc Labonte, CRS Report RL 30634, August 15, 2000.

ENERGY INDEPENDENCE

The analysis above has suggested that energy independence in itself would be unlikely to free the United States from the effects of oil shocks. If domestic production of oil could not help, is there any other way that public policy can lessen the U.S. reliance on foreign oil? It would appear that if alternative non-petroleum energy sources could be developed on a large scale so they could supply a very large portion of U.S. energy demand, then the economy would be less sensitive to oil price shocks. Such a development does not appear to be very likely, at least in the near term. Thus, a case remains for increasing the energy efficiency of the economy as one of the best ways to contain the effect of oil price shocks.

Advanced Vehicle Technologies: Energy, Environment, and Development Issues

Brent D. Yacobucci

Introduction

Technology using electrical energy to power automobiles has been in existence for over a century. However, for a number of reasons, including the energy density of petroleum fuels, the internal combustion engine has been the power source of choice for automobiles and most other vehicles. However, with the oil shocks of the past few decades, as well as an increasing awareness of the emissions of air pollutants and greenhouse gases from cars and trucks, interest in the use of electrical power train systems has grown. While there are other potential replacements for the internal combustion engine, such as compressed air, these other technologies have not been the subject of much interest scientifically or politically.

Much of the advanced vehicle research has come through the Partnership for a New Generation of Vehicles (PNGV), a consortium of the Federal Government and the "Big Three" American automobile manufacturers, established in 1993.[1] PNGV's goal is for each of these manufacturers to produce a prototype of a mid-sized passenger car capable of achieving 80 miles per gallon fuel economy, without compromising emissions standards, safety, affordability, or comfort.[2]

The United States is not alone in pursuing these new technologies. Two major Japanese manufacturers have introduced compact cars that can achieve two to three times the fuel economy of the standard conventional vehicle.[3] The development of these vehicles is a response to global pressures to lower emissions and improve fuel economy. In that context, it is worth noting that in

---

[1] The original PNGV agreements only allowed federal research and development money to go to U.S. owned and operated car companies. When Chrysler merged with Daimler-Benz (a German company), this crated policy concerns, which have since been resolved.

[2] The Partnership for a New Generation of Vehicles, *Program Plan*. November 29, 1995.

[3] Eric C. Evarts, "First fleet of 'green' cars about to hit the road," *Christian Science Monitor*. January 11, 2000.

most developed countries, gasoline and diesel fuel prices re considerably higher than they are in the United States. In Europe, for example, gasoline prices range from 3 to 5 dollars per gallon.

The three most promising advanced technologies are electric vehicles, hybrid vehicles, and fuel cell vehicles. In an electric vehicle, the vehicle runs exclusively on electricity which is supplied from an electric utility provider, eliminating combustion on-board the vehicle. A hybrid vehicle integrates an electrical system with an internal combustion engine to utilize the benefits of each system. In a fuel cell vehicle, instead of combustion, a chemical conversion process is used, leading to higher levels of efficiency. In addition to altering the power train, many other efficiency-related technologies, such as improved aerodynamics and low-resistance tires can be incorporated into both new and conventional vehicles.

While these various technologies are promising, they must overcome certain obstacles before they will be competitive in the marketplace. There are three main barriers to their widespread use: cost, infrastructure, and performance. Cost is a factor since without subsidies, consumers are unlikely to purchase new vehicles in large numbers if the new vehicles are not cost competitive with conventional vehicles. Also, convenient infrastructure must exist for both the fueling and maintenance of these vehicles. Finally, the performance of the new vehicles must be comparable to that of conventional vehicles.

ELECTRIC VEHICLES

An electric vehicle (EV) is powered by an electric motor, as opposed to a gasoline or diesel engine. Power is supplied to the motor by batteries, which are charged through a central station (which can be installed in the owner's garage) or through a portable charger on board the vehicle, which is plugged into a standard outlet. Because no fuel is consumed in EVs, and the vehicles therefore do not produce emissions, they are considered to be zero emission vehicles (ZEVs) in certain air quality control regions. Although there are emissions attributable to the production of electricity to charge the vehicles, the overall fuel-cycle of EVs tends to lead to lower levels of toxic and ozone-forming emissions than those of conventional vehicles. Also, since pollution attributable to electric vehicles occurs at power plants, it is generally emitted in areas with relatively low population density.[4]

Another potential public policy benefit of electric vehicles is that they can reduce U.S. dependence on foreign oil, since only about 3% of electricity in the U.S. is generated from petroleum. Furthermore, transportation dependence on all forms of fossil fuels can be reduced, since approximately 30 to 35% of electricity in the U.S. is generated from non-fossil fuels. However, high electricity costs recently, especially in California, have led to questions about the viability of EVs.

Commercially, these vehicles have not been well-received by consumers.[5] By 1998, only about 3,500 privately-owned EVs were on the road, mainly in California. An additional 1,900 were operated by the Federal government and local and state governments.[6] General Motors only

---

[4] However, there may be concerns over increasing pollution in areas near a power generation facility, though it is generally easier to control emissions for a stationary source than from a mobile source.

[5] It is important to note that the technologies discussed in this report are in relatively early stages of research and development and thus are not directly comparable to the internal combustion engine, which has been a mass market product for nearly a century.

[6] Department of Energy, Energy Information Administration (EIA), *Alternatives to Traditional Transportation Fuels, 1998.* [http://www.eia.doe.gov/fuelalternate.html].

produces its electric vehicle in small batches, since consumer demand is too low to support mass-production, whereas Honda Motor Co. has announced that it will discontinue production of its electric vehicle, the EV Plus, due to lack of demand.[7]

Cost

One of the most significant barriers to wide acceptance of electric vehicles is their higher purchase cost. For example, the manufacturer's suggested retail price for a 1999 General Motors EV1 is approximately $33,995,[8, 9] which is considerably higher than a comparable 1999 Chevrolet Cavalier at $13,670.[10]

Table 1. Cost Difference for GM EV 1 (Electric and Chevrolet Cavalier (Gasoline)

EV 1 purchase price (MSRP)	$33,995
Federal Tax credit (10% of purchase price)	$3,400
California incentives	Up to $5,000
Fuel cost savings*	$2,100 to $3,000
EV 1 net cost	$22,595 to $28,495
Cavalier purchase price (MSRP)	$13,670
Net cost difference	$8,925 to $14,825

*Fuel cost savings are those achieved over ten-year ownership (15,000 miles per year), assuming an electricity cost of 10 cents per kilowatt-hour and a gasoline cost of $1.20 per gallon.

However, fuel costs are much lower for EVs than for conventional vehicles. A small conventional vehicle can achieve a fuel cost of approximately $690 per year.[11] An electric vehicle, however, can achieve a considerably lower cost of $390 to $480 per year.[12] This difference, while significant, fails to make up for the additional purchase or lease cost for an electric vehicle. (See **Table 1**.) With increased petroleum prices, the cost savings for EVs may make them more attractive. However, it is unlikely that even a very large increase in petroleum prices would be sufficient to make electric vehicles cost competitive. Another factor is that because electric vehicles have fewer moving parts, maintenance costs may be lower, although certain parts, such as replacement batteries, tend to be expensive.

Currently, there are Federal and state tax credits for the purchase of electric vehicles. The Federal credit is worth 10% of the purchase price of the vehicle, up to $4,000. This credit, which is part of the Energy Policy Act of 1992, will be reduced by 25% each year between 2002 and 2004, and will expire after 2004.[13, 14] In some areas, these vehicles are also exempted from high occupancy vehicle (HOV) lane restrictions, parking restrictions, and/or vehicle registration fees.

---

[7] Honda Stops Making Electric Cars, Roiling California Regulators," *Wall Street Journal.* April 30, 1999. P. B7.

[8] General Motors, *EV1 Electric.* [http://www.gmev.com/].

[9] It must be noted that this vehicle is only available for lease to consumers, currently.

[10] Chevrolet, *Chevrolet Metro.*. [http://www.chevrolet.com].

[11] John DeCicco, Jim Kliesch, and Martin Tomas, *ACEEE's Green Book: The Environmental Guide to Cars & Trucks.* Washington, D.C. 2000.

[12] Ibid.

[13] P.L. 102-486; 26 US.C. 30.

Infrastructure

Another key obstacle to more widespread use of electric vehicles is the lack of fueling (charging) and maintenance infrastructure. For example, in California and Arizona, there are approximately 400 public charging stations,[15] plus approximately 1,100 General Motors chargers installed for private use (generally in owner's garages).[16] This is about 5% of the approximately 8,600 gasoline refueling stations in the two states.[17] The lack of recharging infrastructure is not only inconvenient, but also limits long-distance travel, since Arizona and California account for 69% of all recharging sites currently in operation.

Adding to the problem of fueling infrastructure, is the lack of maintenance infrastructure. Few mechanics have experience servicing EVs, and most work must be done at a certified dealer. For this reason, most EV leases include free dealer maintenance over the period of the contract. On the other hand, one advantage of electric vehicles is that they have fewer moving parts and thus may be more durable, and require less frequent maintenance.

Performance

Another major concern with electric vehicles is their performance. The batteries used to power the vehicles tend to be quite heavy, limiting the range of these vehicles.[18] While a conventional passenger car can travel 300 to 400 miles before refueling, currently available electric cars generally can drive only travel about 100 to 150 miles before needing to be recharged. Furthermore, while refilling the tank of a conventional vehicle requires only a few minutes, a full residential recharge for an electric vehicle can take 5 to 8 hours. Some high-speed chargers can charge a vehicle in 3 to 4 hours, but these quick charges shorten the life of the batteries, which are expensive to replace.[19] For fleet vehicles, or for short-distance commuting, these performance characteristics might not greatly affect their marketability, but the feasibility of EVs for long-distance, inter-city travel is unlikely with current technology, even if the fueling infrastructure is greatly expanded.[20]

A lesser concern with electric vehicles is an unconventional driving style. To provide maximum efficiency and range, the driver must accelerate and brake very smoothly, or range is

---

[14] For a detailed discussion of the EV tax credit, see CRS Report 98-193 E, *Global climate change: the energy tax incentives in the President's FY 2001 budget.*

[15] Department of Energy, Alternative Fuels Data Center (AFDC), *US Refueling Site counts by State and Fuel Type as of 3/8/2001.* [http://www.afdc.nrel.gov/refuel/state_tot.shtml].

[16] General Motors, op. cit.

[17] Department of Commerce, Bureau of the Census, *Country Business Patterns for the United States.* [http://www.census.gov/epcd/cbp/view/cbpview.html].

[18] Battery weight is a major obstacle to improving the range of these vehicles. For this reason, there has been considerable research and development progress, especially with nickel-metal hydride (NiMH) batteries, which have extended EV range significantly.

[19] John O'Dell, "A Clean Air Detour?; Fuel-efficient, Low-emissions Hybrids are Here," *Los Angeles Times.* February 2, 2000. P. G.1.

[20] There has been some research into the use of modular battery packs to eliminate the need for recharging-depleted batteries are exchanged for fully-charged batteries at a service station-but problems with design and feasibility have hindered progress in this area.

significantly diminished. Because of this, some drivers may not be comfortable or proficient operating an electric vehicle.[21]

The greatest performance benefit from an EV is that, as was stated above, there are no emissions from the vehicle itself. Furthermore, the overall toxic and ozone-forming emissions tend to be much lower than with conventional vehicles since it is easier to control emissions at a power plant than it is to control combustion vehicle emissions. An added benefit is a reduction in noise pollution since EVs are significantly quieter than conventional vehicles.

Greenhouse gas emissions caused by EVs may be lower or higher than those from conventional vehicles, depending on the local fuel mix used in power generation[22] and the efficiency of the power distribution grid. Furthermore, if electricity transmission and distribution losses are high, energy consumption by electric vehicles may exceed conventional vehicles.

Other Issues

A major issue for vehicle manufacturers, and a motivation for increased research and development on electric vehicles is California's zero emissions mandate.[23] Starting in model year (Y) 2003, 10% of vehicles sales by major manufacturers – the "Big Three" American manufacturers (Daimler-Chrysler, Ford, and General Motors), and the Japanese "Big Four" (Honda, Mazda, Nissan, and Toyota) – must be certified as zero emissions as zero emissions (ZEV),[24] super-ultra-low-emissions vehicles (SULEV),[25] or other advanced vehicles with extremely low emissions. Furthermore, at least 2% of sales are required to be ZEVs. Members of the auto industry are concerned that demand is too low, and that consumers will not purchase the required number of vehicles. On February 23, 2001, GM sued the California Air Resources Board to stop the requirement.[26] GM claims that it will be too expensive to meet the mandate, and that it creates an "undue burden on interstate commerce."[27]

Approximately 1,650 electric passenger cars and light trucks were made available in 1998 nationwide.[28] During the same year, sales of conventional cars and light trucks in California alone were over 1.6 million.[29] At current sales levels, the 2% mandate could require the sale of approximately 32,000 electric vehicles in 2003. However, if these vehicles achieve a range of 100 miles or greater, then the sale of one vehicle can qualify as the sale of multiple low-range ZEVs. In MY2003, a high-range vehicle can earn up to quadruple credits. The credits are even higher for earlier voluntary compliance. Even with the extended range credits, however, sales of electric

---

[21] In fact, these techniques can also affect the range and fuel economy of conventional vehicles, but to a much lesser degree.

[22] This is especially true of the high greenhouse gas emissions from coal-fired power plants.

[23] *California Code of Regulations.* Section 1962(e), title 13.

[24] A ZEV has no evaporative or exhaust emissions.

[25] A SULEV has 71% to 89% lower ozone-forming emissions, and no higher particulate emissions, than a California certified Low Emissions Vehicle (2004 standards).

[26] *General Motors Corp. v. California Air Resources Board,* Cal. Super. Ct., No. C 01-00741. February 23, 2001.

[27] Carolyn Whetzel, "General Motors Challenges State Rule to Mandate Sales of Zero Emission Vehicles," *Daily Environment Report.* March 2, 2001, p. A-3.

[28] EIA, op. Cit.

[29] Ward's Communications, *Ward's Automotive Yearbook 1999.* Southfield, Michigan. 1999.

vehicles will have to increase sharply, since electric vehicles are currently the only ZEVs on the market.

The original legislation required 2% of MY 1998 vehicle sales to be ZEVs and SULEVs, and 5% of MY 2001 sales, but these initial requirements were removed in 1996 to encourage market-based introduction of ZEVs. Other states have adopted the California market percentage program, including New York, Maine, Massachusetts, New Jersey, and Maryland.[30]

Congressional Action

In the 107th Congress, three bills concerning EVs have been introduced. H.R. 377 (Serrano) would provide tax credits for the use of EVs and other clean fuel vehicles in certain areas. S. 388 (Murkowski) would allow EVs and other alternative fuel vehicles (AFVs) to use high occupancy vehicle (HOV) lanes regardless of the number of passengers. S. 389 (Murkowski) would provide the above exception to HOV restrictions, and would also expand the EV tax credit to $4,250, with an added credit of $2,125 if the vehicle has a range of 100 miles or more on a single charge. All three bills are currently in committee.

Some bills were introduced in the 106th Congress that would have amended the Energy Policy Act to extend the expiration date of the EV tax credit, eliminate the phase-down of the credit, increase the allowable credit, and/or eliminate the credit. None of these bills were passed out of committee.

Hybrid Electric Vehicles

A type of vehicle that may address many of the problems associated with electric vehicles is a hybrid electric vehicle (HEV). HEVs combine an electric motor and battery pack with an internal combustion engine to improve efficiency. In an HEV, the batteries are recharged during operation, eliminating the need for an external charger.

The combustion and electric systems of HEVs are combined in various configurations. In one configuration (series hybrid), the electric motor supplies power to move the wheels, while the combustion engine is connected to a generator which powers the motor and recharges the batters. In another configuration (parallel hybrid), the combustion engine provides primary power, while the electric motor adds extra power for acceleration and climbing, or the electric motor is the primary power source, with extra power provided by the engine. In some parallel hybrid systems, the engine and electric motor work in tandem, with either system providing primary or secondary power depending on driving conditions.

The hybrid drive train can lead to significantly higher levels of vehicle system efficiency. The higher efficiency of these vehicles allows them to achieve very high fuel economy and lower emissions. For example, the hybrid Honda Insight achieves a city fuel economy rating of 61 miles per gallon (mpg), and a highway rating of 70 mpg. A gasoline-fueled Honda Civic Hatchback, by comparison, achieves a rating of 32 mpg city and 37 mpg highway.[31] Fuel economy improvements can help cut demand or foreign petroleum, and the higher efficiency enables hybrid

---

[30]In New Jersey and Maryland, the program will be adopted only if neighboring states also adopt the program.

[31]DeCicco, et al., op. cit.

vehicles to attain, and even surpass, the range of conventional vehicles, even with a smaller fuel tank. Furthermore, since these vehicles utilize conventional fuel, there are none of the fueling infrastructure problems associated with electric vehicles.

The only hybrid vehicles currently available in the U.S. market are the Honda Insight, and the Toyota Prius. In early 2000, Ford, GM, and DaimlerChrysler introduced hybrid concept cars- the Prodigy, Precept, and ESX3, respectively.

Currently, HEVs are treated as conventional vehicles because they run on gasoline or diesel fuel. However, there is interest in reclassifying these vehicles as alternative fuel vehicles or creating a separate distinction for them, in order to promote their unique characteristics.

Cost

One of the key selling points for hybrids is that while they are more expensive than conventional vehicles, they are much less expensive than pure electric vehicles. However, these vehicles are still relatively expensive. Both of the current Honda and Toyota vehicles, which are compact cars, are currently priced several thousand dollars above comparable conventional vehicles, despite being heavily subsidized by the manufacturers.[32]

The higher purchase price of these vehicles is offset, to some degree, by lower fuel costs. Due to the higher fuel efficiency of hybrids, fuel costs are significantly lower with hybrids than with conventional vehicles. Depending on fuel prices, these savings could be $250 or more per year.[33] (See Table 2.) These savings, along with possible tax credits for the purchase of hybrids, may cover the incremental cost of purchasing a hybrid as opposed to a conventional vehicle. Furthermore, some consumers may be willing to pay a premium to drive a "different" kind of car.

Table 2. Cost Difference for Honda Insight (Hybrid) and Honda Civic Hatchback (Gasoline)

Insight purchase price (MSRP)*	$18,880
Fuel cost savings**	$2,500
Insight net cost	$16,380
Civic purchase price (MSRP)	$12,100
Net cost difference	$4,280

*This price has been subsidized by the manufacturer to motivate sales.
**Fuel cost savings are over ten-year ownership (15,000 miles per year), at a gasoline price of $1.20 per gallon.

Infrastructure

Another key advantage of hybrid vehicles over pure electrics is that no new fueling infrastructure must be installed, since the vehicles are fueled by gasoline or diesel. This will allow

---

[32]"Science and Technology: Hybrid Vigour?," *The Economist.* January 29, 2000, p. 94.
[33]DeCicco, et al., op. cit.

hybrid owners to purchase and operate these vehicles anywhere in the country, and long-distance travel will not be limited by the fueling infrastructure. Furthermore, maintenance of the combustion components in the vehicle can rely on the existing serve infrastructure.

However, as with pure electric vehicles, maintenance of the electric components in hybrid vehicles will most likely need to occur at licensed dealers, who will have first access to the technology. This may limit the acceptability for rural customers who may live a good distance from the dealership, but is less likely to harm acceptance of urban and suburban customers.

Performance

The most notable features of hybrid vehicles are higher fuel economy and extended range. The efficiency of the hybrid drive system allows for two to three times the fuel economy of conventional vehicles, cutting fuel costs. Also, the improved fuel economy means that vehicle range is greatly extended with hybrids, even if a slightly smaller fuel tank is used. This higher efficiency also leads to lower emissions of greenhouse gases, as well as lower emissions of toxic and ozone-forming pollutants.

Congressional Action

No bills have been introduced in the 107th Congress concerning hybrid electric vehicles. In the 106th Congress, bills were introduced to provide tax credits for HEVs. However, none of these bills were passed out of committee.

FUEL CELL VEHICLES

A third type of new vehicle is a fuel cell vehicle (FCV). A fuel cell can be likened to a "chemical battery." Unlike a battery, however, a fuel cell can run continuously, as along as the fuel supply is not exhausted. In a fuel cell, hydrogen reacts with oxygen to generate an electric current. Hydrogen is supplied to the fuel cell as either pure hydrogen, or a through hydrogen-rich fuel (such as methanol, natural gas, or gasoline) which is processed (reformed) on-board the vchicle. There is a physical limit to the voltage that one fuel cell can provide, so fuel cells are arranged in "stacks" to generate a high voltage which is used to power an electric motor.

This chemical process eliminates the need for charging a battery, which is necessary with electric vehicles, while producing much lower emissions than combustion vehicles. In fact, if pure hydrogen fuel is used, the only product from the reaction will be water. With hydrogen fuel, an FCV would qualify as a zero emission vehicle.[34] Using other fuels,[35] while the vehicle is no longer a ZEV, emissions would still be drastically cut as compared to conventional vehicles. Furthermore, because over the long term, the eventual fuel supply for FCVs will likely be natural

---

[34]Like electric cars, however, there will be emissions due to the production and distribution of the fuel.

[35]In these cases, an extra component, called a reformer, is used to separate hydrogen from the fuel.

gas, methanol or pure hydrogen-the latter two produced from natural gas[36] - another potential benefit from fuel cells will be their ability to reduce the transportation demand for foreign petroleum.[37] However, it is likely that the first commercially-available FCVs will be gasoline - or diesel-powered.

While not currently available to consumers, fuel cells have been touted as likely to be one of the most important technologies in the history of the automobile.[38] They are currently very expensive, and thus there has been a great deal of interest in research and development to improve their marketability.

Cost

Arguably, the largest barrier to the production of FCVs is cost. It currently costs approximately $2,000 to $3,000 to produce a gasoline engine for a conventional passenger car.[39] A comparable fuel cell stack costs around $35,00, according to industry estimates, but a leading producer of fuel cells estimates that costs could be cut $3,500 in the future.[40] Since there are fewer moving parts in a fuel cell vehicle, Development costs would likely be lower, so the added cost of the fuel cell system may be offset by lower development costs. Further research and development would be necessary to achieve these benefits.

Another key cost issue will be fuel costs. Fuel costs are a concern because there is no hydrogen infrastructure currently, and the use of methanol and natural gas as transportation fuels is extensive.[41] Consumers might have to pay a premium for these fuels, in order to support a growing infrastructure. However, since hydrogen fuel and methanol would likely be produced from natural gas, price fluctuations caused by changing supply in petroleum markets could be dampened, although natural gas price fluctuations would certainly have an effect.

Infrastructure

Another major barrier to the use of FCVs is that there are no infrastructures for the distribution of hydrogen, and little methanol or natural gas infrastructure for transportation. As of 1998, there were only 91 methanol refueling sites in the U.S., and only 1,754 natural gas sites. The feedstock for methanol, and the likely feedstock (in the near future) for hydrogen fuel is natural gas, although other feedstocks, such as biomass or coal, could be used.[42] Hydrogen derived from solar energy could also be possible in the future, but that technology is far from commercialization.

---

[36]The eventual goal is to produce hydrogen fuel from renewable sources, but that technology not yet marketable.

[37]Recent high natural gas prices have led to questions of the viability of natural gas as a fuel source for FCVs.

[38]Environmental and Energy Study Institute (EESI), *Fuel Cell Fact Sheet.* February, 2000.

[39]GM's Fuel-Cell-Powered Precept Hyped as Efficient and Fast." *The Salt Lake Tribune.* January 12, 2000, p. D9.

[40]"Ballard Reduces Fuel Cell Costs." *Detroit News.* November 30, 1999.

[41]Expanding current natural gas or methanol infrastructure will likely be less expensive than comparable hydrogen infrastructure.

[42]Department of Energy, Alternative Fuels Data Center, *Hydrogen General Information.* [http://www.afdc.doe.gov/altfuel/hyd_general.html].

Until the distribution infrastructure for hydrogen, methanol, or natural gas is developed, it is likely that gasoline will be the fuel of choice in FCVs. However, gasoline fuel cell systems are not as efficient as other systems. For this reason, gasoline systems are seen as a stepping-stone to other, more efficient fuel cell systems in the future.

As with electric vehicles, no Development infrastructure exists for servicing these vehicles. The technology is radically different from conventional vehicles, and most development would likely have to occur at certified dealers.

Performance

One limit on the performance of fuel cell vehicles has been their weight. Fuel cells have been demonstrated on larger vehicles, such as buses, but few passenger car prototypes exist, because the necessary stacks have been too heavy to incorporate into smaller vehicles. Furthermore, reformers for converting gasoline or other fuels to hydrogen are also very heavy. Therefore, much research has focused not only on cutting the cost of fuel cell systems, but decreasing their weight, as well.

Another performance concern is one of fuel storage. Since hydrogen is not very dense, the fuel must be highly concentrated, and must be compressed (requiring a high-pressure tank), liquified (requiring a high-pressure tank), liquified (requiring a cooling system for the storage tank), or chemically bonded with a heavy storage material (such as a metal hydride). Each of these storage systems has problems, such as added weight, safety risks, or expensive raw materials that limit their acceptability.[43] Therefore, research is currently being conducted on improving both the storage capacity and safety of hydrogen fuel. Some of the same problems are associated with natural gas storage, although to a lesser degree. For these reasons, there has been more interest in using methanol or gasoline, since these fuels are easier to deliver and to store.

On the environmental side, the emissions from fuel cell vehicles are extremely low. Using hydrogen, there are no emissions of toxic or ozone-forming pollutants. Using other fuels, the reformer limits the efficiency of the fuel cell system, but emissions are still much lower than with conventional engines. Depending on the emissions attributable to the production and distribution of the fuel, FCVs may prove to have better environmental performance than any other technology for all types of emissions, including greenhouse gases. In addition, with their higher efficiency, even fuel cells run on gasoline will result in lower emissions than conventional vehicles.

Other Issues

Currently, the main issue for FCVs is research and development (R&D). All major automobile manufacturers are spending considerable amounts of money on fuel cell R&D. The Federal Government, to a smaller degree, has also supported fuel cell R&D through PNGV.

---

[43]It must be noted that high-pressure on-board storage of hydrogen will likely be safer than current gasoline tanks.

Congressional Action

No bills specifically targeted to transportation fuel cells have been introduced in the 107th Congress. In the 106th Congress, bills were introduced to promote fuel cell R&D for both transportation and stationary purposes. In addition, bills were introduced to provide tax credits for providers of hydrogen fuel.

COMPONENT TECHNOLOGIES

Another way to improve the fuel economy and emissions characteristics of vehicles is to use advanced components that reduce friction, decrease vehicle weight, or improve system efficiency. Most high-technology vehicles that are available to the public utilize these technologies, but some of these technologies could also be incorporated into the design of conventional vehicles.

Lightweight Materials

An effective way to improve efficiency is to simply reduce the weight of the vehicle. However, simply reducing weight while using the same materials a structural design can compromise passenger safety. Therefore, newer vehicles are making extensive use of advanced materials such as composite or plastic body panels, and high-strength, lightweight aluminum structural components. The use of some of these materials may even make a vehicle more recyclable.[44] Furthermore, conventional materials can improve safety while reducing weight, if more sophisticated structural designs are used.

Decreased Resistance

Another way to improve efficiency is to decrease resistance, both from drag and from friction between the wheels and the road. Wind resistance can be decreased through redesigning the body to a more aerodynamic shape. In addition, the use of "slippery" body panels[45] can further decrease drag, as can decreasing the profile of parts such as side-view mirrors, tires, and the radio antenna. Rolling friction can be limited through the use of low-resistance tires.

Regenerative Braking

A key component in the efficiency of electric vehicles (including hybrids and fuel cell vehicles) is a regenerative braking system. This system allows some of the vehicle's kinetic energy to be recaptured as electricity when the brakes are applied. In braking, the motor acts as a

---

[44]Automobiles are currently one of the most recycled consumer products with over 65% of vehicle mass (mostly steel)reused.

[45]These are made from plastics with a very low coefficient of friction.

generator, taking kinetic energy from the wheels and converting it to electrical energy which is fed back to the batteries.[46] This technology is already available on consumer EVs and HEVs.

CONCLUSIONS

The use of advanced vehicle technologies can help curb consumption of fossil fuels, especially petroleum, and reduce emissions of toxic and ozone-forming pollutants, as well as greenhouse gases. In general, the most promising technologies incorporate electric motors and batteries in their design, while all take advantage of new design techniques and advanced materials to reduce resistance, cut vehicle weight, and better conserve energy. However, these technologies are still in various stages of development and have not yet proven marketable to most consumers.

The three key issues of the marketability of advanced technology vehicles are cost, infrastructure, and performance. Consumers must be willing and able to purchase the vehicles, so purchase cost and overall life-cycle cost of these vehicles must be competitive. In addition, consumers must be able to expect that refueling and servicing these vehicles will be relatively convenient. Finally, the overall performance of the vehicles - in terms of fuel economy, range, driveability, safety, and emissions - must be acceptable.

While most advanced vehicle technologies meet some of these requirements, no new vehicle has yet met all of them. Therefore, research and development has been a key issue in the discussion of these vehicles, as have efforts to make the vehicles more affordable and the infrastructure more accessible. These vehicles may help the Federal Government in its role of promoting energy security and environmental protection if research and development can bring them to a point where they can be successfully marketed to American consumers.

---

[46]In fact, the efficiency of the regenerative braking system is a key factor in the amount of credit available in the Administration's proposed tax credit for hybrid vehicles.

NUCLEAR ENERGY POLICY

Mark Holt and Carl E. Behrens

SUMMARY

Nuclear energy policy issues facing Congress include questions about radioactive waste management, research and development priorities, power plant safety and regulation, nuclear weapons proliferation, nuclear weapons facilities cleanup, and technology for producing nuclear fuel.

Federal funding for nuclear energy research and development was substantially reduced by the Clinton Administration, which placed a higher priority on energy efficiency and alternative energy technologies. However, the Department of Energy (DOE) sought, and Congress provided, $ 35 million in FY2001 for the Nuclear Energy Research Initiative, which focuses on advanced nuclear technology research.

Disposal of highly radioactive waste has been one of the most controversial aspects of nuclear power. The Nuclear Waste Policy Act requires DOE to begin detailed physical characterization of Yucca Mountain in Nevada as a permanent underground repository for high-level waste.

Legislation was introduced in the 106th Congress (H.R. 45, S. 608) to establish an interim storage facility for nuclear waste at Yucca Mountain. But the Clinton Administration opposed temporary storage at the site. In response, the Senate approved an alternative measure February 10, 2000, to authorize DOE to store waste at Yucca Mountain only after receiving a construction permit for a permanent repository (S.1287). The House passed the bill without amendment March 22, 2000, but President Clinton vetoed it April 25, 2000. A Senate effort to override the veto fell short on May 2, 2000, by a vote of 64-35.

Whether progress on nuclear waste disposal and other congressional action will revive the U.S. nuclear power industry's growth will depend on economic considerations. Natural gas- and coal-fired power plants currently are favored over nuclear reactors for new generating capacity. However, the nuclear industry believes that simpler, safer versions of today's commercial reactors could eventually be built in the United States.

Concern about the spread, or proliferation, of nuclear weapons throughout the world has risen sharply since longtime rivals India and Pakistan conducted competing nuclear weapons tests in May 1998. The heightened tensions in Southeast Asia have focused attention on the effectiveness of the international nuclear nonproliferation regime. Potential nuclear weapons development by North Korea and Iran have also recently raised considerable U.S. concern.

Cleaning up severe environmental problems at U.S. nuclear weapons production facilities, owned by DOE, is expected to cost about $ 150 billion over the next several decades. After sharp growth in the early 1990's, DOE environmental cleanup funding under the Clinton Administration has been nearly flat. Congress approved about $6.4 billion for the program in FY2001.

The enrichment of natural uranium to make nuclear fuel, formerly a government activity, now is carried out by the newly privatized U.S. Enrichment Corporation (USEC). USEC was privatized in a $1.9 billion initial public stock offering that was completed July 28, 1998. USEC announced June 21, 2000, that it would close one of its enrichment plant by June 2001.

BACKGROUND AND ANALYSIS

Overview of Nuclear Power in the United States

The U.S. nuclear power industry, while currently generating about 20% of the nation's electricity, faces an uncertain future. No nuclear plants have been ordered since 1978 and more than 100 reactors have been canceled, including all ordered after 1973. No units are currently under active construction; the Tennessee Valley Authority's Watts Bar 1 reactor, ordered in 1970 and licensed to operate in 1996, was the last U.S. nuclear unit to be completed. The nuclear power industry's troubles include high nuclear power plant construction costs, public concern about nuclear safety and waste disposal, and regulatory compliance costs.

High construction costs are perhaps the most serious obstacle to nuclear power expansion. Construction costs for reactors completed since the mid-1980s have ranged from $2-$6 billion, averaging about $3000 per kilowatt of electric generating capacity (in 1995 dollars). The nuclear industry predicts that new plant designs could be built for about have that amount, but their total generating costs would still exceed currently projected costs for new coal- and gas-fired plants.

Nevertheless, all is not bleak for the U.S. nuclear power industry, which currently comprises 103 licensed reactors at 65 plant sites in 31 states (NRC data on each site, by state, is available at [http://www.nrc.gov./AEOD/pib/pib.html]). Electricity production from U.S. nuclear power plants is greater than that from oil, natural gas, and hydropower, and behind only coal, which accounts for 55% of U.S. electricity generation. Nuclear plants generate more than have the electricity in six states.

Average operating costs of U.S. nuclear plants dipped substantially during the 1990's, and costly downtime has been steadily reduced. Licensed commercial reactors generated electricity at a record-high average of nearly 85% of their total capacity in 1999, according to industry statistics. The Calvert Cliffs nuclear plant received the first 20-year license extension from the Nuclear Regulatory Commission (NRS) in March 2000, and several more extensions are pending. Industry consolidation could also help existing nuclear power plants, as larger nuclear operators purchase plants from utilities that run only one or two reactors. Several such sales have been announced, including the planned sale of the Millstone plant in Connecticut to Dominion Energy for a record $1.2 billion. The merger of two of the nation's largest nuclear utilities, PECO energy and Unicom, completed in October 2000, consolidated the operation of 17 reactors under a single corporate entity, Exelon Corporation.

Existing nuclear power plants appear to hold a strong position in the ongoing restructuring of the electricity industry. In most cases, nuclear utilities have received favorable regulatory treatment of past construction costs, and average nuclear operating costs are currently estimated to be lower than those of competing technologies.[1] Although eight U.S. nuclear reactors have permanently shut down since 1990, recent reactor sales could indicate greater industry interest in nuclear plants that previously had been considered marginal. Despite the shutdowns, total U.S. nuclear electrical output increased nearly 25% from 1990 to 1999, according to the Energy Information Administration. The increase resulted primarily from reduced downtime at the remaining plants, the startup of five new units, and reactor modification to boost capacity.

Global warming that may be caused by fossil fuels - the "greenhouse effect" - is cited by nuclear power supporters as an important reason to develop a new generation of reactors. But the large obstacles noted above must still be overcome before electric utilities will risk ordering new nuclear units. The Energy Information Administration forecasts that no new U.S. reactors will become operational before 2010, at the earliest.

Nuclear Power Research and Development

Under the Clinton Administration, development of advanced reactors has largely ended, although some research is continuing. In FY1995, Congress accepted the Administration's plan to halt development of the advanced liquid metal reactor (ALMR), also called the Integral Fast Reactor (IFR). For FY1996, Congress agreed to terminate research on the gas turbine modular helium reactor (GT-MHR), although $5 million was provided in FY1999 for a joint U.S.-Russian program to develop the GT-MHR for destruction of surplus weapons plutonium. Congress and the Administration continued funding for improved versions of today's light water reactors (LWRs) through FY1997. But the Administration's FY1998 request declared the program completed and provided only $5.5 million in termination costs for advanced LWR development.

The Clinton Administration's FY2001 budget request included $40 million for new LWR programs in DOE, which started in FY1999 and FY2000. The "nuclear energy plant optimization" (NEPO) program, for which $5 million was requested, is intended to improve the economic competitiveness of existing nuclear power plants. The "nuclear energy research initiative" (NERI), with a $35 million funding request, is designed to support innovative nuclear energy research projects. The FY2001 Energy and Water Development Appropriations bill (P.L. 106-377) provides the full request for both programs, plus $7.5 million for studies of advanced nuclear power technologies.

DOE justifies its efforts to encourage the continued operation of commercial U.S. nuclear plants as an important element in meeting national goals for reducing carbon dioxide emissions. Because nuclear plants directly emit no carbon dioxide, the continued operation of existing U.S. reactors avoids more than 620 million tons of carbon dioxide emissions each year, according to the FY2000 DOE budget justification. Opponents have criticized the nuclear energy research proposals as providing wasteful subsidies to an industry that they believe should be phased out.

Shutting down the ALMR program and its associated research facilities, particularly the Experimental Breeder Reactor II (EBR-II) in Idaho, is expected to take several years. Some ALMR facilities are being used for electrometallurgical treatment of EBR-II fuel, for which $45 million was appropriated in FY1999. Opponents of the program have expressed concern that such activities could help keep the ALMR/IFR program alive and have called for Congress to halt further funding. Supporters contend that the technology could convert unstable fuel elements into

---

[1]"Production Costs Made Nuclear Cheapest Fuel in 1999, NEI Says" *Nucleonics Week,* January 11, 2001, p. 3.

safer forms for storage and disposal. DOE issued a Record of Decision September 19, 2000, to use the electrometallurgical process for full-scale treatment of spent fuel at the Idaho site.

Nuclear Power Plan Safety and Regulation

Safety

Controversy over safety has dogged nuclear power throughout its development, particularly following the 1979 Three Mile Island accident in Pennsylvania and the April 1986 Chernobyl disaster in the former Soviet Union. In the United States, safety-related shortcomings have been identified in the construction quality of some plants, plant operation and maintenance, equipment reliability, emergency planning, and other areas. In addition, mishaps have occurred in which key safety systems have been disabled. NRC's oversight of mishaps have occurred in which key safety systems have been disabled. NRC's oversight of the nuclear industry is an ongoing issue; nuclear utilities often complain that they are subject to overly rigorous and inflexible regulation, but nuclear critics charge that NRC frequently relaxes safety standards when compliance may prove difficult or costly to the industry.

Domestic Reactor Safety. In terms of public health consequences, the safety record of the U.S. nuclear power industry in comparison with other major commercial energy technologies has been excellent. In more than 2,250 reactor-years of operation in the United States, the only incident at a commercial power plant that might lead to any deaths or injuries to the public has been the Three Mile Island accident, in which more than half the reactor core melted. Public exposure to radioactive materials released during that accident is expected to cause fewer than five deaths (and perhaps none) from cancer over the following 30 years. An independent study released in September 1990 found no "convincing evidence" that the TMI accident had affected cancer rates in the area around the plant. However, a study released in February 1997 concluded that much higher levels of radiation may have been released during the TMI accident than previously believed.

The relatively small amounts of radioactivity released by nuclear plants during normal operation are not generally believed to pose significant hazards. Documented public exposure to radioactivity from nuclear power plant waste as also been minimal, although the potential long-term hazard of waste disposal remains controversial. There is substantial scientific uncertainty about the level of risk posed by low levels of radiation, the assumed risk of low-level exposure has been extrapolated mostly from health effects documented among persons exposed to high levels of radiation, particularly Japanese survivors of nuclear bombing.

The consensus among most safety experts is that a severe nuclear power plant accident in the united States is likely to occur less frequently than once every 10,000 reactor-years of operation. These experts believe that most severe accidents would have small public health impact, and that accidents causing as many as 100 deaths would be much rarer than once every 10,000 reactor-years. On the other hand, some experts challenge the complex calculations that go into predicting such accident frequencies, contending that accidents with serious public health consequences may be more frequent.

Reactor Safety in the Former Soviet Bloc. The Chernobyl accident was by far the worst nuclear power plant accident to have occurred anywhere in the world. At least 31 persons died quickly from acute radiation exposure or other injuries, and between 5,000 and 45,000 fatal cancers may result over the next 40 years from radiation released during the accident. Those cancers would represent an increase in the cancer rate of about half a percent among the 75 million people in the western part of the former Soviet Union and a smaller increase in non-Soviet Europe, with a higher increase possible in the contaminated region around the plant.

The 10-year anniversary of the Chernobyl accident prompted renewed interest in the disaster's long-term consequences. According to a November 1995 report by the Organization for Economic Cooperation and Development (OECD), the primary observable health consequence of the accident has been a dramatic increase in childhood thyroid cancer. About 1,000 cases of childhood thyroid cancer have been reported in certain regions surrounding the destroyed reactor – a rate that is as much as a hundred times the pre-accident level, according to OECD. The death rate for accident cleanup workers has also risen measurably, the organization reported. Other recent studies have found increased genetic mutations among children born in contaminated regions.

Environmental contamination from the accident was widespread. The OECT report estimated that about 50,000 square miles of land in Belarus, Ukraine, and Russia were substantially contaminated with radioactive cesium. Significant levels of radioactive strontium, plutonium, and other isotopes were also deposited. Although radiation levels have declined during the past decade, land-use restrictions in the most contaminated areas may remain indefinitely, according to OECD.

World concern in recent years has focused on the safety of 13 other Chernobyl-type reactors (called RBMKs) that are still operating in the former Soviet Union (the last operating Chernobyl unit was permanently closed at the end of 2000). Despite safety improvements made after the Chernobyl disaster, the RBMKs remain inherently unstable and dangerous, according to many western experts. Also still operating in the former Soviet bloc are 10 early-model Soviet light water reactors (LWRs), which are similar to most Western reactors but suffer from major safety deficiencies, such as the lack of Western-style emergency cooling systems. More than two dozen new Soviet-designed LWRs that are currently operating are substantially safer than the earlier models but still do not meet all Eastern standards.

Immediate shutdown of the Soviet-designed reactors appears impractical because of the ex-Soviet bloc's critical need for electricity. Western help has been proposed for developing replacement power sources, allowing shutdown of the riskiest nuclear units, as well as funding for short- and long-term safety improvements. Russian leaders have estimated that total costs of the effort could range as high as $40 billion.

The United States is providing direct assistance for upgrading the safety of Soviet-designed reactors, a program being coordinated by DOE, NRC, the Agency for International Development (AID), and the Department of State. DOE was appropriated $45 million in FY1997 for improving the operation and physical condition of Soviet-designed nuclear power plants. The program was appropriated $35 million in FY 1999, and Congress provided $15 million for FY2000. For FY2001, the Energy and Water Development Appropriations bill provides $20 million for the program.

The General Accounting Office estimates that $1.93 billion had been provided through November 1999 by the United States and other industrialized nations to improve the safety of Soviet-designed reactors. Of that amount, $753 was contributed by the European Union, $532 by the United States, $43 million by the International Atomic Energy Agency (which receives much of its funding from the United States), and the remainder from 14 other countries.

Regulation

For many years a top priority of the nuclear industry was to modify the process for licensing new nuclear plants. No electric utility would consider ordering a nuclear power plant, according to the industry, unless licensing became quicker and more predictable, and designs were less subject to mid-construction safety-related changes ordered by NRC. The Energy Policy Act of 1992 largely implemented the industry's licensing goals.

Nuclear plant licensing under the Atomic Energy Act of 1954 (P.L. 83-703; U.S.C. 2011-2282) had historically been a two-stage process. NRC first issued a construction permit to build a plant, and then, after construction was finished, an operating permit to run it. Each stage of the licensing process involved complicated proceedings. Environmental impact statements also are required under the National Environmental Policy Act.

Over the vehement objections of nuclear opponents, the Energy Policy Act (P.L. 102-486) provides a clear statutory basis for one-step nuclear licenses, allowing completed plants to operate without delay if construction criteria are met. NRC would hold preoperational hearings on the adequacy of plant construction only in specified circumstances.

A fundamental concern in the nuclear regulatory debate is the performance of NRC in issuing and enforcing nuclear safety regulations The nuclear industry and its supporters have regularly complained that unnecessarily stringent and inflexibly enforced nuclear safety regulations have burdened nuclear utilities and their customer with excessive costs. Moreover, the nuclear industry is concerned about the size of NRC's own budget, because that agency is required to cover most of its costs through annual fees imposed on commercial reactors. But many environmentalists, nuclear opponents, and other groups charge NRC with being too close to the nuclear industry, a situation that they say has resulted in lax oversight of nuclear power plants and routine exemptions from safety requirements.

Primary responsibility for nuclear safety compliance lies with nuclear utilities, which are required to find any problems with their plants and report them to NRC. Compliance is also monitored directly by NRC, which maintains at least two resident inspectors at each nuclear power plant. The resident inspectors routinely examine plant systems, observe the performance of reactor personnel, and prepare regular inspection reports. For serious safety violations, NRC often dispatches special inspection teams to plant sites.

The House and Senate Appropriations Committees have been strongly urging NRC to reduce the cost of nuclear regulation. The Senate Committee report on the FY1999 Energy and Water Development Appropriations Bill sharply criticized NRC for allegedly failing to streamline its regulatory system in line with improvements in nuclear industry safety. The Committee contended, among other problems, that NRC's regional offices were inconsistent with one another, that NRC was inappropriately interfering with nuclear plant management, and that numerous NRC review processes were outdated and unnecessary. The House panel directed NRC to "reduce its workforce, reduce the regulatory burdens on licensees, and streamline its adjudicatory process."

In response, NRC has begun reorganizing and overhauling many of its procedures. The Commission is moving toward "risk-informed regulation," in which safety enforcement is guided by the relative risks identified by detailed individual plant studies. NRC began implementing a new reactor oversight system April 2, 2000, that relies on a series of performance indicators to determine the level of scrutiny that each reactor should receive. However, the Union of Concerned Scientists issued a report August 17, 2000, that questioned the validity of the individual plant studies on which risk-informed regulation is based.

The House and Senate Appropriations committees have expressed general satisfaction with the NRC's new regulatory program, and Congress approved nearly the full NRC FY2000 funding request, except for a $1 million cut for the NRC Inspector General. For FY2001, the final Energy and Water appropriation provides the full NRC request, with a $700,000 reduction in the Inspector General's request.

Decommissioning and Life Extension

When nuclear power plants end their useful lives, they must be safely removed from service, a process called decommissioning. NRC requires nuclear utilities to make regular contributions to special trust funds to ensure that money is available to remove all radioactive material from reactors after they are closed. Because no full-sized U.S. commercial reactor has yet been completely decommissioned, which can take several decades, the cost of the process can only be estimated. Decommissioning cost estimates cited by a 1996 DOE report, for one full-sized commercial reactor, ranged from about $150 million to $600 million in 1995 dollars. Disposal of large amounts of low-level waste, consisting of contaminated reactor components, concrete, and other materials, is expected to account for much of those costs.

For planning purposes, it is generally assumed that U.S. commercial reactors could be decommissioned at the end of their 40-year operating licenses, although several plants have been retired before their licenses expired and others could seek license renewals to operate longer. NRC rules that took effect June 13, 1992, allow plants to apply for a 20-year license extension, for a total operating life of 60 years. On March 23, 2000, the Calvert Cliffs nuclear plant in Maryland became the first U.S. plant to receive a license extension. Several other license-extension applications are pending, and more are expected to be filed. Assuming a 40-year lifespan, without life extension, m ore than half of today's 103 licensed reactors could be decommissioned by the year 2016.

Nuclear Accident Liability

Liability for damages to the general public from nuclear accidents is controlled by the Price-Anderson Act (Section 170 of the Atomic Energy Act of 1954, 42 U.S.C. 2210). The act is up for reauthorization on August 1, 2002, but existing nuclear plants will continue to operate under the current Price-Anderson liability system if no extension is enacted.

Under Price-Anderson, the owners of commercial reactors must assume all liability for accident damages to the public. To pay any such damages, each licensed reactor must carry the maximum liability insurance available, currently $200 million. Any damages exceeding that amount are to be assessed equally against all operating commercial reactors, up to $83.9 million per reactor. Those assessments – called "retrospective premiums" – would be paid at an annual rate of no more than $10 million per reactor, to limit the potential financial burden on reactor owners following a major accident.

For each accident, therefore, the Price-Anderson liability system currently would provide up to $8.84 billion in public compensation. That total includes the $200 million in insurance coverage carried by the reactor that had the accident, plus the $83.9 million in retrospective premiums from each of the 103 currently licensed reactors. On top of those payments, a 5% surcharge may also be imposed. Under Price-Anderson, the nuclear industry's liability for an accident is capped at that amount, which varies depending on the number of licensed reactors, the amount of available insurance, and an inflation adjustment that is made every five years. Payment of any damages above that liability limit would require congressional action.

The same total liability limit (whatever it may be at any given time) also applies to contractors who operate hazardous DOE nuclear facilities. Price-Anderson authorizes DOE to indemnify its contractors for the entire amount, so that damage payments for accidents at DOE facilities would ultimately come from the Treasury. However, the law also allows DOE to fine its contractors for safety violations.

The mechanism for imposing fines on DOE contractors has become controversial since the 2000 startup of the national Nuclear Security Administration (NNSA) within DOE to administer the Department'' nuclear defense programs. In approving legislation to clarify the situation (H.R. 4446), the House Commerce Committee recommended that the DOE Assistant Secretary for Environment, Safety, and Health continue to directly impose Price-Anderson fines on DOE contractors who are now managed by NNSA (H.Rept. 106-694, Part 1), while the House Armed Services Committee recommended that such fines be imposed only through the NNSA Administrator (H.Rept. 106-694, Part 2).

The Price-Anderson Act's limits on liability were crucial in establishing the commercial nuclear power industry in the 1950s. Supporters of the Price-Anderson system contend that it has worked well since that time in ensuring that nuclear accident victims would have a secure source of compensation, at little cost to the taxpayer. However, opponents contend that Price-Anderson subsidizes the nuclear power industry by protecting it from some of the financial consequences of the most severe conceivable accidents.

Two bills were introduced in the 106th Congress to extend the Price-Anderson Act (S. 2162 and S. 2292), although no further action was taken. Without an extension, any commercial nuclear reactor licensed after August 1, 2002, could not be covered by the Price-Anderson system, although existing reactors would continue to be covered. Because no new U.S. reactors are currently planned, the lack of an extension would have little short-term effect on the nuclear power industry. However, if Price-Anderson expired, DOE would have to use alternate indemnification authority for hazardous nuclear contracts signed after that time. NRC issued a report to Congress in October 1998 recommending that Price-Anderson be extended for another 10 years and that the annual per-reactor limit on retrospect premiums be doubled to $20 million. A DOE report on Price-Anderson extension is available at [http://www.gc.doe.gov].

Nuclear Waste Management

One of the most controversial aspects of nuclear power is the disposal of radioactive waste, which can remain hazardous for thousands of years. Each nuclear reactor produces an annual average of about 20 tons of highly radioactive spent nuclear fuel and 50-200 cubic meters of low-level radioactive waste. Upon decommissioning, contaminated reactor components are also disposed of as low-level waste.

The federal government is responsible for permanent disposal of commercial spent fuel (paid for with a fee on nuclear power) and federally generated radioactive waste, while states have the authority to develop disposal facilities for commercial low-level waste. Spent fuel and other highly radioactive waste is to be isolated in a deep underground repository, consisting of a vast network of chambers carved from rock that has remained geologically undisturbed for hundreds of thousands of years.

DOE is studying Nevada's Yucca Mountain as the site for such a geologic repository, as required by the Nuclear Waste Policy Act of 1982 (NWPA, P.L. 97-425) as amended. DOE issued a "viability assessment" in December 1998 that found no insurmountable problems with the site, but a final recommendation on the site's suitability is not expected until 2001. DOE contends that it will need its full FY2001 budget request of $437.5 million to keep the program on schedule. The final FY2001 Energy and Water appropriations bill provides $391 million for the program, plus another $10 million that DOE can use upon written certification that it is necessary to complete the site suitability recommendation by 2001. The extra $10 million comes from $85 million in FY1996 appropriations for interim storage, which was contingent on enactment of legislation that was vetoed by President Clinton. The remaining $75 million would be rescinded.

As originally enacted, the 1982 nuclear waste law established procedures and timetables for DOE to examine candidate sites for at least one deep repository for commercial spent fuel (with the option of also taking government high-level waste), to begin operating by January 31, 1998. Nuclear utilities were required to sign a contract with DOE for disposal services. The Nuclear Waste Fund, consisting of revenues from a fee on nuclear power, was created to pay for the disposal program. However, DOE could not spend money from the fund without annual congressional appropriations. The waste repository was required to meet Environmental Protection Agency (EPA) standards and be licensed by the Nuclear Regulatory Commission (NRC).

Controversy over implementation of the waste law led to fundamental revisions included in the Omnibus Budget Reconciliation Act of 1987 (P.L. 100-203). The revised waste law singled out Yucca Mountain as the only candidate site for a permanent waste repository.

With no federal storage or disposal facility available by the nuclear waste law's 1998 deadline, nuclear power plants must continue storing their waste at reactor sites much longer than originally anticipated. Most are expected to build additional on-site storage facilities, a move that has drawn strong state and local opposition in several recent cases. A federal appeals court ruled August 31, 2000, that nuclear power plant owners could sue DOE for damages resulting from the missed 1998 disposal deadline.

Interim Storage Legislation

DOE's current goal for opening the Yucca Mountain waste repository is 2010 – 12 years later than required by NWPA. The nuclear industry and state utility regulators are urging Congress to authorize waste to be stored at an interim facility near Yucca Mountain until the permanent respository is ready.

Legislation to establish a Yucca Mountain nuclear waste interim storage facility was introduced in both Houses in the 106th Congress (H.R. 45, S. 608), but Clinton Administration veto threats stalled the idea. In an effort to reach a compromise, an alternative bill was developed in the Senate (S. 1287) that would allow waste to be shipped to Yucca Mountain after NRC granted a repository construction permit – as early as 2007, under the bill's schedule. In addition to authorizing expedited waste shipments, the bill would bar EPA from issuing final environmental standards for the repository until June1, 2001. The Senate approved S. 1287 by a vote of 64-34 on February 10, 2000, and the House passed the same bill without amendment March 22, 2000, by 253-167, but President Clinton vetoed it.

H.R. 45 was approved by the House Commerce Committee's Subcommittee on Energy and Power on April 14, 1999, by a vote of 25-0, with full Committee approval following on April 21, 1999, by a 40-6 vote. The Committee-passed version would have required an interim storage facility at Yucca Mountain to open by June 2003 and required work on a permanent repository to move forward at the same time. To pay for both activities, the bill would have exempted the program's spending from budget ceilings while maintaining utility fees at the current level.

Several key Commerce Committee leaders spoke out against the move to bring S. 1287 to the House floor rather than H.R. 45.

The Clinton Administration opposed the sitting of an interim storage facility at Yucca Mountain before more technical study of the site's suitability for a permanent repository was completed. Administration veto threats blocked the proposal in the 104th and 105th Congresses. Before the Energy and Power Subcommittee markup of H.R. 45, Energy Secretary Richardson reiterated the Administration's opposition.

The Senate Energy Committee marked up S. 1287 on June 16, 1999, including provisions that would have authorized DOE to take title to spent fuel at commercial reactor sites and pay for storage costs, and eliminated EPA's role in setting repository standards, in addition to authorizing early waste shipments to the repository site (S. 1287, S. Rept. 106-98). Environmental and anti-nuclear groups staunchly oppose any proposal that would hasten waste shipments to Yucca Mountain, charging that the risks of transporting unprecedented amounts of high-level radioactive waste across the country are unwarranted. Supporters of the various nuclear waste bills contend that minimal transportation risks would be outweighed by the margin of safety gained by removing spent fuel from multiple reactor sites.

Supporters of S.1287 made further changes on the Senate floor in an effort to win enough votes to override a presidential veto. The EPA role in setting environmental standards for the repository was restored, but the agency was barred from issuing final standards until June 1, 2001, after an new Administration would be in place. The provision allowing DOE to take title to nuclear waste at reactor sites was dropped, in response to concerns that DOE might keep the waste at reactor sites indefinitely.

Despite the changes, President Clinton vetoed S. 1287 on April 25, 2000, contending that it would interfere with EPA rulemaking and undermine public confidence in the repository program. An effort in the Senate to override the veto fell short of the necessary two-thirds majority, 64-35, on May 2, 2000.

Low-Level Waste Facilities

Disposal facilities for commercially generated low-level radioactive waste – from nuclear power plants, hospitals, universities and industry – are a state responsibility. The Low-Level Radioactive Waste Policy Amendments Act of 1985 (P.L. 299-240) gave state and regions until the beginning of 1993 to begin operating their own low-level waste disposal facilities before potentially losing access to outside waste sites.

Only two commercial low-level sites, in South Carolina and Washington, are currently operating. Certain types of low-activity waste are also accepted by a Utah disposal facility, which has applied for a license to receive all three major classes of low-level waste. Access to the Washington site is allowed only to states in the Pacific Northwest and Rocky Mountain regions. A planned disposal facility at Wad Valley, California, for use by the Southwestern disposal region received a state license in 1993, but the facility's operation has been blocked by the federal government's refusal to transfer the federally owned site to the State of California. California Governor Davis established an advisory panel in June 1999 to study alternative waste management strategies.

Congress approved a disposal compact among Texas, Maine and Vermont September 2, 1998 (P.L. 105-236), which allows waste from the three states to go to a site to be developed in Texas and the exclusion of waste from other states. The South Carolina site is currently open nationwide, but South Carolina joined a compact with Connecticut and new Jersey on July 1, 2000, that will allow access outside those three states to be phased out.

Nuclear Weapons Proliferation

Nuclear technology was first used to make nuclear weapons, initially by the United States, and subsequently in Russia, England, France and China. Peaceful nuclear energy followed the development of nuclear weapons. The nuclear tests carried out by India and Pakistan in May 1998, combined with proliferation problems in Iraq, North Korea, Iran, and Russia, intensified longstanding concerns about worldwide nonproliferation regime and U.S. policy re receiving attention from many directions.

The discovery following the Gulf War in 1991 that Iraq had been near success in developing nuclear weapons led to efforts to strengthen inspection and enforcement of the Nuclear Nonproliferation Treaty (NPT). The NPT is nearly universal, with 187 members. The International Atomic Energy Agency (IAEA) operates a global safeguards system that monitors nuclear technology and materials to deter and detect diversions from peaceful to military uses. Detection by the IAEA of undeclared nuclear activities in North Korea – like Iraq, a member of the NPT – triggered efforts to halt nuclear weapons development in that nation as well.

The United States contuse to be a leading proponent of the international non-proliferation regime. It also has a system of export control and licensing laws covering transfers of nuclear technology or materials. There are also laws requiring sanctions against countries that obtain or test nuclear weapons, which were applied against India and Pakistan.

In addition to broad questions about the effectiveness of international nonproliferation efforts, Congress is sometimes faced with the repercussions of nonproliferation policy in specific instances, particularly with respect to sanctions and controls that do not solve proliferation problems but still have negative effects on bilateral relations and trade.

South Asia

The sanctions imposed on India and Pakistan included a prohibition on export credits, including export credits for agricultural projects. The 105th Congress passed separate legislation exempting credits, guarantees, and financial assistance to support purchase of food or agricultural commodities from the mandated sanctions. In addition, the Omnibus FY1999 Appropriations Act (P.L. 105-277) gave the President authority to waive some sanctions for a year. President Clinton used the new authority by lifting some of the sanctions on India and Pakistan November 6, 1998, to encourage the two countries to halt further testing, establish effective export controls, and begin bilateral discussions on nuclear weapons. There has since been little progress or restraint, despite further lifting of sanctions and the President's visit to India and Pakistan in March 2000. Restrictions on transfers of nuclear technology, however, remain in place.

The Middle East

The ongoing confrontation between certain Middle East countries and Israel has long had a nuclear undercurrent. Israel has made no official acknowledgment of a weapons program, but is widely considered to have developed nuclear weapons. Israel's weapons program has led to calls in Arab states for development of an "Islamic bomb." Iraq, before its defeat in the Gulf War in 1991, actively pursued nuclear weapons development. Iran declares it has no nuclear weapons program, but the United States claims that it does. The Clinton Administration has not succeeded in efforts to dissuade Russia from selling nuclear reactors to Iran. It is feared that such assistance could be a cover for weapons-related activities.

China

China has long been a nonproliferation concern. It was the major supplier to Pakistan's nuclear weapons program in the 1980s and early 1990s and also supplied technology to Iran and Algeria. However, China has gradually taken steps to join international nonproliferation agreements, and the 105th Congress approved a U.S. agreement for nuclear cooperation with China. However, the projected demand for U.S. nuclear technology sales to China has not materialized.

North Korea

North Korea had an active nuclear weapons program in the early 1990s. In October 1994, the United States signed an agreement with North Korea to exchange its existing nuclear reactors and reprocessing equipment for light water reactor technology that is less suited to making bombs. The agreement has had a difficult history, with funding being a continuing issue. A House amendment to the Foreign Operations Appropriations Bill for FY2000 (H.R. 2606) put new conditions on aid to the Korea Peninsula Energy Development Organization (KEDO), which is building the nuclear power plant in North Korea. Conditions include a new certification for U.S.-North Korean nuclear cooperation. The Clinton Administration waived parts of the certification when it was submitted February 24, 2000.

Russia

Maintaining control over the storage and disposal of Russian nuclear materials is also a nonproliferation issue. The Departments of Energy, Defense, and State are involved in the Cooperative Threat Reduction (Nunn-Lugar) program to improve the security of Russian nuclear material, technology, and expertise. In February 1993 the United states agreed to buy 500 metric tons of highly enriched uranium (HEU) from dismantled Russian weapons to use in commercial nuclear power reactors. Implementation of the purchase by the newly privatized U.S. Enrichment Corporation has faced numerous hurdles, however. Disposal of plutonium from weapons is a more difficult problem; President Clinton and Russian President Boris Yeltsin signed a joint statement September 2, 1998, calling for the elimination of 50 metric tons of weapons plutonium by each nation. The Department of Energy plants to "burn" part of the excess plutonium as fuel in existing civilian power reactors, but the plan is expensive and controversial.

Environmental Problems at Nuclear Weapons Facilities

The aging U.S. nuclear weapons production complex, managed by the Department of Energy, faces long-term problems with environmental contamination, radioactive waste disposal, and other environmental risks. DOE's Environmental Management Program, which is responsible for cleaning up the nuclear weapons complex, has grown into DOE's largest activity since its formal establishment in 19898. For FY2000, DOE was appropriated $6 billion for the program, excluding the Uranium Enrichment Decontamination and Decommissioning Fund. The FY2001 Energy and Water Development Appropriations bill provides about $6.4 billion for the program.

A DOE proposal for accelerating the cleanup program, issued in June 1998, estimated that total costs could reach about $150 billion through 2070, with cleanup completed at 41 of 53 major sites by 2006. DEO managers contend that substantial long-term savings can be gained by focusing on completing work at those sites, allowing the earliest possible termination of infrastructure costs.

The bulk of the EM privatization funding was intended to go toward the Hanford Tank Waste Remediation System, consisting of a "vitrification" plant what would turn liquid high-level waste into radioactive glass for eventual disposal. However, high costs estimates prompted DOE to decide in May 2000 to switch the project to traditional contracting methods. Other major privatized project include a project to treat "mixed" radioactive and hazardous waste at the Idaho National Engineering and Environmental Laboratory, and waste treatment storage, and disposal facilities at Oak Ridge, Tennessee.

The EM privatization effort is intended to reduce costs by increasing competition for cleanup work and shifting a portion of project risks from the federal government to contractors. Profits to contractors would depend on their success in meeting project schedules and holding down costs; potentially, profits could be substantially higher than under traditional DOE contracting arrangements.

Uranium Enrichment

Only 0.7% of the uranium found in nature is the fissile isotope uranium-235 (U-235). The remaining 99.3% is U-238. Before uranium is enriched in the United States for commercial reactors at plants originally built for the nuclear weapons program. Until July 1, 1993, the enrichment program was run by DOE.

The Energy Policy At of 1992 (EPACT) established the U.S. Enrichment Corporation (USEC), a wholly owned government corporation that took over operation of DOE's uranium enrichment facilities and enrichment marketing activities. EPACT authorized the sale of USEC to the private sector and required the corporation to prepare a privatizatin continuing appropriations bill for FY1996 sign by President Clinton April 26, 1996 (P.L. 104-134.

The USEC privatization was completed July 28, 1998, with an initial public offering of stock that raised an estimated $1.9 billion for the federal government. The privatized USEC leases its enrichment plants at Portsmouth, Ohio, and Paducah, Kentucky, from DOE. Controversy over the privatized corporation has focused on whether USEC will continue purchasing highly enriched uranium (HEU) from dismantled Russian nuclear weapons (under an agreement, negotiated in 1993), and future sales of Usee's large inventories of natural uranium. Under the HEU agreement, USEC receive enriched uranium from Russian nuclear weapons and, in addition to its payment for the material, returns an equivalent amount of natural (enriched) uranium to Russia to sell on the world market.

USEC's board of directors voted June 21, 2000, to close the Portsmouth enrichment plant by June 2001, leaving the company with only the Paducah plant. The USEC privatization agreement requires the company to operate both plants until 2204, unless certain financial problems rise. USEC says it is facing such problems, making a plant shutdown necessary. Opponents of the shutdown contend that it will leave the United States vulnerable to foreign suppliers.

DOE, which retains ownership of the Portsmouth plant, announced a plan October 6, 2000, to maintain part of the facility in standby condition for possible restart. The plan also calls for construction of a new enrichment plant at the site to demonstrate advanced gas centrifuge enrichment technology. Maintaining the Portsmouth plant in cold standby and building a centrifuge demonstration plant are estimated by DOE to cost $468 million over the next five years, with funding coming from a Treasury account for USEC privatization expenses. At the same time, DOE plans to accelerate the cleanup of the parts of the Portsmouth plant that will not be kept in standby condition.

Federal Funding for Nuclear Energy Program

The following tables summarize current finding for DOE nuclear fission programs and uranium activities, and for the NRC. The sources for the funding are Administration budget requests and committee reports on the Energy and Water Development Appropriations Acts, which fund all nuclear programs. President Clinton's funding request for FY2001 was submitted to Congress February 7, 2000, and the House passed the FY2001 Energy and Water measure June 27, 2000. The Senate approved its version of the FY2001 spending bill September 28, 2000, and by the Senate October 2, 2000. President Clinton vetoed the measure October 7, 2000, primarily over a waterway management provision.

Table 1. Funding for the Nuclear Regulatory Commission
(budget authority in millions of current dollars)

	FY2000 Approp.	FY2001 Request	FY2001 House	FY2001 Senate	FY2001 Conf.
Nuclear Regulatory Commission					
Reactor Safety	210.7	217.2	--	--	--
Nuclear Materials Safety	53.3	57.4	--	--	--
Nuclear Waste Safety	52.4	57.8	--	--	--
Defense and International	4.7	4.8	--	--	--
Management and Support	143.8	144.7	--	--	--
Inspector General	5.0	6.2	5.5	5.5	5.5
Total NRC Budget Authority*	**469.9**	**488.1**	**487.4**	**487.4**	**487.4**

*Entirely offset by fees on NRC licensees through FY2000, plus payments from the Nuclear Waste Fund for repository licensing. FY2001 conference total is offset 98%. Subtotals in House and Senate bills not specified.

Table 2. DOE Funding for Nuclear Activities
(budget authority in millions of current dollars)

	FY2000 Approp.	FY2001 Request	FY2001 House	FY2001Senate	FY2001 Conf.
Nuclear Energy (selected programs)					
Advanced Radioisotope Power Systems	34.5	30.9	29.2	34.2	32.2
Program Direction	24.7	27.6	25.9	24.7	22.0
University Reactor Assistance	12.0	12.0	12.0	12.0	12.0
Nuclear Energy Plant Optimization	5.0	5.0	5.0	5.0	5.0
Nuclear Energy Research Initiative	22.5	34.9	22.5	41.5	35.0
Nuclear Energy Technologies	--	--	--	--	7.5
Uranium Programs.	41.9	53.4	--	--	--
Isotope Support	20.5	16.7	15.2	21.2	19.2
Accelerator Transmutation of Waste	9.0	0	--	5.0	3.0*
International Nuclear Safety**	15.0	20.0	20.0	20.0	20.0
Total, Nuclear Energy	288.7	288.2	231.8	262.1	259.9
Uranium Facilities Maintenance and Remediation			301.4		393.4
Nuclear Waste Activities					
Environmental Management, Defense	5,716.0	6,159.7	5,864.0	6,042.1	6,122.2
Env.Mgmnt., Non-Defense	332.4	282.8	281.0	309.1	277.8
Uranium Enrichment D&D Fund	249.2	294.6	--	297.8	--

Nuclear Waste fund Activities***	347.2	437.5	413.0	351.2	401.1

*Funded under "Advanced Accelerator Applications" under "Other Defense Activities."

**Funded under "Defense Nuclear Nonproliferation."

*** Funded by a 1-mill-per-kilowatt-hour fee on nuclear power, plus appropriations for defense waste disposal. FY2000 request excludes $39 million in previous appropriations for interim storage.

LEGISLATION (106TH CONGRESS)

P.L. 106-377 H.R. 5483

Energy and Water Development Appropriations Bill for FY2001. Introduced October 18, 2000, as successor to the vetoed H.R. 4733. Incorporated by reference in conference report on the appropriations bill for the Departments of Veterans Affairs and Housing and Urban Development and other agencies (H.R. 4635, H. Rept. 106-988). H.R. 4635 approved by House and Senate October 19, 2000. Signed into law October 27, 2000.

H.R. 45 (Upton) S. 608 (Murkowski)

Rewrites Nuclear Waste Policy Act of 1982 and mandates construction of an interim storage site for spent nuclear fuel at Yucca Mountain, Nevada. House bill introduced January 6, 1999; referred to Commerce Committee, with sequential referrals to the committees on Resources and Transportation and Infrastructure. Approved 25-0 by Energy and Power Subcommittee on April 14, 1999. Senate bill introduced March 15, 1999; referred to committee on Energy and Natural Resources.

H.R. 43877 (Packard)

Energy and Water Development Appropriations Bill for FY2001. Provides funding for DOE nuclear-related programs. House Appropriations Committee reported June 23, 2000, and House approved June 27, 2000 (H.Rept. 106-693). Approved by Senate Appropriations Committee July 18, 2000 (S.Rept. 106-395), and by the Senate September 7, 2000. Conference report passed by the House September 28, 2000, and by the Senate October 2, 2000, Vetoed October 7, 2000. Superseded by H.R. 5483.

S.1287 (Murkowski)

Nuclear Waste Policy Amendments Act of 2000. Authorizes DOE to receive spent fuel at Yucca Mountain site after NRC issues a construction permit for a permanent repository. Reported as an original bill by Senate Energy and Natural Resources Committee (S. Rept. 106-98) June 24, 1999. Approved by the Senate February 10, 2000, by vote of 634-34. Approved by the House, 253-167, on March 22, 2000. Vetoed April 25, 2000, Senate defeated veto override May 2, 2000, by vote of 64-35.

S. 2162 (Bingaman)

Extends authority under the Price-Anderson Act for DOE to indemnify its contractors and for NRC to indemnity commercial nuclear plants, and amends DOE authority to impose fines on nonprofit contractors. Introduced March 2, 2000; referred to Senate Committee on Energy and Natural Resources.

S. 2292 (Inhofe)

Extends authority for NRC to indemnify commercial nuclear plants under the Price-Anderson Act. Introduced March 23, 2000; referred to Senate Committee on Environment and Public Works.

INDEX